D1247087

STRATEGIC COPYWRITING

STRATEGIC COPYWRITING

How to Create Effective Advertising

Edd Applegate

ROWMAN & LITTLEFIELD PUBLISHERS, INC.
Lanham • Boulder • New York • Toronto • Oxford

ROWMAN & LITTLEFIELD PUBLISHERS, INC.

Published in the United States of America
by Rowman & Littlefield Publishers, Inc.
A wholly owned subsidiary of
The Rowman & Littlefield Publishing Group, Inc.
4501 Forbes Boulevard, Suite 200, Lanham, MD 20706
www.rowmanlittlefield.com

P.O. Box 317, Oxford OX2 9RU, UK

British Library Cataloguing in Publication Information Available

Library of Congress Cataloging-in-Publication Data

Applegate, Edd.
Strategic copywriting : how to create effective advertising / Edd Applegate.
p. cm.
Includes bibliographical references and index.
ISBN 0-7425-3067-1 (cloth : alk. paper) — ISBN 0-7425-3068-X (pbk. : alk. paper)
1. Advertising copy. 2. Copy writers—Vocational guidance—United States. I. Title.
HF5825.A66 2004
659.1—dc22

2004006896

Printed in the United States of America

The paper used in this publication meets the minimum requirements of American National Standard for Information Sciences—Permanence of Paper for Printed Library Materials, ANSI/NISO Z39.48-1992.

Contents

Detailed Contents

Tables, Figures, and Boxes

TABLES

FIGURES

BOXES

Preface and Acknowledgments

David Ogilvy (Ogilvy & Mather) died in July 1999. It seems that advertising as we know it died with him. Indeed, the advertising we grew to know typically contained features and *benefits* about the products and services. Today, much of advertising, especially television commercials, contains neither.

In his book *The End of Advertising As We Know It*, Sergio Zyman, the former marketing director at Coca-Cola, writes, "The goal of advertising is to sell more stuff to more people more often for more money."[1] Advertising agencies used to produce advertisements that did just that. However, something went wrong. As Zyman points out, "Instead of focusing on their clients' consumers, ad agencies and advertising executives at companies fell in love with themselves."[2] In essence, they focused on producing award-winning advertisements that bordered on being nothing more than works of art instead of "works of communication."[3] According to Zyman, in order to work, advertising must tell consumers to buy a product or service and provide reasons for doing so.[4] In short, advertising should provide benefits—that is, express what the product or service will do for the consumer.

This book focuses primarily on advertising copywriting. Unlike some texts, which discuss this aspect of advertising from the perspective that Ogilvy and Zyman would find suspect, I approach the subject from a more traditional and sound perspective—a perspective that Ogilvy and Zyman would approve.

There is a major reason for this perspective: it is the perspective that is based on principles that have been shown to work in advertising time after time. Furthermore, students and other novices must know these principles that have guided advertising for decades before they even consider testing these principles or altering these principles in any way.

In chapter 1 we examine the importance of research—from research about the client to research about the consumer. In addition to providing additional information about research, chapter 2 provides insight into the creative strategy. In chapter 3 we examine headlines and slogans—elements that not only are important in advertisements but often are all the copy that consumers read. We look at body copy, including the various types, in chapter 4. In chapter 5 we examine the elements of advertising design, including the frequently used designs found in print advertisements. We look at newspaper advertising, especially retail, in chapter 6. In chapter 7 we examine magazine advertising, including consumer, business to business, industrial, trade, and farm or agriculture. We look at radio advertising, including the types of commercials, in chapter 8. In chapter 9 we examine television advertising, including what a good commercial must have. We look at direct mail advertising, including letters, brochures, and folders, in chapter 10. In chapter 11 we examine Internet advertising, including the various kinds. We look at other media advertising, including outdoor, point of purchase, and the *Yellow Pages*, in chapter 12. In chapter 13 we examine public relations and corporate advertising. We look at advertising copy research, including pretests and posttests, in chapter 14. And chapter 15 offers information and advice on how to get a job in advertising.

ACKNOWLEDGMENTS

I wish to thank the following individuals at Middle Tennessee State University for their help and encouragement:

- Dr. Richard Campbell, former director of the School of Journalism, College of Mass Communication, for his understanding and help
- Dr. Donald Parente, a colleague, for his friendship over the years
- Dr. Glenn Himebaugh, a colleague who enjoys writing, for his friendship over the years
- The individuals who served on the Non-instructional Assignment Committee during spring 2002 and who provided me the opportunity to begin this project

In addition to the above, thanks go to the following individuals and firms for their support of my questions and requests:

Art Johnsen, formerly the chief operating officer at BOHAN Advertising/Marketing, Nashville, Tennessee, now a managing partner at Locomotion Creative, Nashville. Art, a friend, helped secure materials that personnel at BOHAN Advertising/Marketing produced. In addition, he provided information and leads to other advertising agencies.

David Bohan, the chairman and CEO of BOHAN Advertising/Marketing, Nashville, for providing permission to use advertisements that personnel at BOHAN Advertising/Marketing produced for various clients and for the personal note

Dennis Walker, creative group head for the Richards Group, Dallas, for providing numerous advertisements that personnel at the Richards Group developed for various clients as well as permission

Sarah Avery, in public relations at the Richards Group, Dallas, for her help and information

Veronica Gotway, the PR coordinator for the Richards Group, Dallas, for her help and information

Debra Weiss, the vice president of Metro Creative Graphics, Inc., New York, for providing permission to use several advertisements that personnel at Metro Creative Graphics developed

Roanna Lee, the marketing manager for Metro Creative Graphics, Inc., New York, for providing information about Metro Creative Graphics as well as providing numerous advertisements that personnel at Metro Creative Graphics developed

Kristen Thomas, a consultant at SRI Consulting Business Intelligence, Menlo Park, California, for her help and permission to use the VALS Segment Profiles and framework

Barbara Dunlap-Berg, United Methodist Communications, Nashville, Tennessee, for permission to use the creative strategy for Nestle Crunch

Craig Wood, the president of MONITOR MindBase, Yankelovich, Inc., Chapel Hill, N.C., for permission to use material from Yankelovich Partners' MONITOR MindBase

Jeff Holmes, the CEO/creative director for 3 Marketeers Advertising, Inc., San Jose, California, for providing several advertisements that personnel at 3 Marketeers Advertising developed for several clients as well as permission

Robert A. Gavin, the CEO of Gavin & Gavin Advertising, Inc., San Diego, for providing an advertisement that personnel at Gavin & Gavin Advertising developed for a client as well as permission

Ford Wiles, the senior vice president (Creative) for O2 ideas, Birmingham, Alabama, for providing several advertisements that personnel at O2 ideas developed for clients as well as permission

Hope Butler, the manager of member services for the Outdoor Advertising Association of America, Inc., Washington, D.C., for her help and information about the outdoor advertising industry

Kathy Curtis, the senior vice president (Knowledge Management) for POPAI, Washington, D.C., for her help and information about the point-of-purchase advertising industry

Peter Himler, the managing director of media relations for Burson-Marsteller, New York, for his help concerning public relations and press releases

Roger Hurni, Off Madison Ave, Tempe, Arizona, for providing several advertisements that personnel at Off Madison Ave developed for clients

Shelly Moss, the art director for Off Madison Ave, Tempe, for her help and information

Peter Verrengia, the regional president and general manager of Fleishman Hillard, New York, for his help concerning public relations and press releases

Rochelle Amos and the American Marketing Association, Chicago, for permission to use material that appeared in the October 1961 *Journal of Marketing* (Vol. 25, No. 6)

Alan Rosenspan, the president of Alan Rosenspan & Associates, Newton, Massachusetts, for providing several direct mail advertisements that personnel at Alan Rosenspan & Associates developed for clients and permission

Susan Kaplan, the director of rights/clearances for VNU Business Media, Inc., New York, for permission to use material that appeared in the May 15, 1995, *Brandweek* (Vol. 36, No. 20)

Cynthia Passarelli, the assistant to the vice president of IDI Group, Ste-Anne-de-Bellevue, Canada, for providing a photograph of a point-of-purchase display that personnel at IDI Group developed for a client as well as permission

Melissa Stallings, the federation membership manager for the Newspaper Association of America, Vienna, Virginia, for her help and information about newspaper advertising, including the "One-Item Ads," "Two-Item Ads," and "Three-Item Ads" sections that appear in chapter 6

Alex Konanykhin, the president of KMGI Studios, Inc., New York, for providing information about KMGI Studios and permission to use several advertisements that had been developed for clients

Gary A. Johnston, the brand manager for DuPont Textiles & Interiors—Residential Flooring, Kennesaw, Georgia, for his help and permission to use the advertising copy for Stainmaster carpet

Bob McKeon, the manager of media relations for ConAgra Foods, Inc., Omaha, for his help in securing permission to use the advertising copy for Egg Beaters

Jean Skornicka, the brand manager for ConAgra Dairy Foods, Downers Grove, Illinois, for her help and permission to use the advertising copy for Egg Beaters

Rick Colby, the president/executive creative director of Colby & Partners, Santa Monica, for providing numerous advertisements that personnel at Colby & Partners had developed for several clients. Mr. Colby and several of his employees, including Paul Izenstark and Angie Mosier, deserve credit for securing permission to use some of these advertisements.

Alan Bethke, the advertising and sales training manager for the American Suzuki Motor Corporation, Brea, California, for securing permission to use several advertisements that were created for the American Suzuki Motor Corporation by personnel at Colby & Partners

Ken Brown and Kathy Triolo of the Reader's Digest Association, Inc., Pleasantville, New York, for providing several direct mail advertisements as well as permission

Lisa Castaldo, in public relations for the Pepsi-Cola Company, Purchase, New York, for help in securing permission to use one of the company's press releases

James R. Huges Jr., the president and creative director of the Martin Agency, Richmond, Virginia, for his assistance

Patty Roberts, the creative resources coordinator for the Martin Agency, Richmond, Virginia, for providing advertisements that had been produced by personnel of the Martin Agency and for help in securing permission to use some of the advertisements

Celeste Speier, the public relations manager for the American Suzuki Motor Corporation, Brea, California, for her assistance in gaining permission to use several advertisements

Jeffrey Buntin Sr., the president and chief operating officer of the Buntin Group, Nashville, Tennessee, for his assistance

Karen Baker, the director of public client relations for the Buntin Group, Nashville, for providing advertisements and public relations that had been produced by personnel at the Buntin Group. Ms. Baker was also helpful in securing permission.

Pete Samuels, of PING, Phoenix, for securing permission to use the advertisement about PING golf clubs that had been produced by personnel at the Martin Agency, Richmond, Virginia

Thomas McNaught, of the JFK Library Foundation, Boston, for securing permission to use the advertisement about the JFK Library that had been produced by personnel at the Martin Agency, Richmond, Virginia

Janet Hoppe, in public affairs for Frito-Lay, Inc., Dallas, for securing permission to use the press release about Frito-Lay

Michael Bolig, a marketing assistant for the Radio Advertising Bureau (RAB), New York, for securing permission to use at least two tables from one of the RAB's publications

Nicole Kaplan, the vice president of marketing and promotion for the Magazine Publishers of America (MPA), New York, for securing permission to use one table from one of the MPA's publications

Deb Martin, the director of information services for MPA, New York, for her assistance

Carie Arseneau, an information specialist for MPA, New York, for securing permission to use one table from one of the MPA's publications

Cristina J. Santos, the manager of communications for MPA, New York, for her assistance

Hope Etheridge, the vice president of finance and administration for the Television Bureau of Advertising (TVB), New York, for securing permission to use two tables from one of TVB's publications

David Friedman, of TVB, New York, for his assistance

Richard Gordon, the permissions editor for *Advertising Age*, Chicago, for securing permission to use one table from one of Crain Communications' publications

Kitty Munger, the manager of communications for Wendy's International, Inc., Dublin, Ohio, for her assistance in securing permission to use the press release about Wendy's Old Fashioned Hamburgers

Denny Lynch, the senior vice president of corporate communications for Wendy's International, Inc., Dublin, Ohio, for permission to use the press release about Wendy's Old Fashioned Hamburgers

Without the cooperation of the individuals mentioned above, most of the figures, tables, and advertising copy found on the following pages would not appear here. The editors, the publisher, and I thank these individuals for their help.

NOTES

1. Sergio Zyman (with Armin Brott), *The End of Advertising As We Know It* (Hoboken, NJ: John Wiley and Sons, Inc., 2002), p. 14.
2. Zyman, *The End of Advertising As We Know It*, p. 14.
3. Zyman, *The End of Advertising As We Know It*, p. 14.
4. Zyman, *The End of Advertising As We Know It* p. 26.

CHAPTER 1

Research

Before we discuss how to write copy for advertisements, we need to understand what advertising is. Basically, *advertising is placing a message about an idea, product, or service in one or more media (newspapers, television, magazines, radio, outdoors, point of purchase, and direct mail), for which the advertiser pays a fee.* Today, in addition to the media mentioned, businesses and organizations are using the World Wide Web as a medium in which to place advertisements.

Who creates these advertising messages? Usually, professional men and women who work in advertising agencies, specialty firms, or the media create these messages. Sometimes they work in the client's advertising or marketing department. How do they create these commercial messages? They do so by first understanding their client, their client's product or service, and their client's intended consumer.

THE CLIENT

Many businesses and organizations—both large and small—have marketing departments usually headed by marketing directors. These directors, together with members of their departments, typically produce marketing plans. A thorough marketing plan will discuss the overall business or organization, its sales or growth, its competition, its customers, its future projections, its various objectives, its marketing strategy, its marketing programs including advertising and promotion, its financial situation, and its contingency plans.

Most marketing plans contain the following headings or something similar:

I. Executive Summary
II. Situational Analysis
  A. The External Environment
  B. The Internal Environment
III. The Target Market
IV. Problems and Opportunities
V. Marketing Objectives and Goals
VI. Marketing Strategy
VII. Marketing Tactics
VIII. Implementation and Control
IX. Summary
X. Appendixes

The Executive Summary section is a synopsis of the overall marketing plan. The Situational Analysis section examines in depth the major competition; the economic conditions of the nation, the state, and the community; the political landscape; the legal and regulatory factors; technological changes; cultural trends; current and potential customers; current and anticipated organizational resources; and current and anticipated cultural and structural issues.

The Target Market section describes the target market in terms of demographics, psychographics, geographics, and lifestyles. The Problems and Opportunities section identifies each problem and what is intended to solve it. Also, each opportunity is identified and explained.

The Marketing Objectives and Goals section discusses each marketing goal's respective objectives in terms of sales volume and market share. The Marketing Strategy section examines the target market(s), the major consumer reactions, and the major competitor reactions. The Marketing Tactics section discusses the structural issues, the marketing strategy(ies) in terms of the marketing mix (the four Ps: place, price, product, and promotion), and how each will be implemented.

The Implementation and Control section discusses current costs, current gross margins, projected costs, projected gross margins, input control mechanisms, and output control mechanisms. And the Summary section presents the advantages, costs, profits, and differential advantage of the marketing plan versus the competition's.[1]

Basically, the marketing director of the firm has identified the firm's marketing problem(s) in the marketing plan. A marketing plan can help advertising personnel learn about their client, their client's product or service, their client's consumers, and even their client's marketing problem(s). Consequently, the marketing plan becomes a valuable resource to advertising personnel, especially if they have been given the task of developing an in-depth advertising plan or integrated marketing communications plan, which typically includes the following headings or something similar:

- I. Executive Summary
- II. Situation Analysis
  - A. Company Analysis
  - B. Product Analysis
  - C. Consumer Analysis
  - D. Market Analysis
  - E. Competitive Analysis
  - F. Problems and Opportunities
- III. Target Market Profile
- IV. Advertising Objectives
  - A. Primary or Selective Demand
  - B. Direct or Indirect Action
- V. Advertising (Creative) Strategy
  - A. Objectives
  - B. Product Concept
  - C. Target Audience
  - D. Message
- VI. Advertising Media
- VII. The Advertising Budget
  - A. Method of Allocation
- VIII. Testing and Evaluation
  - A. Advertising Research
  - B. Pretesting and Posttesting

The Executive Summary section encapsulates the advertising plan. The Situation Analysis section reviews the major topics that were presented in the marketing plan. The Target Market Profile section briefly describes the primary (and secondary) target market(s).

The Advertising Objectives section examines the specifics of what the advertising should accomplish. The Advertising or Creative Strategy section discusses the creative effects—that is, what the advertising and forms of promotion are supposed to do. If the plan includes other marketing communications, such as sales promotion, public relations, or direct marketing, then each would be listed followed by similar subheads.

The Advertising Media section identifies and provides explanations for the media in which the advertising message will appear. The Advertising Budget section discusses the amount of money that has been allocated to the advertising. Finally, the Testing and Evaluation section identifies the research techniques that will be used to measure the advertising's effectiveness.[2]

The following is a hypothetical example of an advertising or integrated marketing communications plan for Burger King:

I. Executive Summary
II. Situation Analysis
   A. Company Analysis
   B. Product Analysis
   C. Consumer Analysis
   D. Market Analysis
   E. Competitive Analysis
   F. Problems and Opportunities
III. Target Market
   A. Primary Market
   B. Secondary Market
IV. Campaign Objectives
   A. Overall Objectives
V. Creative Strategy (Advertising)
   A. Objectives
   B. Strategy
   C. Target Audience
   D. Manner
   E. Tone
   F. Creative Tactics
VI. Media Strategy
   A. Objectives
   B. Strategy
   C. Mix
   D. Allocation
   E. Flow Chart
VII. Marketing Communications Strategy (Sales Promotion, Public Relations, etc.)
   A. Objectives
   B. Strategy
   C. Tactics
VIII. Budget
   A. Budget Allocation
IX. Campaign Evaluation
X. Appendixes
   A. Appendix A: Primary Research
   B. Appendix B: Creative Executions

Advertising agency personnel would conduct the secondary and primary research, develop the overall campaign objectives, plan the media mix, create the advertisements, and calculate the expenditures.

Advertising copywriters would work with the layout artists, graphics personnel, and other creative individuals to develop the print advertisements and broadcast commercials that would be placed in the various media. Specifically, the copywriters would be concerned with the Creative Strategy section of the advertising plan. In addition to understanding the client's product or service, copywriters would have to understand who make up the target market(s)—that is, the consumers who would be inclined to purchase the product. After all, the advertisements and commercials would have to be directed to these individuals.

WHO ARE THE CONSUMERS?

According to the U.S. Census Bureau, there are more than 281 million people in the United States. Although every state experienced growth during the last decade, growth rates in states differed. For instance, Nevada grew 66 percent, whereas North Dakota grew 1 percent. The highest growth rates occurred in the western and southern states. The population in the western states grew 19.7 percent, and the population in the southern states grew 17.3 percent.[3]

Demographic Segmentation

THE AFRICAN AMERICAN MARKET There are almost 35 million African Americans, totaling slightly more than 12 percent of the country's population. This group has a purchasing power of more than $570 billion. In the past, African American households spent more on apparel, telephone services, and natural gas than other American households. They also spent a higher proportion of their after-tax income on housing, electricity, transportation, and food consumed at home. The majority of African American families rent apartments or houses. African Americans are becoming more conscious about education, even though less than 15 percent have a college degree.[4] (See table 1.1.)

THE ASIAN AMERICAN MARKET There are more than 10 million Asian Americans, totaling almost 4 percent of the country's population. This group has a purchasing power of more than $250 billion. In fact, this group's purchasing power has grown faster than that of any other group in the United States. The primary reason for this is that Asian Americans are better educated than the average American. Indeed, almost 45 percent have a college education. Consequently, a large proportion of them hold top-level jobs in management or professional specialties.[5] (See table 1.1.)

TABLE 1.1 *Breakdown of the U.S. Population by Race*

RACE	TOTAL	PERCENT
One race	274,595,678	97.6
White	211,460,626	75.1
Black or African American	34,658,190	12.3
American Indian and Alaska Native	2,475,956	0.9
Asian	10,242,996	3.6
Native Hawaiian and Other Pacific Islander	398,835	0.1
Other	15,359,073	5.5
Two or more races	6,826,228	2.4
Race alone or in combination with one or more other races		
White	216,930,975	77.1
Black or African American	36,419,434	12.0
American Indian and Alaska Native	4,119,301	1.5
Asian	11,898,826	4.2
Native Hawaiian and Other Pacific Islander	874,414	0.3
Other	18,521,486	6.6
Hispanic or Latino (of Any Race)	35,305,818	12.5
Total	**281,421,906**	**100.0**

Source: U.S. Census Bureau.

TABLE 1.2 *Breakdown of the U.S. Population by Age*

AGE	TOTAL	PERCENT
Under 5 years	19,175,798	6.8
5 to 9 years	20,549,505	7.3
10 to 14 years	20,528,072	7.3
15 to 19 years	20,219,890	7.2
20 to 24 years	18,964,001	6.7
25 to 34 years	39,891,724	14.2
35 to 44 years	45,148,527	16.0
45 to 54 years	37,677,952	13.4
55 to 59 years	13,469,237	4.8
60 to 64 years	10,805,447	3.8
65 to 74 years	18,390,986	6.5
75 to 84 years	12,361,180	4.4
85 years and over	4,239,587	1.5
Median age (years)	35.3	

Source: U.S. Census Bureau.

THE HISPANIC AMERICAN MARKET There are more than 35 million Hispanic or Latino Americans, totaling more than 12 percent of the country's population. This group rivals the African American group for being the largest minority group in the United States.

Although Hispanic Americans can be found across the country, about two million reside in New York City. Other large pockets of Hispanics can be found in California, Florida, Illinois, and Texas. Overall, this group has a purchasing power of more than $425 billion. In fact, this group's purchasing power has grown faster than that of the African American group.

Hispanic Americans earn less than other groups, but they spend more on food consumed at home, telephone services, and apparel. They also spend a higher proportion of their after-tax income on housing, personal care products, and services. However, they spend less on reading material, education, tobacco, health care, and entertainment. The majority of Hispanic households rent apartments or houses.[6] (See table 1.1.)

THE AMERICAN INDIAN AND ALASKA NATIVE MARKET There are more than two million American Indian and Alaska natives in the United States, totaling almost 1 percent of the country's population. Most American Indians live on reservations, where most of their business and leisure activity occurs. Alaska natives reside in the Northwest, primarily in Alaska. These groups do not fare as well as other groups, economically speaking, although certain subgroups within each have seen improvement.[7] (See table 1.1.)

THE YOUTH MARKET There are almost 40 million boys and girls under the age of 10 and another 40 million-plus from 10 to 19 years of age in the United States, for almost 29 percent of the population. There are more than eight million children enrolled in preschool or kindergarten. There are almost 33

TABLE 1.3 *Breakdown of Family Households in the United States*

HOUSEHOLDS BY TYPE	TOTAL	PERCENT
Family households (families)	71,787,347	68.1
With own children under 18	34,588,366	32.8
Married-couple family	54,493,232	51.7
With own children under 18	24,835,505	23.5
Female householder, no husband present	12,900,103	12.2
With own children under 18	7,561,874	7.2
Nonfamily households	33,692,754	31.9
Householder living alone	27,672,706	25.8
Householder 65 years and over	9,722,857	9.2
Households with individuals under 18	38,022,115	36.0
Households with individuals 65 years and over	24,672,706	23.4
Average household size	2.59	
Average family size	3.14	

Source: U.S. Census Bureau.

million children enrolled in elementary school, almost 16 million children enrolled in high school, and almost 16 million enrolled in college or graduate school.[8]

THE YOUNG MATURE MARKET There are almost 59 million men and women between the ages of 20 and 35 in the United States, for almost 21 percent of the country's population.[9] (See table 1.2.)

THE MATURE MARKET There are almost 83 million men and women between the ages of 35 and 55 in the United States, totaling almost 30 percent of the country's population. There are more than 24 million men and women between the ages of 55 and 65 in the United States, for almost 9 percent of the country's population.[10] (See table 1.2.)

THE "GOLDEN YEARS" MARKET There are almost 35 million men and women who are in their "Golden Years"—that is, 65 years of age and older in the United States, totaling more than 12 percent of the country's population.[11] (See table 1.2.)

HOUSEHOLDS IN THE UNITED STATES The average household in the United States has 2.59 individuals. The average family household in the United States has 3.14 individuals.[12] See table 1.3. There are more than 71 million family households in the United States, making up more than 68 percent of the total households in the country. Married couples head more than 54 million, or 51.7 percent, of these family households, whereas only females head almost 13 million, or 12.2 percent, of these family households. There are more than 38 million households, or 36 percent, that have individuals under 18 years of age, and there are more than 24 million households, or 23.4 percent, that have individuals 65 years of age and over.[13] (See table 1.3.)

EMPLOYED POPULATION 16 YEARS AND OVER More than 40 million people work in management or some other professional field, and almost 35 million work in sales or some related field. More than 19 million work in service fields, and more than 19 million work in production and transportation fields.[14] (See table 1.4.)

INCOME AND BENEFITS FOR ALL HOUSEHOLDS More than 10 million households earn less than $10,000 a year, whereas more than 20 million households earn between $50,000 and $75,000. More than 27 million households earn between $15,000 and $35,000. The median household income is $41,349, and the mean household income is $55,263.[15] (See table 1.5.)

TABLE 1.4 *Breakdown of the U.S. Employed Population 16 Years and Over by Occupation, Industry, and Class of Worker*

OCCUPATION, INDUSTRY, OR CLASS OF WORKER	ESTIMATED TOTAL
Occupation	
Management, Professional, and Related	43,380,156
Service	19,672,918
Sales and Office	34,735,733
Farming, Fishing, and Forestry	960,317
Construction, Extraction, and Maintenance	12,355,807
Production, Transportation, and Material Moving	19,132,137
Industry	
Agriculture, Forestry, Fishing, and Hunting	1,873,713
Mining and Utilities	1,684,241
Construction	8,873,677
Manufacturing	18,508,011
Wholesale Trade	5,000,281
Retail Trade	15,507,231
Transportation, Warehousing, Information, and Communication	9,671,996
Finance, Insurance, Real Estate, and Leasing	8,961,233
Services	53,987,168
Public Administration	6,169,516
Class of Worker	
Private Wage and Salary	103,599,330
Government	18,376,263
Self-employed	7,278,574
Unpaid Family	982,900

Source: U.S. Census Bureau.

TABLE 1.5 *Income and Benefits for All Households in the United States*

INCOME	ESTIMATED TOTAL
Less than $10,000	10,022,803
$10,000 to $14,999	6,995,026
$15,000 to $24,999	13,994,472
$25,000 to $34,999	13,491,042
$35,000 to $49,999	17,032,000
$50,000 to $74,999	20,017,509
$75,000 to $99,999	10,479,853
$100,000 to $149,999	8,125,132
$150,000 to $199,999	2,336,503
$200,000 or more	2,239,229
Median household income	$41,349
Mean household income	$55,263

Source: U.S. Census Bureau.

LANGUAGE SPOKEN FOR THOSE FIVE YEARS AND OVER Almost 210 million people in the United States speak only English, and almost 45 million people speak a language other than English. Almost 27 million people speak Spanish.[16]

THE EDUCATED MARKET There are almost 16 million people in the United States with a graduate or professional degree and another 28 million-plus people with a bachelor's degree. More than 11 million have an associate's degree, and more than 36 million have some college credit. More than 52 million have a high school diploma. Fewer than 33 million people have less than a high school diploma in the United States.[17] (See table 1.6.)

Although none of the information above should be used alone to determine consumers for a specific target market, advertising copywriters may use much of it as well as the following information to determine the warm and hot prospects for a client's product or service.

Generational Segmentation

THE GENERATION Y MARKET This group includes those born between 1980 and 1995 and is 60 million-plus strong—or three times larger than the so-called Generation X group. Marketers pay particular attention to those who are in their teens, about 31 million individuals.

Generation Y is the fastest growing demographic group under 65 years of age in the United States, and its members spend about $275 billion a year. Not necessarily eager to conform, this group has a tendency to try what is new. Members purchase online primarily because they grew up with the Internet, and they usually have the latest electronic innovations in their rooms. Unlike Generation X, this group has preferred khakis instead of jeans for years. Many have had VCRs or DVD players and a remote for their televisions. They are more racially diverse than members of Generation X, and one in three is not white. One in four lives in a single-parent household. Three in four have working mothers. Until September 11,

2001, war was unknown to them. They have never experienced a major recession. As a result, their attitude is buy now and pay later. They are not as devoted to their jobs as members of Generation X. In fact, they are not afraid to quit their jobs for others. Although younger members of this group have a weekly allowance that varies from $25 to $175, the majority receives about $50 a week.

Contrary to popular opinion, these members save and even invest some of their money. For years, advertisers had a difficult time selling their brands to this group, but today that has changed. In fact, boys and girls prefer certain brands, including Tommy Hilfiger, Old Navy, Abercrombie & Fitch, Limited Too, American Eagle, Borders, and Best Buy.

This generation also influences what their mothers or fathers purchase at the grocery store. If both parents work, then some of the members of this group do some of the grocery shopping for the family.

Members of Generation Y are aware of their world and enjoy being entertained. They are concerned about the environment. They do not like to see others belittle people. They have seen violence at school, in Oklahoma City, and in New York City. They have seen so-called reality television. They like to communicate via cell phones and computers. They even like to learn via computers. They expect feedback and rewards for what they do.[18]

THE GENERATION X MARKET Born between 1965 and 1979, this group of almost 50 million individuals was raised on television and computers. Unlike Generation Y, however, this group is more cynical, primarily because of growing up when the country faced economic and social problems such as a major economic recession, which in turn caused corporations to downsize, parental separation or divorce, and, of course, the AIDS epidemic. This group has been saturated with advertising; consequently, its members do not necessarily react positively toward a lot of the advertising they view, read, or hear.

This group uses the computer and enjoys listening to music. A greater proportion of this group is unemployed or underemployed. A greater share is also living at home.

This group spends a greater proportion of its income on eating out, alcohol, clothes, and electronics. Members of this group desire a home of their own, a lot of money, a swimming pool, and a vacation

TABLE 1.6 *Educational Attainment of Citizens in the United States*

LEVEL OF EDUCATION	ESTIMATED TOTAL
Less than 9th grade	12,328,762
9th to 12th grade, no diploma	20,364,795
High school graduate (including equivalency)	52,427,005
Some college, no degree	36,456,924
Associate degree	11,493,115
Bachelor's degree	28,563,252
Graduate or professional degree	15,929,046
Percent high school graduate or higher	81.6
Percent bachelor's degree or higher	25.1

Source: U.S. Census Bureau.

home. This group has $125 billion of discretionary income. Its members desire the prestigious brands that offer the most value for the money. Members of this group have discriminating tastes and do not care for being labeled by marketers. Nor do they care for companies that promote their products with exaggerated claims. They appreciate advertisements that contain humor. However, they desire, if not demand, to be informed about products or services as well as to be given reasons as to why they should purchase products or services. To them, products have to fulfill a practical need, whether it is social, psychological, or financial. Members of this group consider themselves experimenters—that is, they gather information from various sources, not just the traditional media. Therefore, advertisers, if they desire to reach members of this group, have to use newer media such as the Internet.

On the other hand, the older and more educated segments of Generation X tend to become loyal to specific brands, much like those classified as baby boomers. Also, they tend to be more conservative, and, to a certain extent, they conform in order to achieve what they desire or feel they need in life.

Although it has been reported that they are environmentalists, they are less likely than baby boomers to use recycled products. This does not necessarily mean that they are not concerned about the planet; it simply means that they believe that one individual cannot make much of a difference. Nonetheless, many actually recycle glass, magazines, newspapers, and plastic. Many Generation Xers prefer smaller, fuel-efficient cars and trucks. Few prefer larger, gas-guzzling cars and trucks.

Members of this group tend to marry later. Indeed, many remain single until they reach their thirties. However, when compared with members of other groups, they tended to take on greater responsibilities during their teenage years. They also enjoy greater autonomy.

Many in this group are concerned about their personal appearance; consequently, they purchase large quantities of cosmetics and other grooming products. They also purchase more clothing than they need. However, they prefer natural fibers. For instance, females prefer cloth coats to fur, T-shirts or sweatshirts to blouses, and skirted suits to pants. Males and females prefer workout clothes to specialty clothes such as leotards and tennis outfits. Basically, they prefer comfort instead of glamour.

They enjoy traveling, especially the college-educated segment, and they use travel agents, airlines, and hotels, much like baby boomers. They travel within the United States and abroad, and no matter where they go they tend to locate individuals who are in their age groups.

Many Generation Xers have given up on Social Security, believing that it will not be available when they retire. As a result, they have opened individual retirement accounts. Many have given up on Medicare, too, believing that it will not be available when they retire. Consequently, many believe that they will have to pay for their medical coverage after they retire.

Many in this group desire to work for themselves, not for others. Many are opening their own businesses. Capitalism is popular but not that popular. They do not desire the same material goods and services as their parents and grandparents, for instance.

The members of this group do not vote in presidential elections as often as members of other groups; however, those who do usually vote for the more liberal and Democratic candidates. In 1992, they cast a higher percentage of votes for Ross Perot than any other group did.

Although they prefer designer jeans and designer athletic shoes, they do not cater to network news programs or major daily newspapers. Skepticism and disillusionment are part of their psychological makeup. However, they tend to be happier in their jobs than baby boomers. They may be cynical when it comes to government and other established institutions, but they are optimistic when it comes to their own selves. According to a survey by Yankelovich Partners, members of Generation X fall into four distinct groups based on attitudinal factors:

Yup and Comers: This group accounts for 28 percent of Generation X and has the highest levels of education and income. They focus on intangible rewards, not material wealth, and they are confident about themselves and their future.

Bystanders: Primarily female African Americans and Hispanics, this group represents 37 percent of Generation X. This group works hard, favors established brands, enjoys shopping, and desires romance.

Playboys: This mostly single, white, and male group accounts for 19 percent of Generation X. Self-absorbed, fun-loving, and impulsive, this group prefers pleasure and material goods.

Drifters: This group represents 16 percent of Generation X. This group is the least educated, and its members are frustrated with their lives. Members of this group seek security and status and choose brands that offer a sense of belonging and self-esteem.[19]

Many members of Generation X continue to receive financial help from their parents, especially for emergency situations. Many feel obligated to repay their parents for the help they have provided. Many, even those who have moved out on their own, continue to keep in contact with their parents, sisters, brothers, half sisters, half brothers, stepfathers, stepmothers, grandparents, aunts, uncles, cousins, and friends.[20]

THE BABY BOOMER MARKET Baby boomers were born between 1946 and 1964, after World War II, and include almost 78 million individuals in the United States. They account for almost 50 percent of the dollars spent each year. They have reached their forties and fifties. Many do not consider themselves as senior citizens until they have reached 60 or even 70 years of age.

Baby boomers are self-absorbed and self-assured, probably because they are better educated than their predecessors. They consider themselves to be culturally sophisticated and environmentally conscious. They desire convenience. Home delivery and take-out goods and services have been developed and marketed successfully in response to this desire. Portable items have been developed and marketed successfully as well.

Baby boomers were encouraged by their parents to get a college education and a good job. Competitiveness and individualism are more important to these people than cooperativeness. As a result, businesses have offered individual-minded baby boomers customized products and services at a reasonable price. As the baby boomers age, they will need higher priced furniture, bigger cars and trucks, investment advice, insurance advice, and wellness centers, among other products and services.

Unlike Generation Xers, baby boomers married at a younger age and often put considerable space between their spouses and their parents. Women in this group helped make certain products popular, including the so-called power suits and particular brands of cars, such as BMW.

Baby boomers are more loyal to specific brands than members of other groups. They understand success and are proud of what they have accomplished. Probably as a result of their nonconformist attitude, they are willing to take greater risks than members of other groups.

Environmentalism is important to baby boomers, especially when it comes to purchasing products and services. In fact, they prefer environmentally safe products and services and will purchase recycled products.

Baby boomers are idealistic; they tend to believe that there are easy solutions to problems. Although many have high incomes, they do not necessarily overindulge in material goods and services. Many are conservative and family oriented. They are concerned about the community in which they live. They are not as cynical as members of other groups. They enjoy reading, gardening, various crafts, and the media and are receptive to electronic innovations. Some are not necessarily interested in style or fashion. They are somewhat selfish with their time when they are away from their jobs.[21]

THE SENIOR MARKET There are more than 34 million individuals in the United States who are 65 years of age and over. They represent more than 12 percent of the country's population. This figure will increase each year. By 2030, about 70 million individuals will be 65 years of age or over.

Older male members of this group are much more likely to be married than older female members. In 1999, for instance, 77 percent of the older males were married, compared with 43 percent of the older females. Almost half (45 percent) of all older females were widows. More than half (52 percent) lived in nine states: California, Florida, New York, Texas, Pennsylvania, Ohio, Illinois, Michigan, and New Jersey. About 50 percent lived in the suburbs. Compared with other segments, the elderly are less likely to move, primarily because the majority (77 percent) owns a home mortgage free. In fact, in 1997, 37 percent of these homeowners spent more than one-fourth of their income on remodeling, compared with 30 percent of homeowners less than 65 years of age. These individuals reported a median income of $33,148 in 1999, and 46.9 percent earned more than $35,000. Only 9.7 percent were below the poverty level; many of these were living alone or with nonrelatives. Hispanic women who lived alone experienced the highest poverty rates.

The members of this segment are not sedentary. They do not necessarily stay at home. They travel. They volunteer their time and energy for worthy causes such as at low-income urban centers, where they help students who are struggling in school. They enroll in courses at community colleges, colleges, and universities. In response to their interest in learning, institutions of higher education have developed special programs for them. Those who had completed high school rose from 28 percent to 68 percent between 1970 and 1999. About 15 percent had a bachelor's degree or higher the latter year.

Some even return to work on a part-time or full-time basis, primarily because of their desire to keep active, not because they need the income. In 1999, for instance, four million were working full-time.

Although many believe that senior citizens are in poor health, are sedentary, have a difficult time thinking, and purchase products and services based on price, these are misconceptions. Marketers need to understand that members of this segment have an active lifestyle, read more than members of any other segment, and purchase products and services based on value, not just price. They readily accept change. After all, they have witnessed more change in their lifetimes than members of any other segment. They are more loyal to brands than members of other segments. Unfortunately, for years marketers have ignored this large segment or have focused exclusively on remedy-type products. Only lately have advertisers realized that this segment is active, progressive, and even desires to look appealing, especially to members of the opposite sex. In short, they are romantic. This is one reason advertisers now use attractive, middle-aged models in the advertisements targeting this market.

However, just like in the previous demographic segments, members who are considered seniors are not homogeneous—that is, they should not be stereotyped. They are different in age. In fact, the U.S. Census Bureau divides seniors into four age groups. These age groups differ considerably in terms of lifestyles, needs, and wants. For instance, some in this segment do not have color televisions or even Touch-Tone telephones, let alone cell phones. Others have color televisions, Touch-Tone telephones, and cell phones. Many have computers and surf the Internet. Indeed, this segment spends more time at the computer than any other segment, regardless of age.

Today, some marketers have segmented the senior market by putting its members into one of three categories, depending on their age: young-old (65–74), old (75–84), and old-old (85 and older). Of course, other marketers use other means to segment this group.[22]

As you can determine, copywriters have their hands full when trying to write advertisements for these different groups. However, the task may not be as difficult as you might think. For instance, if a copywriter is writing an advertisement about life insurance, the copywriter does not necessarily desire to attract young people. Consequently, a word or phrase in the headline may identify the target market desired, such as "Retired?" or "Are You 55 Years of Age or Older?" Or the visual could be a photograph of a senior male, female, or couple.

Psychographic Segmentation

Demographic factors are not usually enough for marketers to identify a market. Psychographic factors are also considered. Generally, psychographics include consumers' activities, interests, and opinions (AIO), and these AIO items are used to construct a consumer psychographic profile. Usually, marketing research firms are hired by clients to conduct psychographic studies that have been tailored to the clients' product categories. However, several firms have developed psychographic profiles of individuals that are not necessarily related to any product or service category. For instance, the Stanford Research Institute, or SRI, Consulting Business Intelligence developed the "VALS: Values and Lifestyles Psychographic Segmentation" system, which was revised in 1989 to VALS 2. Today, it is known as VALS. VALS typology claims that consumer behavior is motivated by three self-orientations: principle, status, and action. According to SRI, "Principle-oriented consumers are guided in their choices by abstract, idealized criteria, rather than by feelings, events, or desire for approval and opinions of others. Status-oriented consumers look for products and services that demonstrate success to their peers. Action-oriented consumers are guided by a desire for social or physical activity, variety, and risk taking."[23]

VALS also segments by resources, which refer to psychological, physical, demographic, and material means that are available to consumers. The resources continuum (minimal at the bottom to abundant at the top) encompasses education, income, self-confidence, health, eagerness to buy, intelligence, and energy level. As figure 1.1 shows, there are eight segments:

Actualizers: These people are successful, sophisticated, and active. They have high self-esteem and numerous resources. They seek to develop, explore, and grow. They desire to express themselves in a variety of ways. Image is important as an expression of independence and character. They do not necessarily conform to principle-, status-, or action-oriented behavior. They appreciate the finer things in life.

Fulfilleds: These people are mature, comfortable, and reflective. They value knowledge, order, and responsibility. Most are well educated and work in professional fields. They base their decisions on principles. They are self-assured. They take personal risks but are averse to societal risks. They are content with their careers and family and are open-minded to new ideas. They are conservative consumers, looking for durability and value in the products they purchase.

Believers: These people are conventional and conservative. They believe in family, community, the nation, and the church. They favor domestic products and well-known brands. They have a modest education and income, but both are sufficient to meet their needs. They have regular routines.

Achievers: These people are successful in their careers. They are also in control of their lives and are committed to their families. They value structure and stability and enjoy their jobs. Their lives are conventional, and they respect the status quo primarily because they are conservative. They favor major brand products and services that will illustrate their success.

Strivers: These people desire approval from those around them. They have fewer economic, social, and psychological resources. They understand that money signifies success. They try to emulate those who have more, and what they wish for is usually out of their reach. They are impulsive and unsure of themselves. Many desire to be stylish.

Experiencers: These people are young, impulsive, enthusiastic, and even rebellious. Action-oriented individuals who enjoy affecting their environment, these individuals seek excitement. They enjoy shopping for clothing, music, movies, and fast food. They enjoy exercise, sports, and social activities. They are uninformed and politically uncommitted.

Makers: These people are practical and value self-sufficiency and family. They enjoy working on houses, raising children, and repairing cars. They purchase products that have a practical or functional purpose such as fishing equipment, trucks, and tools. They are conservative and respect governmental authority, although they resent government intrusion on individual rights.

Strugglers: These people have limited economic, social, and psychological resources and suffer from poor health. They believe that the world is difficult. They do not think about the future; rather, they focus on the present. They are cautious when it comes to purchasing goods and services. They are concerned about feeling safe and secure.[24]

Marketers can use VALS to market their products and services. Advertising copywriters can use VALS, too, in identifying segments within the overall market.

Another system is Yankelovich Partners' MONITOR MindBase, which helps clients target specific consumers. In the MONITOR MindBase, eight major groups of consumers have been identified by their attitudes and motivations:

Up and Comers: This group accounts for 16 percent of the population in the United States. These individuals are young singles and couples without children. They are self-focused and enjoy adventure. They are socially conscious. They enjoy technology, especially computers and the Internet. They are open to new ideas and are positive about the world. They are creative and self-confident. They are not concerned about the latest trends or fashions. They enjoy cultural events, camping, hiking, shopping, sports, and watching television. They are not concerned about their financial future. They are concerned about their health. They tend to be single nonparent Generation Xers.

Aspiring Achievers: This group accounts for 8 percent of the population in the United States. This group is concerned about financial success. These individuals are cynical and socially concerned about the world. They are self-focused, and style is important. They purchase brands that reflect success. They are adventurous, but they are not practical. They tend to be religious and family oriented. They enjoy shopping and sports. They do not enjoy cooking, gardening, reading, or watching television. They are not necessarily concerned about their physical health or their financial future. They are not necessarily concerned about being in debt. They are not conservative when they invest. Although they accept technology, they feel stressed by it. They tend to be single nonparent Generation Xers.

Realists: This group represents 12 percent of the population in the United States. They enjoy excitement but worry about their lives. They desire more time and less stress. They are overwhelmed by the technology and information that are available to them. Many do not own computers, even though many use computers at their jobs. They tend to be optimistic about the world. They desire personal and spiritual health. They play games, read books about parenting, watch movies, and spend time with friends. They are not socially conscious. They enjoy shopping, even though they have low incomes and are in debt. They do not try to live within their financial means. They are concerned about the latest trends and fashions. They tend to be ethnically diverse parents of children under 18 years of age.

New Traditionalists: This group represents 14 percent of the population in the United States. This group is family oriented. They create positive environments for their children. Success equals a solid marriage and healthy children. They are socially conscious and very religious. They appreciate technology and are optimistic about the world. They are open to new ideas. They are ambitious. They enjoy cooking, decorating, gardening, playing games, reading, and watching television. They enjoy their computers. They enjoy shopping, especially for new products and services discussed in *Consumer Reports*. They manage their finances and are planning for their retirements. They desire to live within their financial means. They tend

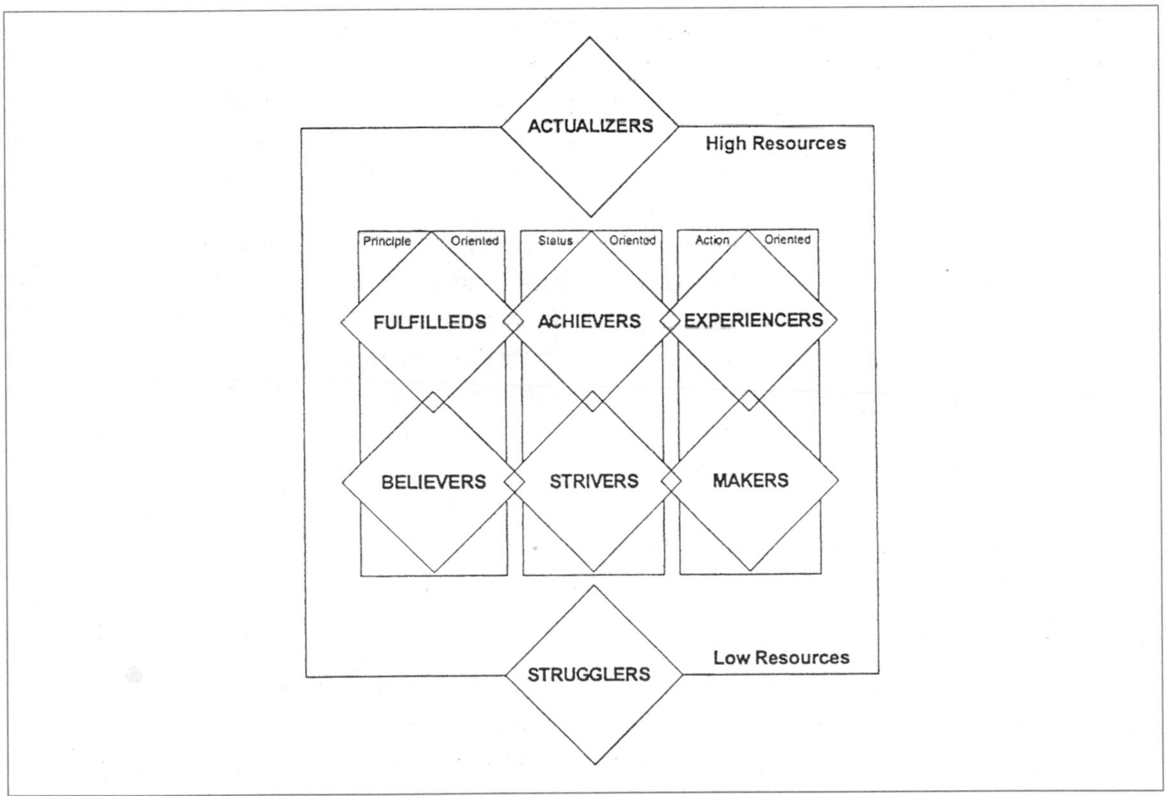

FIGURE 1.1 VALS Typology. *Courtesy of SRI Consulting Business Intelligence.*

to be married baby boomers with children under 18 years of age. They are well educated and have good incomes. They are not necessarily interested in acquiring material goods.

Family Centereds: This group accounts for 14 percent of the population in the United States. They focus on their families, not on themselves or their friends. They do not devote a lot of time to socially conscious activities. They are somewhat cynical about the world. They respect businesses that are honest and ethical. They enjoy family-type activities such as sports. They are not concerned about the latest fashions and trends. They are not concerned about cultural activities, movies, shopping, or traveling. They are concerned about their debt and financial affairs. They do not enjoy investing in bonds or stocks. They view technology as a means to accomplishment. They tend to be baby boomer parents.

Individualists: The members of this group are dedicated to their jobs. They are not necessarily concerned about family or society. They do not desire adventure or excitement. They enjoy listening to classical music, reading, and taking a brief trip. They consider themselves to be individualists. They are receptive to technology and enjoy the Internet. They have average incomes, and they enjoy investing and saving for their futures. They have little debt. They do not focus on their health. They do not have much stress. They have the highest educations of any MindBase segment. They tend to be single baby boomers. Half of the members in this group are parents, but none of them have children under 18 years of age.

Renaissance Masters: This group accounts for 13 percent of the population in the United States. They are family and socially oriented. They are concerned about the environment, older people, and privacy. They view themselves as practical and responsible. They are religious and attend church. They enjoy antiquing, cooking, decorating, gardening, reading, and watching television. They are concerned about their health in the future. They eat well and watch their weight. They try alternative therapies. They enjoy learning about style and fashion from reading magazines and newspapers. Many own businesses and have substantial incomes. They enjoy managing their money and investing it for their futures. They try to live within their financial means. They tend to be active older married individuals with grown independent children.

Maintainers: This group represents 17 percent of the population in the United States. They tend to be traditional and content. They view themselves as neighborly, old-fashioned, personal, and sincere. They do not seek adventure. They are not concerned with the latest styles or material goods. They enjoy their homes. They enjoy working in the garden or yard. They keep current by reading newspapers or watching television news programs. They are conservative about their money and live within their means. They are not interested in technology—to them it is inhuman. They tend to be older adults with a cynical view of the world. Many are parents and grandparents.

These major consumer groups have been separated into 32 distinct segments. Some have more segments than others.[25]

Geodemographic Segmentation

Geodemographics, a conjunction of geography and demography or demographics, is based on the notion that people who live in similar neighborhoods or even postal ZIP-code zones are inclined to have similar demographics, attitudes, interests, and opinions. In short, they will have similar lifestyles and consumption patterns.

Several marketing research firms have developed geodemographic market clusters for the country's 250,000-plus neighborhoods. Specifically, these clusters represent people who have similar demographics and lifestyles. For instance, in the early 1970s Claritas created PRIZM, which is one of the most widely used lifestyle segmentation systems in the United States. Based on the adage "Birds of a feather flock together," PRIZM applies this notion by assigning every neighborhood in the country to one of 62 clusters. Each cluster describes the demographics and lifestyles of the people living in that neighborhood.[26]

Other Forms of Segmentation

In addition to demographic, psychographic, and geodemographic segmentation, marketers have identified markets by geography, by sociology and culture, by product usage, and even by the product or service's benefits to consumers. No matter which is used to identify segments, however, advertising copywriters must be informed; otherwise, what they write will not necessarily reflect the segment's interests or beliefs. Consequently, the advertisements will not be effective.

MOTIVATING CONSUMERS

Advertising copywriters must understand that every individual has needs. According to Dr. Abraham Maslow, a psychologist, individuals have basic needs in the order listed in box 1.1. Maslow claimed that most normal individuals are partially satisfied and unsatisfied in all their basic needs. In other words, it is difficult for one to satisfy every need, especially as one moves from the first to the fifth level. In fact, many individuals have trouble feeling secure, loved, appreciated, and fulfilled. Some have trouble feeling nourished. Maslow claimed that any given behavior tends to be determined by several or all of the basic needs simultaneously rather than by only one.[27]

BOX 1.1 *Maslow's Hierarchy of Needs*

1. Physiological or Basic Needs
- Food
- Shelter
- Drink
- Sex

2. Security Needs
- Self
- Family
- Society

3. Belongingness or Social Needs
- Position in society
- Position in group
- Love/affection

4. Esteem (Ego) Needs
- From self (strength, achievement, adequacy, mastery, competence, confidence, independence, freedom)
- From others (reputation, dominance, recognition, attention, importance, appreciation)

5. Self-actualization
- Self-fulfillment

Adapted from Abraham H. Maslow, "A Theory of Human Motivation," *Psychological Review*, Vol. 50 (1943): pp. 370–396; Abraham H. Maslow, "'Higher' and 'Lower' Needs," *Journal of Psychology*, Vol. 25 (1948): pp. 433–436; and Abraham H. Maslow, *Motivation and Personality* (New York: Harper and Row, 1954).

TABLE 1.7 *Behavioral Dimensions Model*

RELATED BEHAVIORAL DIMENSIONS	MOVEMENT TOWARD PURCHASE	RELEVANT EXAMPLES OF PROMOTION OR ADVERTISING TYPES
• Conative • The realm of motives • Ads stimulate or direct desires	• PURCHASE	• Point of purchase • Retail store ads • Deals • "Last-chance" offers • Price appeals • Testimonials
• Affective • The realm of emotions • Ads change attitudes and feelings	• CONVICTION • PREFERENCE	• Competitive ads • Argumentative copy • "Image" ads • Status, glamorous appeals
• Cognitive • The realm of thoughts • Ads provide information and facts	• LIKING • KNOWLEDGE	• Announcements • Descriptive copy • Classified ads • Slogans • Jingles • Sky writing • Teaser campaigns
	• AWARENESS	

Source: Robert J. Lavidge and Gary A. Steiner, "A Model for Predictive Measurements of Advertising Effectiveness," *Journal of Marketing*, Vol. 25, No. 6 (October 1961). © 1961 by the American Marketing Association, Chicago. Reprinted by permission.

Advertising copywriters must be able to recognize one or more needs that consumers in a particular segment have and, if possible, develop messages that address these needs. This may not be an easy task, especially if the client's marketing plan is not available or if the advertising agency has not developed an advertising plan or integrated marketing communications plan.

Although trying to fill one or more needs may motivate individuals into behavior of some kind, there are other factors that influence behavior, including *perception* and *learning*. Basically, *perception is the process by which one assigns meaning to information*. Usually, the meaning assigned will be based on sensory impressions and experience. Because of the amount of stimuli that one views, reads, and hears in a typical day, advertisers have a difficult time getting attention. In addition, individuals use selective exposure—that is, they choose which messages to view, read, hear, or remember. Unfortunately, most do not wish to view, read, hear, or remember advertisements.

Learning is related to perception. Consumers cannot learn unless they have perceived stimuli and assigned meaning to it. Basically, *learning causes changes in one's physical and mental behavior*. Advertisers attempt to change consumers' behavior by informing them and persuading them to purchase products or services.

Hierarchy-of-Effects Models

Advertising copywriters are asked to develop commercial messages that have an effect on consumers. These messages should persuade consumers to think favorably about a brand or preferably purchase a brand.

Over the years several persuasive communication models have been used in advertising. Russell Colley presented one model in the 1960s in his book *Defining Advertising Goals for Measured Advertising Results*. Practitioners familiar with the book use the acronym DAGMAR. Basically, *DAGMAR suggests that consumers climb a mental ladder before they purchase products or services: unawareness, awareness, comprehension/image, conviction or attitude, and action*. Whatever advertisers do to promote their products or services helps move consumers up the ladder toward "action."[28]

A second model was developed by Robert Lavidge and Gary Steiner and includes six levels. These levels are divided into the three components that make up one's attitudes. The first level consists of "Awareness" and "Knowledge"; these are comparable to the "Cognitive" or "Knowledge" component of one's attitudes. The second level consists of "Liking" and "Preference"; these are comparable to the "Affective" component of one's attitudes. The third level consists of "Conviction" and "Purchase"; these are comparable to the "Conative" component of one's attitudes. (See table 1.7.)

The model seems to be linear, but consumers do not necessarily make decisions in this order. Usually, which decision they make first, second, third, and so on depends on the product or level of involvement. For instance, a consumer may actually skip "Awareness" and "Knowledge" when purchasing a soft drink or some other convenience product. We focus on copy research and the creative strategy in the next chapter.

EXERCISES

1. Use the Internet to look up the following: U.S. Census Bureau, Yankelovich Partners (MONITOR MindBase), Stanford Research Institute Consulting Business Intelligence (VALS), and Claritas (PRIZM).
2. Use the Internet to look up "advertising plan" and "marketing plan."

NOTES

1. William A. Cohen, *The Marketing Plan*, 3d ed. (New York: John Wiley and Sons, Inc., 2001), p. 8. See also O. C. Ferrell, Michael Hartline, and George Lucas, "Marketing Plan Worksheet," in *Marketing Strategy*, 2d ed. (Cincinnati, OH: South-Western Publishing, 2002).
2. William F. Arens, "Advertising Plan Outline," in *Contemporary Advertising*, 8th ed. (New York: McGraw-Hill/Irwin, 2002), Appendix B. Also Donald Parente, "Exhibit 1-2: An Outline for a Marketing Communication Plan," in *Advertising Campaign Strategy: A Guide to Marketing Communication Plans*, 2d ed. (Orlando, FL: Harcourt, Inc., 2000), p. 21.
3. Alison Stein Wellner, "The Census Report," *American Demographics*, Vol. 24, No. 1 (January 2002), p. S4.
4. Jeffrey M. Humphreys, "African-American Buying Power by Place of Residence: 1990–1999," available at www.selig.uga.edu/forecast/totalbuy/afr-amerBlack%20Buying%201999%20text.html. Also U.S. Census Bureau, "DP-1. Profile of General Demographic Characteristics: 2000" (Washington, DC: U.S. Census Bureau, 2000).
5. Jeffrey M. Humphreys, "Asian-American Buying Power by Place of Residence: 1990–1999," *Georgia Business and Economic Conditions*, Vol. 59, No. 1 (January–February 1999), pp. 1–7. Also U.S. Census Bureau, "DP-1."
6. Jeffrey M. Humphreys, "Hispanic Buying Power by Place of Residence: 1990–1999," *Georgia Business and Economic*

Conditions, Vol. 58, No. 6 (November–December 1998), pp. 1–8. Also Wellner, "The Census Report," p. S5; U.S. Census Bureau, "DP-1."

7. U.S. Census Bureau, "DP-1."
8. U.S. Census Bureau, "DP-1."
9. U.S. Census Bureau, "DP-1."
10. U.S. Census Bureau, "DP-1."
11. U.S. Census Bureau, "DP-1."
12. U.S. Census Bureau, "DP-1."
13. U.S. Census Bureau, "DP-1."
14. U.S. Census Bureau, "QT-03. Profile of Selected Economic Characteristics: 2000" (Washington, DC: U.S. Census Bureau, 2000).
15. U.S. Census Bureau, "QT-03."
16. U.S. Census Bureau, "QT-02. Profile of Selected Social Characteristics: 2000" (Washington, DC: U.S. Census Bureau, 2000).
17. U.S. Census Bureau, "QT-02."
18. See "To Arms, to Arms, Generation Y Is Advancing on the Aftermarket," *Aftermarket Business*, July 1999; Alf Nucifora, "Pay Attention: Generation Y Is Looming," *Business Journal*, May 19, 2000; "Generation Y Challenges Retailers," *USA Today*, December 2000; Ken Gronback, "Marketing to Generation Y," *DSN Retailing Today*, July 24, 2000; Haidee E. Allerton, "Generation Why: They Promise to Be the Biggest Influence Since the Baby Boomers," *Training and Development*, November 2001.
19. Karen Benezra, "Don't Mislabel Gen X," *Brandweek*, Vol. 36, No. 20 (May 15, 1995), p. 32.
20. See Margot Hornblower, "Great Xpectations: Slackers? Hardly. The So-called Generation X Turns Out to Be Full of Go-getters Who Are Just Doing It—But Their Way," *Time*, Vol. 149, No. 23 (June 9, 1997), pp. 58–63, 66–68; Karen Ritchie, "Why Gen X Buys Brand X," *Brandweek*, Vol. 36, No. 20 (May 15, 1995), pp. 22–23, 26–27, 29, 31; Lori Tieszen, "The X Market," *Beverage World*, Vol. 115, No. 1630 (December 15, 1996), pp. 98–100; Karen Ritchie, "Marketing to Generation X," *American Demographics*, Vol. 17, No. 4 (April 1995), pp. 34–39.
21. See Hornblower, "Great Xpectations"; Ritchie, "Why Gen X Buys Brand X"; Ritchie, "Marketing to Generation X."
22. See U.S. Department of Health and Human Services, "A Profile of Older Americans: 2000" (Washington, DC: U.S. Department of Health and Human Services, 2000), pp. 1–13; Rebecca Gardyn, "Retirement Redefined," *American Demographics*, Vol. 22, No. 11 (November 2000), pp. 52, 54–57.
23. SRI Consulting Business Intelligence, "The VALS Segment Profiles" (333 Ravenswood Avenue, Menlo Park, CA).
24. See SRI Consulting Business Intelligence, "The VALS Segment Profiles."
25. Yankelovich Partners, "Yankelovich MONITOR MindBase" (200 West Franklin Street, Chapel Hill, NC).
26. Claritas Inc., "PRIZM," 2001, available at www.claritas.com.
27. Abraham H. Maslow, "A Theory of Human Motivation," *Psychological Review*, Vol. 50 (1943), pp. 370–396; Abraham H. Maslow, "'Higher' and 'Lower' Needs," *Journal of Psychology*, Vol. 25 (1948), pp. 433–436; Abraham H. Maslow, *Motivation and Personality* (New York: Harper and Row, 1954.).
28. Russell H. Colley, *Defining Advertising Goals for Measured Advertising Results* (New York: Association of National Advertisers, 1961).

CHAPTER 2

Creative Strategy

In this chapter I discuss topics that relate to the creative strategy and then present an example of a creative strategy. Finally, we examine the "big idea."

CREATIVE STRATEGY RESEARCH

If the client's marketing plan is not available or if it does not contain enough information about the product or service, the consumer or target market, the media that has been used or should be used, or the purpose of the advertising, then advertising personnel will have to research these and other topics before they attempt to develop a creative strategy and advertising for the client. Otherwise, the advertising copywriter will not know enough about the above to write advertisements that are effective.

This research is usually termed *secondary* and *primary*. *Secondary research is perusing sources that are readily available in publications, on CD-ROM, or on the World Wide Web. Primary research is conducted either by advertising personnel or a specialty firm and usually includes survey questionnaires, personal interviews, focus group sessions, and so on.* Advertising personnel should not do any primary research until secondary research has been conducted, primarily because in many instances answers to questions or needed information can be found in secondary sources. Also, conducting primary research may be more expensive and time consuming than conducting secondary research. (In most instances, primary research will not be performed unless the client agrees to pay for it.) Of course, secondary research sources must be available and relevant to the research task at hand. In addition, these sources must be accurate and current.

A sound creative strategy should address the following: primary and secondary target markets (consumers), product or service, distinctive product feature and benefit (key selling point), competing product(s)/brand(s), advertising problem(s), advertising objective(s), unique selling proposition or positioning (if applicable), and the creative tactics such as the advertising concept or theme and supporting selling points. Information for these topics may be combined and put under one heading, as the sample creative strategy on p. 34 illustrates.

Secondary Research about Consumers

FROM ACADEMIC JOURNALS For information about consumers, peer-reviewed scholarly journals may be examined. Such journals include the following:

- *Advances in Consumer Research*
- *Journal of Advertising*
- *Journal of Advertising Research*
- *Journal of Consumer Affairs*
- *Journal of Consumer Marketing*
- *Journal of Consumer Psychology*
- *Journal of Consumer Research*
- *Journal of Direct Marketing*
- *Journal of Public Policy and Marketing*
- *Psychology and Marketing*
- *Public Opinion*
- *Public Opinion Quarterly*

Of course, there are other peer-reviewed scholarly journals that may be useful. Some of these may be on the World Wide Web. Most are available in college and university libraries.

FROM BOOKS There are several books that provide information about consumers:

- *Lifestyle Market Analyst: A Reference Guide for Consumer Market Analysis* (published annually)
- *Lifestyle Market Segmentation*, by Ronald D. Michman (1991)
- *The Official Guide to Household Spending: The Number One Guide to Who Spends How Much on What* (published biennially—every two years)
- *The Sourcebook of ZIP Code Demographics* (published annually)
- *Why We Buy: The Science of Shopping*, by Paco Underhill (1999, 2000)

There may be others; check *Books in Print* for possible titles.

FROM THE FEDERAL GOVERNMENT The various branches of the federal government publish numerous volumes and put much, if not all, of this information on the World Wide Web. One of these reports is *Economic Indicators*, a publication from the Council of Economic Advisers, which contains data about personal consumption as well as economic trends.

The federal government, through the U.S. Bureau of the Census, publishes the most accurate and current information about the country's population. This information is available in the annual *Statistical Abstract of the United States* as well as on the World Wide Web.

The U.S. Bureau of Labor Statistics provides information based on the Consumer Expenditures Survey, which is conducted by the U.S. Bureau of the Census. The Consumer Expenditures Survey provides information about consumers and the products and services they purchase. Much of this data can be obtained in published reports or on the World Wide Web. For other reports published by the federal government, see the *Catalog of Public Documents*, the *Monthly Catalog of United States Government Publications*, or the *Subject Guide to Major United States Government Publications*.

FROM MAGAZINES Similar information can be found in magazines. These include the following:

- *American Demographics*
- *Business Week*
- *Forbes*
- *Fortune*
- *Time*
- *U.S. News & World Report*
- *Newsweek*

- *Sales and Marketing Management* (S&MM—this publication includes the "Survey of Buying Power," in at least one of its monthly issues. The survey provides statistics on the United States, individual states, metropolitan statistical areas, counties, and cities. S&MM also publishes the "Survey of Media Markets," which offers statistics on geographical areas.)

There may be other magazines, but the above should be examined before others are searched.

FROM NEWSPAPERS Similar information can be found in major newspapers such as the *New York Times* and the *Wall Street Journal*.

FROM RESEARCH FIRMS Simmons Market Research Bureau and Mediamark Research Inc. gather in-depth information about consumers and what they purchase. This information is presented either on CD-ROM or in volumes. Information Resources Incorporated publishes reports that provide thorough information about consumer expenditures and brand sales based on audits. There are, of course, other research firms that gather and publish similar information.

FROM SURVEYS There are research firms that learn about consumers' lifestyles. The Roper Center for Public Opinion Research offers various reports, and Yankelovich Partners provides the Yankelovich *Monitor*. Both make available valuable information. Roper ASW provides articles about consumers based on surveys. These articles are insightful.

The National Opinion Research Center, University of Chicago, offers the annual "General Social Survey." The Survey Research Center of the Institute for Social Research, University of Michigan, offers several annual surveys, including the "Surveys of Consumers." The Gallup Organization offers the "Gallup Poll Analyses," which concern all kinds of information based on various surveys.

FROM THE WORLD WIDE WEB LEXIS-NEXIS provides abundant information about consumers and other topics. Of course, there are other databases and search engines that can be used.

Secondary Research about Businesses, Products, and Services

FROM ACADEMIC JOURNALS For information about businesses, products, and services, peer-reviewed scholarly journals may be examined. These include the following:

- *Journal of Business*
- *Journal of Business Research*
- *Journal of Marketing*
- *Journal of Marketing Research*

Of course, those listed earlier as well as other scholarly journals may have articles that are relevant.

FROM BROKERAGE REPORTS AND BOOKS Information about specific companies, products, and services can be found in in-depth reports such as *The Wall Street Transcript*, which provides information about several hundred companies. Other sources include Moody's (now Mergent) manuals and Standard and Poor's data. Mergent publishes numerous volumes that contain financial and other information for thousands of companies and government bodies. Each manual is published annually; updates are available almost every week. Some include:

- *Moody's Bank and Finance Manual*
- *Moody's Industrial Manual*
- *Moody's Municipal and Government Manual*
- *Moody's Transportation Manual*
- *Moody's Public Utility Manual*

Standard and Poor's provides financial information on thousands of publicly owned companies. Each volume is published annually. Some Standard and Poor's volumes include the following:

- Standard & Poor's Corporation Records
- Standard & Poor's Industry Surveys
- Standard & Poor's Stock Reports: American Stock Exchange
- Standard & Poor's Stock Reports: New York Stock Exchange

Another valuable resource is *Market Share Reporter*, which contains information about several thousand product and service categories.

FROM COMPANIES Information about companies, products, and services can be found in annual reports, catalogs, house organs, informational brochures or pamphlets, press kits or releases, sales presentation material, sales reports, technical papers or reports, and on websites.

FROM THE FEDERAL GOVERNMENT The federal government publishes numerous volumes that contain information about businesses, products, and services as well as the economy. Two of these include:

- *Business Conditions Digest*, a monthly publication from the U.S. Department of Commerce, concerning business trends; and
- *Survey of Current Business*, a monthly publication from the U.S. Bureau of Economic Analysis, concerning the country's output and wealth.

Additional information from the federal government can be found at STAT-USA Internet (www.stat-usa.gov). Of course, there are other federal government websites, but this one provides useful information about business and the economy. In addition to the above, the federal government publishes information about the wholesale, retail, and service industries:

- *Census of Wholesale Trade* provides sales, expenses, and other information about the wholesale industry.
- *Monthly Wholesale Trade: Sales and Inventories* provides current data for the wholesale industry.
- *Census of the Retail Trade* provides sales, payroll, and other information about the retail industry.
- *Monthly Retail Sales and Inventories* provides current data for the retail industry.
- *Census of Service Industries* provides sales, payroll, and other information about retail service companies.
- *Monthly Selected Services Receipts* and *Service Annual Survey* provide current data for service providers.

FROM MAGAZINES Information about businesses, products, and services can be found in magazines such as the following:

- *Barron's*
- *Business Week*
- *Forbes*
- *Fortune*
- *Harvard Business Review*
- *Mediaweek*

There may be other magazines that contain articles about companies, products, and services. Check the directories that were mentioned earlier in the chapter for additional titles.

FROM NEWSPAPERS Similar information can be found in newspapers such as the *New York Times* and the *Wall Street Journal*, as well as *Investor's Business Daily*.

FROM TRADE ASSOCIATIONS Trade associations are voluntary organizations; members work in the same type of business or industry. Usually, trade associations conduct research about their respective types of businesses or industries. Various trade associations can be found in the *Encyclopedia of Associations*, the *Directory of National Trade Associations*, and the *National Trade and Professional Associations of the United States*.

FROM TRADE PUBLICATIONS Information about specific companies, products, and services can be found in trade publications. There are trade publications for practically every type of business or industry. These publications can be found in *The Standard Periodical Directory*, *Ulrich's International Periodicals Directory*, and the *Business Publication Advertising Source*.

Secondary Research about Advertising and Marketing

FROM ACADEMIC JOURNALS Information about advertising and marketing (objectives, creative concepts, creative strategies, creative tactics, etc.) can be found in peer-reviewed scholarly journals such as the following:

- *Advances in Consumer Research*
- *Journal of Advertising*
- *Journal of Advertising Research*
- *Journal of Business and Industrial Marketing*
- *Journal of Consumer Research*
- *Journal of Direct Marketing*
- *Journal of Marketing*
- *Journal of Marketing Communications*
- *Journal of Marketing Research*
- *Journal of Professional Services Marketing*
- *Journal of Retailing*
- *Journal of Services Marketing*

There may be others such as those that deal with global or international advertising or marketing, but the above should be examined first. Some of the above may be on the World Wide Web. Most are available in college and university libraries.

FROM BOOKS In addition to textbooks about advertising and marketing, there are trade and reference books about these subjects. Some of these include the following:

- *Butterfly Customer: Capturing the Loyalty of Today's Elusive Consumer*, by Susan M. O'Dell and Joan A. Pajunen (1997, 2000)
- *Differentiate or Die: Survival in Our Era of Killer Competition*, by Jack Trout with Steve Rivkin (2000)
- *Environmental Marketing: Positive Strategies for Reaching the Green Consumer*, by Walter Coddington (1993)
- *Marketing to Generation X*, by Karen Ritchie (1995)
- *Marketing to the Mind: Right Brain Strategies for Advertising and Marketing*, by Richard C. Maddock and Richard L. Fulton (1996)

- *Multicultural Marketing: Selling to a Diverse America*, by Marlene L. Rossman (1994)
- *Rocking the Ages: The Yankelovich Report on Generational Marketing*, by J. Walker Smith and Ann Clurman (1998)
- *Segmenting the Mature Market: Identifying, Targeting and Reaching America's Diverse Booming Senior Markets*, by Carol M. Morgan and Doran J. Levy (1993, 1996)
- *Segmenting the Women's Market: Using Niche Marketing to Understand and Meet the Diverse Needs of Today's Most Dynamic Consumer Market*, by Janice E. Leeming and Cynthia F. Tripp (1994)
- *Target Marketing: Researching, Reaching, and Retaining Your Target Market*, by Linda Pinson and Jerry Jinnet (1996)
- *Targeting Families: Marketing to and through the New Family Structure*, by Robert Boutilier (1993)
- Check *Books in Print* for additional books about advertising and marketing.

FROM MAGAZINES Information about advertising and marketing may be found in the following magazines:

- *Business Week*
- *Forbes*
- *Fortune*
- *Harvard Business Review*
- *Mediaweek*
- *Potentials*
- *Sales and Marketing Management*

Check the directories for more titles that may contain articles about these topics.

FROM REPORTS The publisher of *Adweek* publishes the *Adweek Client/Brand Directory*, which presents expenditures for advertising thousands of brands. The Arbitron Company and Radio's All-Dimension Audience Research provide information about radio ratings. And Jupiter Media Metrix provides information about businesses and the Internet.

Leading National Advertisers, Inc., publishes quarterly and annual reports about advertising expenditures. For instance, the *Company/Brand $* presents advertising expenditures by company and brand. The *Class/Brand QTR $* presents expenditures by industry, company, and brand. The *Class/Brand Year-to-Date* reports current expenditures by industry, company, and brand. The *Ad $ Summary* summarizes expenditures for advertising brands.

Nielsen Media Research provides information about television ratings. Roper Starch Worldwide offers reports about readers of advertisements that have appeared in specific magazines. And Standard Rate and Data Service (SRDS) provides current advertising rates for various media, including magazines and newspapers, in several volumes. SRDS also publishes a number of volumes that concern nontraditional media such as direct mail and out-of-home varieties. Usually, these volumes can be found in college and university libraries.

FROM TRADE PUBLICATIONS Information about advertising and marketing can be found in trade publications such as the following:

- *Advertising Age*
- *Adweek*
- *Brandweek*
- *Mediaweek*
- *Marketing News*

There may be others that contain articles about advertising and marketing. Check the directories mentioned earlier in this chapter for other titles.

FROM THE WORLD WIDE WEB "Adnews On-line Daily" provides advertising and marketing information, and "Adtrack" presents advertisements of a quarter page or larger from more than 100 business and consumer magazines. The Department of Advertising at the University of Texas in Austin has "Advertising World: The Ultimate Marketing Communications Directory" (http://advertising.utexas.edu/world) available on the World Wide Web. This directory contains numerous subjects.

The Department of Communication Studies at the University of Iowa lists resources in advertising that are available online. The website is www.uiowa.edu/~commstud/resources/advertising.html. The John W. Hartman Center for Sales, Advertising and Marketing History at Duke University provides "Ad Access" (http://scriptorium.lib.duke.edu/adaccess), which features over 7,000 ads dating between 1911 and 1955.

Abundant information about advertising and marketing can be found at LEXIS-NEXIS as well as on other search engines. In addition, college and university libraries have indexes such as the *Business Periodicals Index* as well as computer databases that list articles in periodicals.

Primary Research

Primary research may be *qualitative* or *quantitative*, depending on the type of information needed.

QUALITATIVE RESEARCH Qualitative research is appropriate when in-depth information about consumers cannot be found. Qualitative research includes focus group sessions and personal interviews.

Focus group sessions usually are made up of a skilled moderator and from 8 to 12 individuals who represent the intended target market. The moderator has certain topics that he or she wishes for the participants to discuss. These topics may concern an evaluation of creative executions (advertisements); an evaluation of the product's packaging; the perception of the product or service; the positioning of the product or service; and the participants' attitudes, beliefs, motivations, needs, and wants.

Personal interviews (one-on-one or depth interviews) are structured conversations between a skilled interviewer and a respondent. Primarily because of the time involved, the number of individuals interviewed will be low, usually about 10. Therefore, it is crucial that these respondents or sample represent the intended target market. Although both forms of qualitative research can provide useful information, focus group sessions usually provide more information about individuals than personal interviews, primarily because of the individuals' interaction.

QUANTITATIVE RESEARCH Quantitative research provides statistical information such as averages and percentages that represent a population even though only a sample of the population has been used. Quantitative research includes observation research, in which people's behavior is recorded; physiological research, in which a person's response to a stimulus is recorded; and survey research, in which individuals respond to questionnaires. The latter is the most popular form of quantitative research.

Observation research may be natural (real world) or contrived (artificial), depending on the observer's level of participation in monitoring people's behavior. Physiological research includes brain pattern analysis, eye movement analysis, galvanic skin response analysis, and voice pitch analysis. Survey research includes Internet surveys, mail surveys, personal interviews, and telephone surveys. Each type of survey has advantages and disadvantages, such as accuracy, cost, time required, number of questions, and response rates. These advantages and disadvantages as well as the characteristics of the sample should be considered when deciding on which type to use.

THE CREATIVE STRATEGY

Once information about the company, the product, the competition, the consumer, and the advertising has been gathered, answers to the following questions will guide the eventual development of the creative strategy and consequently the advertising.

Questions about the Company

1. What is the company's name?
2. Where is the company located?
3. What is the company's history?
4. Is the company financially sound?

Other questions may come to mind when you study the information about the company.

Questions about the Product

1. What is the product's brand name?
2. What is the product's history?
3. How is the product manufactured?
4. Is the product manufactured well?
5. What are the product's components? What are the product's most significant features?
6. How is the product designed?
7. What are the product's shape and size?
8. How many models and colors of the product are available?
9. What options can be added to the product?
10. How is the product packaged?
11. Does the product operate well?
12. Has the product earned any awards?
13. Does the product come with a warranty or guarantee?
14. How is the product distributed? To wholesalers? To retailers? To consumers?
15. Where is the product purchased? What type of store?
16. How much does the product cost?
17. Is the product's price competitive?
18. When and how often is the product purchased?
19. Where and how often is the product used?
20. What does the product do for the consumer? What are the product's benefits?

21. Is the product in the introduction, growth, maturity, or decline stage of the life cycle?
22. How does the product compare with its competition?
23. Is the product the leading selling brand?
24. What unique feature does the product have that its competition does not?

Other questions may come to mind when you are studying the information about the product or examining the product itself.

Questions about the Competition

1. What companies are considered the competition?
2. What products (brands) do these companies manufacture?
3. Which of these products compete directly with the client's product?
4. Are any of these products the leading selling product (brand)?
5. Which of these products (brands) follow the leading selling product (brand)?
6. Do these products have significant features that are different from the client's product? If so, what are these significant features?
7. Do these products cost about the same as the client's product? Less? More?

There may be other questions that come to mind when you study the information about the competition.

Questions about the Consumer

1. What type of consumer purchases the product?
2. When does the consumer purchase the product? For instance, is the product purchased during a specific season?
3. Where does the consumer purchase the product?
4. Why does the consumer purchase the product?
5. How does the consumer purchase the product? Cash? Credit card? Loan?
6. What is the consumer's attitude toward the product?
7. Does the consumer believe that the product provides a benefit? If so, what is this benefit?
8. Does the consumer prefer the client's product or some other manufacturer's product (brand)? Or does the brand matter?
9. What are the demographics of the consumer? Age? Education? Ethnicity? Gender? Income? Marital status? Occupation? Political orientation? Religious orientation? Social class or status?
10. What are the psychographics of the consumer? Attitudes? Interests? Needs? Opinions? Wants?
11. What media or media channels/programs does the consumer listen to, read, and view?
12. What major products (brands) does the consumer own?
13. Is the consumer politically or economically conservative?
14. Is the consumer concerned about the environment?
15. Is the consumer interested in exciting or adventurous activities?
16. Is the consumer impulsive when shopping?
17. Is the consumer influenced by family members, friends, and/or the media, including advertising?
18. Is the consumer conscious about current fashions or styles and trends?

Of course, there may be other questions that come to mind when you study information about the consumer.

Questions about the Media and Advertising

1. What media have been used to advertise the product?
2. What media should be used to advertise the product?
3. What are the media's strengths and weaknesses when (or if) advertising the product?
4. What is the purpose of the advertising? To inform the consumer about the product? To persuade the consumer to purchase the product? To improve the image of the company that manufactures the product? To improve the image of the product?

There may be other questions that come to mind when studying the information about the media or advertising.

What Is in a Creative Strategy?

A creative strategy is basically a blueprint for creative directors, advertising copywriters, advertising layout artists, and advertising graphics personnel. It identifies the target market (consumers) and explains who these consumers are; it identifies the product or service and presents its major characteristics and major benefits. It expresses the objective(s) of the advertising; it discusses the advertising message strategy (affective, brand image, generic, positioning, preemptive, resonance, unique selling proposition, etc.) that will be used for the advertising and, depending on the strategy, may address the product's major benefit as well as provide a "reason why" this benefit is important to the consumer. It discusses the product's personality that will be developed in the advertising, usually over the advertising campaign's duration; and it presents the tactics or the specifics of the advertising.

In short, a creative strategy should discuss the following:

- Target Audience
- Objective
- Major Benefit
- Supporting Information
- Product's or Service's Personality

For years, employees of Young & Rubicam, a large international advertising agency that is a member of the WPP Group, have used the "Y & R Creative Work Plan," which includes the following:

1. Key Fact
2. Consumer Problem the Advertising Must Solve
3. Advertising Objective
4. Creative Strategy
   - The Prospect Definition
   - Principal Competition
   - Consumer Benefit
   - Reason Why
5. (If Necessary) Mandatories and Policy Limitations

The key fact is the most relevant to the advertising of the product (brand). According to Hanley Norins, "It must be a fact upon which advertising can take action."[1] The consumer problem the advertising must solve should relate to the key fact. It should be stated from the consumer's perspective.

The advertising objective should specifically state how the advertising proposes to solve the consumer's problem.

The creative strategy should define the intended consumer, the major competition, the major benefit to the intended consumer, and the specific reason for what has been claimed about the major benefit. The mandatories and policy limitations should not be filled in unless something has to be done or not done. Such may be legalities, medical restrictions, or media mandatories or limitations.[2] As the above illustrates, creative strategies differ in form and terminology, but the general strategy basically covers the topics mentioned earlier.

THE ADVERTISING MESSAGE STRATEGY

The advertising message strategy drives the creative executions—the advertisements and broadcast commercials. There are several strategies from which advertising personnel may choose. However, advertising personnel should choose a strategy that is based on primary and secondary research, the identified target market, and the objective. The more popular advertising message strategies include the following:

Affective or Emotion: This strategy employs an emotional message that arouses the consumer's feelings. Ambiguity and humor are used primarily to capture attention.

Brand Image: This strategy employs psychological appeals or brand characteristics primarily to differentiate the brand by creating an image or personality for it.

Generic: This strategy employs a claim about a product's benefit to the consumer. It does not differentiate the brand or claim that the brand is superior to its competitors. In short, the message could be used for any product in the category.

Preemptive: This strategy employs a claim about an attribute or benefit that could apply to any product in the category. Yet, because this claim has not been used for other products in the category, the brand stands out. Its competitors are forced into using a "me-too" strategy.

Positioning: This strategy attempts to "position" the brand in relation to its competitors in the consumer's mind. Usually, this strategy focuses on how the brand is different from and superior to its competitors.

Resonance: Closely related to "Affective or Emotion," this strategy employs emotions, lifestyles, or situations that the consumer can understand or has experienced and links these emotions, lifestyles, or situations with the product or service.

Unique Selling Proposition: This strategy claims that the product or service is unique. The uniqueness is based on a characteristic or benefit that the product or service has or provides. Usually, the uniqueness will imply that the product or service is superior to its competitors.[3]

Unique Selling Proposition

Let us examine the last item in depth. For national advertisements, advertising copywriters can use physical attributes of the product such as color, flavor, or form to help them identify something that is unique about the product. They can also use the advantages resulting from the manufacturing or the advantages relating to the marketing strategy to help them identify something that sets the product or service apart from its competitors. For instance, advantages resulting from manufacturing could include packaging, process, or size, and the advantages relating to the marketing strategy could include convenience, exclusiveness, guarantee, or price.

Advertising copywriters can use unique selling propositions in advertisements for local advertisers such as retail stores. Usually, these advertisements are different from advertisements for national advertisers. Local advertisements are more current and focus on price. Advertising copywriters can use one or more of the following to help them identify a unique selling proposition:

- Coupon offered
- Credit offered
- Exclusive availability
- First time offered
- Live demonstration
- Promotional event
- Special purchase
- Special sale
- Special service offered
- Spectacular event

Advertising copywriters can use unique selling propositions in advertisements that are aimed at professional working men and women. Usually, these advertisements inform professionals how to do their jobs better, easier, or faster. These ways of doing jobs can be used as unique selling propositions in advertisements.

Industrial advertisements are created for manufacturers that produce products that other manufacturers need. Usually, these advertisements discuss how the advertised products will help manufacturers decrease costs or improve products. Advertising copywriters can use one of these to help them identify a unique selling proposition.

Trade advertisements are created for manufacturers that sell products to wholesalers, retailers, or other buyers. These advertisements attempt to persuade potential buyers that their businesses will benefit by stocking the manufacturer's product line or brand. Advertising copywriters can use one or more of the following to help them identify a unique selling proposition for trade advertisements:

- Cooperative advertising program
- Fast delivery on orders
- National consumer advertising program
- Point-of-purchase display program
- Sales incentives offered
- Unique packaging
- Unique deals
- Unusual profit margin

Remember, all of the above are for identifying unique selling propositions, not for any of the other advertising message strategies. However, one or more of these may help spark an idea even if another advertising message strategy is selected.

The Emotional Selling Proposition

In addition to the unique selling proposition, there exists what has been termed the "emotional selling proposition." Basically, this is an advertising message strategy that attempts to change consumers' attitudes toward products or services by manipulating their feelings. Usually, this can only be accomplished over a long period of time. In other words, advertisements do not necessarily focus on a product's features or benefits. Rather, advertisements employ psychological or emotional characteristics that make the product or service different from its competitors.[4]

A WORD ABOUT USING AN EMOTIONAL SELLING PROPOSITION Advertisements should not rely solely on emotion to try to persuade consumers to purchase products or services. As Jack Trout points out, "If an advertisement presents emotion and leaves out a reason to buy, all that emotion is a waste of money."[5] Trout, who has written extensively about advertising and marketing in addition to working with numerous major clients over the years, is critical of advertisements that do not present a reason to purchase. Unfortunately, numerous major advertisers have allowed advertising agencies to create advertisements that are vague. According to Trout, "A large amount of today's advertising has gotten so creative or entertaining that it's sometimes hard to tell what companies are even advertising."[6] Trout believes that these advertisements have failed in their purpose, which is to persuade consumers to purchase products or services.

AN EXAMPLE OF A CREATIVE STRATEGY

See box 2.1 for an example of a creative strategy.

The Big Creative Idea

According to David Ogilvy, the founder of the advertising agency that bears his name, "It takes a big idea to attract the attention of consumers and get them to buy your product. Unless your advertising contains a big idea, it will pass like a ship in the night."[7] George Lois, the chairman and creative director of the advertising agency that bears his name, agrees. He writes, "Great advertising comes down to The Big Idea."[8]

What is the big idea? According to Lois, it is "a surprising solution to a marketing problem, expressed in memorable verbal and/or graphic imagery."[9] Lois believes that advertising personnel must be able to express the big idea in a sentence. If it requires more than a sentence, then it is not a big idea.[10]

Coming up with "big" creative ideas for advertising can be difficult and time consuming. However, there are steps that can be taken to ease some of the difficulty and save time. In fact, advertising personnel and others have discussed numerous structured processes that can be employed to help with finding the big creative idea.

For instance, Graham Wallas, a sociologist in Britain, in his book *The Art of Thought*, which was published in 1926, described one of the earliest creative processes. Wallas discussed four steps: preparation, incubation, illumination, and verification. In the preparation step, the problem is investigated. In the incubation step, the problem is not thought about whatsoever. In the illumination step, an idea relating to the problem suddenly forms. In the verification step, the validity of the idea is tested. Usually, during the last step the idea is reduced to exact form.[11]

James Webb Young, a former vice president of creative at J. Walter Thompson, an advertising agency, explained a more expanded creative process. In his book *A Technique for Producing Ideas*, which was published in 1940, Young claims that "an idea is nothing more or less than a *new combination* of old elements."[12] He writes: "The capacity to bring old elements into new combinations depends largely on the ability to see relationships."[13] Young discussed the following steps:

Step 1: The first step is gathering information.
Step 2: The second step is masticating the information.
Step 3: The third step is rest and relaxation—that is, putting the subject out of your mind by doing something else.

BOX 2.1 *Creative Strategy for Nestlé Crunch Milk Chocolate with Crisped Rice*

This report will serve as the basis for the Nestlé Crunch milk chocolate advertising campaign.

CONSUMER ANALYSIS

Consumers select Nestlé Crunch candy bars for a variety of reasons: to satisfy a craving, to get a burst of positive energy, or to enjoy a treat. According to its manufacturer, Nestlé Crunch is "the crunchy chocolate candy bar that makes milk chocolate more fun to munch."

The most distinct target market for Nestlé Crunch is white women, ages 25–34, who have graduated from high school; are employed full-time at the clerical, sales, or technical level; have a household income of $75,000 or more; are married; are parents of 6 to 11 year olds; and live in the Pacific or Middle Atlantic region of the United States.

PRODUCT ANALYSIS

A 17th-century writer called chocolate "the only true food of the gods." In Switzerland, Henri Nestlé and Daniel Peter invented milk chocolate in 1875. By 1938, when the Nestlé Crunch bar was introduced, the company—now known as Nestlé, S. A.—had established a global distribution network.

Today, the Nestlé candy bar category claims 10 percent of the U.S. market share. Distinctive because of its blend of milk chocolate and crisped rice, Nestlé Crunch comes in several sizes and varieties, including traditional, mocha, white chocolate, Buncha Crunch, and ice cream and frozen novelties. Its chief competitor is Hershey Foods Corporation's chocolate brands, including Hershey Krackel, a chocolate bar with similar ingredients.

Nestlé Crunch is competitively priced; a 1.55-ounce bar costs less than $1.

OBJECTIVES

The primary objectives are to position Nestlé Crunch as the consumer's first choice when she or he looks for milk chocolate and to regain market share lost recently to the newer chocolate-covered wafer bars with the cookie centers.

STRATEGY

In order to achieve this objective, Nestlé Crunch will be positioned as a "delightfully, delectably delicious" snack for persons with an active lifestyle. Advertising will stress that Nestlé Crunch, with its tiny toasted rice "crunchies," offers a better chocolate experience (more chocolate) than the newer "cookie" bars, plus more crunchiness than a plain, solid chocolate bar.

TACTICS

The first television spot will portray three teams of trained laboratory rats engaged in play-offs of "rat basketball." In rat basketball, played on a specially designed miniature court, a rat is given a piece of rice cereal whenever it makes a basket. In this commercial, Team A is rewarded with small pieces of Nestlé Crunch; Team B, with morsels of chocolate-covered wafer bars; and Team C, with tiny bits of plain chocolate. Eager to receive their Nestlé Crunch reward, Team A wins, paws down! The slogan will appear on the screen: "Escape the rat race. Sink your teeth into delightfully, delectably delicious Nestlé Crunch." Additional ads will appear in newspapers and magazines to support the creative theme.

The second TV spot will portray professionals, primarily women, engaged in busy lifestyles. It will show factory workers on a huge, loud, fast-moving assembly line. Suddenly, the forewoman announces a Nestlé Crunch break. Work immediately grinds to a halt as employees begin eating Nestlé Crunch bars. Factory noise is replaced by new sounds: the crinkle of paper and foil packages being unwrapped, the crunch of teeth biting into candy, and the crew's animated conversation. The slogan will appear on the screen: "Delightfully, delectably delicious Nestlé Crunch. Worth stopping for." Additional ads will appear in newspapers and magazines to support the creative theme.

Barbara Dunlap-Berg, "Creative Strategy for Nestlé Crunch Milk Chocolate with Crisped Rice," United Methodist Communications, Nashville, February 2001. Reprinted by permission.

Step 4: The fourth step is the birth of the idea. An idea comes out of nowhere. Usually, the idea occurs when it is least expected.

Step 5: The fifth step is the development of the idea so that it can be used.[14]

Alex F. Osborn, one of the founding members of Batten, Barton, Durstine, and Osborn (BBDO), an advertising agency, developed another creative process that can be employed to help generate a big idea. In his book *Applied Imagination: The Principles and Procedures of Creative Thinking*, which was published in 1953, Osborn explained that creativity usually includes some or all of the following phases:

1. Orientation: Pointing up the problem.
2. Preparation: Gathering pertinent data.
3. Analysis: Breaking down the relevant material.
4. Hypothesis: Piling up alternatives by way of ideas.
5. Incubation: Letting up, to invite illumination.
6. Synthesis: Putting the pieces together.
7. Verification: Judging the resultant ideas.[15]

Osborn also discussed "brainstorming," which he developed and used at BBDO. In advertising brainstorming occurs when a leader and several members engage in a candid discussion about a product or service. A brainstorming session usually begins by the leader introducing the purpose and the problem to the members of the group. Next, the information, especially information about the advertiser, the advertiser's product or service, and the target market, is presented. Then members analyze the information to determine what is relevant to the task at hand. Next, the members offer various ideas. After that, members are encouraged to relax so that a big idea may possibly form in their minds. Next, members examine all of the ideas that are generated and attempt to determine which ideas are the most suitable as well as the best for the task at hand. Finally, the members judge the ideas that have been selected, primarily to determine which one should be used in the advertising.

Osborn believed that in order for a brainstorming session to be productive, the following had to exist:

1. *Judicial judgment* is ruled out. Criticism of ideas must be withheld until later.
2. *"Freewheeling" is welcomed.* The wilder the idea, the better; it is easier to tame down than to think up.
3. *Quantity is wanted.* The greater the number of ideas, the more the likelihood of winners.
4. *Combination and improvement are sought.* In addition to contributing ideas of their own, participants should suggest how the ideas of others can be turned into *better* ideas or how two or more ideas can be joined into still another idea.[16]

Furthermore, in order for a brainstorming session to function properly, there should be a trained facilitator in charge. In addition, there should be no more than 10 members. In fact, a session will be more productive if the number of members is from five to eight. However, a brainstorming session consisting of three individuals—a creative director, a copywriter, and a layout artist or graphics person—can be productive.

In *The Act of Creation*, Arthur Koestler discussed another concept that, if applied, can help generate a big creative idea. Termed "bisociation," the concept refers to two independent matrices of ideas making contact with one another. In short, when two thoughts or ideas collide and combine, another new idea occurs. According to Koestler, creativity is blocked when one focuses on one matrix or frame of reference. It is released when one allows more than one matrix or frame of reference to enter the picture. As a result, associations happen; the dots connect, and the lines take shape.[17]

Edward de Bono discussed another approach that can help generate a big creative idea in his book *Lateral Thinking for Management*, which was published in 1971. According to de Bono, lateral thinking is generative and provocative. Unlike vertical thinking, which is selective, sequential, logical, analytical, and finite, lateral thinking is the opposite—that is, it ignores patterns by being open; it searches among various arrangements or alternatives in order to arrive at a solution or solutions. In short, lateral thinking suggests that one should examine an idea upside down and inside out, not the opposite, which is vertical thinking.[18]

Based on the concepts of Graham Wallas, James Webb Young, and others, Roger von Oech expressed that those who are involved in the creative process must take on four roles. These roles include "Explorer," "Artist," "Judge," and "Warrior."

In the first role, creative people must have information such as facts, concepts, and experiences in order to generate new ideas. In the second role, they must examine the information from different perspectives. In addition, they must experiment and rearrange the information; they must ask questions about it. Then they must come up with an idea. In the third role, the creative people must critically evaluate the idea's worth. For instance, they should ask questions such as, "Is the idea sound?" "How much will it cost?" and "Is it worth the investment?" Eventually, a decision must be made. In the fourth role, the creative people must have the courage to turn the idea into reality—that is, do what is necessary to implement it.[19]

As von Oech points out, a dynamic creative process can only occur when people can adopt all four roles. These people must know when it is appropriate to adopt each role. Also, they must be flexible in moving from one role to another.

In 1999, in *Flash of Brilliance: Inspiring Creativity Where You Work*, William C. Miller identified four strategies for generating creative ideas: *Visioning*, *Modifying*, *Experimenting*, and *Exploring*. He called the model *Innovation Styles*. According to Miller,

> With Visioning, you seek to see the ideal, long-term solution—you *envision* and *idealize*. . . . Visioning helps to provide direction, inspiration, and momentum to creative projects.
>
> With Modifying, you seek to expand and build on what you've already done—you *build* and *optimize*. . . . Modifying helps provide stability and thoroughness to creative endeavors by ensuring that the full potential of an idea gets developed.
>
> With Experimenting, you seek to combine various elements and test out novel solutions—you *combine* and *test*. . . . Experimenting helps you to expand and troubleshoot new possibilities while building a consensus for a solution.
>
> With Exploring, you seek to challenge core assumptions and discover new alternatives—you *challenge* and *discover*. . . . Exploring helps you to open up the possibility for radical breakthroughs.[20]

Of course, there are other means to finding big creative ideas. For instance, merely speaking to a representative of the advertiser or studying the advertiser's product may spark an interesting idea for the advertising. Other means include personal experience, others' experiences, advertiser's problem, advertiser's previous advertising for the product, competitors' advertising, and identifying the target market's problem. If the idea can solve the target market's problem and the advertiser's problem concurrently, then the idea may not only be a big creative idea; it may be the biggest.

Whoever was responsible for designing the Super Wal-Mart stores should have employed some of the above advice before any were built. The typical Super Wal-Mart store has one parking lot, primarily because the usual two entrances are located on one end of the building. How many potential consumers drive onto the parking lot only to realize that the parking lot is almost full and the remaining spaces are half a city block away from the store and consequently drive away, possibly going to a different store? Yet the typical Super Wal-Mart is more than one store. Indeed, it is a mini mall; it has a grocery as well as a department store, not to mention other smaller stores, under one roof. A Super Wal-Mart store should be positioned in the center of its location, with parking lots and entrances on both ends of the building, if not all around the building. Checkouts should be at both ends of the building as well. This would have allowed those consumers who become overwhelmed when they see a large, nearly full parking lot more possible spaces to park in. With at least two parking lots, these extra spaces would have been in all likelihood closer to the entrances of the store.

There are other means for finding ideas. For instance, consider the following: the product's name, the product's purpose, the product's history, where the product is manufactured, how the product is manufactured, the product's packaging, the product's marketing environment, life with the product, or even life without the product. Information pertaining to any of these may spark a big creative idea for the advertising. However, make certain that the big creative idea relates to the creative strategy section of the advertising or integrated marketing communications plan. If it does not, then the idea needs to be changed. The creative strategy should not be changed because it is based on information found in other sections of the advertising or the integrated marketing communications plan. In short, if the creative strategy is changed, it will not necessarily be based on secondary and primary research; consequently, the advertising will in all likelihood misfire and not solve the advertiser's problem. We examine headlines and slogans in the next chapter, primarily because we will be examining print advertising first.

EXERCISES

1. Conduct the research using the sources mentioned in this chapter and then write a brief creative strategy for an ad for Cheerios cereal. You do not have to worry about writing the ad.
2. Choose a popular brand of detergent and then conduct the research using the sources mentioned in this chapter to develop a creative strategy for an ad for the detergent.
3. Write a creative strategy for an energy bar/drink, candy bar, or soft drink of your choice. Make sure that your creative strategy includes the following: a brief statement about the purpose of the creative strategy, consumer analysis, product analysis, objectives, strategy statement, and tactics.

NOTES

1. Hanley Norins, *The Young & Rubicam Traveling Creative Workshop* (Englewood Cliffs, NJ: Prentice-Hall, Inc., 1990), p. 23.
2. Norins, *The Young & Rubicam Traveling Creative Workshop*, pp. 22–34.
3. Henry A. Laskey, Ellen Day, and Melvin R. Crask, "Typology of Main Message Strategies for Television Commercials," *Journal of Advertising*, Vol. 18, No. 1 (Winter 1989), pp. 36–41.
4. Jim Aitchison, *Cutting Edge Advertising: How to Create the World's Best Print for Brands in the 21st Century* (Singapore: Prentice-Hall, 1999), pp. 42–43.
5. Jack Trout with Steve Rivkin, *Differentiate or Die: Survival in Our Era of Killer Competition* (New York: John Wiley and Sons, Inc., 2000), p. 42.
6. Trout with Rivkin, *Differentiate or Die*, p. 37.
7. David Ogilvy, *Ogilvy on Advertising* (New York: Vintage Books, 1985), p. 16.
8. George Lois with Bill Pitts, *What's the Big Idea? How to Win with Outrageous Ideas (That Sell!)* (New York: Plume, 1993), p. 5.
9. Lois with Pitts, *What's the Big Idea?* p. 6.
10. Lois with Pitts, *What's the Big Idea?* p. 272.
11. Graham Wallas, *The Art of Thought* (New York: Harcourt, Brace and Co., 1926), pp. 79–107.
12. James Webb Young, *A Technique for Producing Ideas* (Chicago: Crain Books, 1975 [1940]), p. 25.
13. Young, *A Technique for Producing Ideas*, p. 26.
14. Young, *A Technique for Producing Ideas*, pp. 30–54.
15. Alex F. Osborn, *Applied Imagination: The Principles and Procedures of Creative Thinking* (New York: Charles Scribner's Sons, 1953), p. 125, 131–182.
16. Osborn, *Applied Imagination*, pp. 300–301.
17. See Arthur Koestler, *The Act of Creation* (New York: Macmillan Co., 1964).
18. See Edward de Bono, *Lateral Thinking for Management* (New York: American Management Association, 1971).
19. See Roger von Oech, *A Kick in the Seat of the Pants* (New York: Harper Perennial, 1986).
20. William C. Miller, *Flash of Brilliance: Inspiring Creativity Where You Work* (Reading, MA: Perseus Books, 1999), pp. 64–68.

CHAPTER 3

Headlines and Slogans

In the previous chapter, the creative strategy and various structured processes for creativity were discussed; one of these processes should help in the development of a big creative idea, which is the heart of an advertisement's message. Now, the advertisement needs to be developed.

AIDA

Advertising personnel who have been given the task of developing a print advertisement or a broadcast commercial have been using a formula for years. This formula is known by the acronym AIDA, which was developed in the 1920s and which stands for *Attention*, *Interest*, *Desire*, and *Action*. AIDA suggests that in order to persuade consumers, advertising must attract attention, create interest, stimulate desire, and cause action. AIDA works as follows:

Attention —> Interest —> Desire —> Action

Attention

If consumers are to be persuaded to purchase products or services, advertisers must gain their attention. Advertisers can use attention-getting devices such as the medium (magazine, newspaper, radio, television, etc.), the size of the advertisement or the length of the commercial, and the position of the advertisement. Additional devices include, in print, the headline, illustration or photograph, and copy that features benefits and, in broadcast commercials, sound effects, music, and opening comments. Establishing shots in television commercials can also capture attention. An attention-getting device is used to attract consumers to the rest of the message. Thus, it should relate to the rest of the message. Attention also can be obtained by using a strong creative strategy such as a unique selling proposition. Attention may also be obtained by using one of the following words in the headline:

- Amazing
- Announcing
- At last
- Finally
- Free
- How to
- Introducing
- Latest
- New
- Now
- Presenting
- Revolutionary
- Suddenly
- Today

Of course, one of these words should be used only if it applies. For instance, *Free* should not be used if the advertiser is not giving anything away.

Interest

Advertisements must appeal to consumers' interests or they will not be viewed, read, or heard. Interest can be obtained by understanding the intended consumers and what appeals to them. For instance, one of the following may appeal to them:

- avoiding embarrassment
- avoiding housework
- avoiding pain
- avoiding worry
- being creative
- being a leader
- caring for children
- enjoying comfort
- enjoying cooking
- enjoying leisure activities
- enjoying looking for bargains
- gaining professional and/or social prestige
- getting ahead in a career
- having financial security
- having friends
- having a happy marriage
- having a nice home
- improving one's education
- improving one's health
- improving one's physical appearance
- influencing others
- insuring one's health
- investing money
- making money
- protecting one's family
- reducing weight
- saving money
- winning gifts or money
- winning praise from others

Many print advertisements and broadcast commercials are based on these appeals.

Desire

The advertisement's message should move the reader (viewer or listener) to the point that she or he desires the product or service. This may not be easy. Even if a reader reads a headline of a print advertisement, she or he may not read the body copy. Yet, in many instances, it is the body copy that causes the reader to grow desirous about the product or service, primarily because it elaborates on what has been mentioned in the headline. Perhaps the easiest way of achieving this is by informing consumers that the product or service offers benefits.

Action

The print advertisement or broadcast commercial should move the reader (viewer or listener) to this stage—that is, direct the reader to purchase the product or service now or change the reader's perception of the product or service from neutral to favorable, so that the reader will be inclined to purchase the product when the need occurs. If the advertisement does not do either of the above, then it has failed. Of course, there may be other purposes for advertisements. For instance, the purpose of a network television commercial about a nationally distributed truck may be to inform consumers about the model and brand, especially if it is a new model, not necessarily to get the consumers to purchase the truck. A later network television commercial or magazine advertisement about the truck may have that purpose.

HEADLINES

The typical elements of a print advertisement include the artwork, the headline, the body copy, the slogan, and the logotype. Usually, the headline is the most important element in a print advertisement. (Some who work in advertising insist that artwork is the most important element in a print advertisement. However, people read newspapers and magazines, not just look at the photographs. If they see advertisements, then they probably read the headlines as well as look at the artwork.) If the headline does not get the reader's attention, it has failed to do its job.

Capturing the Reader's Attention

The use of certain words such as those previously mentioned in the discussion about *Attention* as well as *I*, *You*, and *Me* may be one way of getting the reader's attention. How the subject matter is presented may be another. For instance, presenting a problem or a solution to a problem may attract the reader's attention. Or presenting a provocative statement or unusual question may capture the reader's attention. Of course, there are other structures and techniques that can be used so that headlines attract attention, such as certain punctuation marks.

In addition to provoking interest, an advertisement's headline should use language—words and phrases—that is familiar to the reader. Also, the advertisement's headline should be positive, not negative. For instance, if a headline concerns a product such as an underarm deodorant, it should not focus on the negative—body odor; it should focus on the positive—that is, what the product will do for the consumer. After all, this is the major benefit, and this is what the consumer is interested in knowing. In short, the headline should capture attention, be easy to understand, and promise a reward such as a benefit.

David Ogilvy suggested that the brand name be included in the headline because most readers do not read the body copy. Consequently, they will never know what the product is unless they are informed in the headline. Sometimes the brand name is mentioned in a subhead, especially if the subhead immediately follows the headline, or in the company's logo (logotype), particularly when the logo serves as part of the headline.

The Best Headlines

The best headlines appeal to the reader's interests or desires. Other excellent headlines offer the reader news or arouse the reader's curiosity. Good headlines might offer the reader an easy way of doing something. Of course, all of these headlines will have validity or believability.

Look at the following headline:

Now pick up dust,
fingerprints, even grease
without having to pick up all of these.

The full-page advertisement contains a large photograph of a Scotch-Brite High Performance Cleaning Cloth as well as a smaller photograph of a bucket filled with various cleaning supplies such as a sprayer, paper towels, and rubber gloves.

This headline is interesting to the reader who does the cleaning around the house because it presents useful information about a product that has been designed to do tasks that usually require several products. The product should save the reader time and money, which is the implied benefit.

Look at the following headline for Neutrogena, an antiwrinkle cream:

THE SIGNS OF
AGING ARE
WRITTEN ALL OVER
YOUR FACE.

This headline uses fear, another appeal, which is suitable for advertising this product. Most women are concerned about the aging process and its effect on their faces. Is it appropriate to remind them of this concern? Certainly, if you manufacture a product such as Neutrogena, which may slow the aging process or at least reduce lines and wrinkles within a relatively short time, which is the product's benefit.

Kinds of Headlines

NEWS Most of these headlines introduce new products or inform consumers about products that have been improved. For instance, look at the following headlines:

New from Bush's.
Maple Cured Bacon Baked Beans.

This headline uses the word *New* to introduce Bush's Maple Cured Bacon Baked Beans, suggesting to the reader that this product has not been on the market long.

Why can't someone just make a cold sore go away sooner?
Now someone can.
Introducing ABREVA.

This headline uses the word *Introducing* to present a new product for treating cold sores. As before, the headline suggests to the reader that this product has not been on the market long.

HOW-TO These headlines explain how consumers can do something better, easier, faster, or simpler. For instance, look at the following examples:

How to improve your camera's image.

This headline is for Vivitar lenses. If readers desire better photographs, then they may try better lenses such as those by Vivitar.

How To Take Years Off Your
Looks Without Going To A Plastic Surgeon!

This headline is for Parisian Formula Cell Renewal, a facial product for women that supposedly will make women look younger.

COMMAND OR IMPERATIVE These headlines tell consumers what to do. Often forceful sounding, these headlines probably do not work as well as other kinds of headlines. Look at the following examples:

TAKE CHARGE OF
YOUR ACHING JOINTS BEFORE
THEY TAKE CHARGE OF YOU!

This headline is for Flex Able glucosamine and chondroitin products that help build cartilage between joints.

Pick up
Bounty
before
somebody
picks up a
sponge full
of germs.

This headline is for Bounty paper towels, which are apparently healthier to use than a sponge.

QUESTION OR INTERROGATORY Although these headlines usually arouse curiosity, they should ask questions that consumers wish to be answered. In addition, they should state or imply a benefit. Look at the following headlines:

Could aspirin save
your life this year?

This headline is for Bayer, specifically what Bayer terms "aspirin regimen therapy"—that is, a physician-prescribed program that includes diet, exercise, and aspirin to help prevent a heart attack or stroke.

Which home is clean
all the way down to the allergens?

This headline is for Clorox Clean-Up, which destroys almost 100 percent of the allergens found in a typical house.

TESTIMONIAL OR QUOTATION These headlines are in advertisements that usually have photographs of individuals who are supposedly speaking to the reader. The headlines are in quotation marks or, if not, are written as if the persons in the photographs are making the statements. In other words, the headlines sound natural and conversational so that they have validity. In short, these headlines must sound believable. Look at the following examples:

"I'll give you my $30 Car Vac
absolutely free just for
trying my 8-lb. Oreck XL."

This advertisement has a photograph of David Oreck positioned beside the headline. In addition, his signature is written and positioned beneath it. The headline makes an interesting proposition to the reader. Indeed, whoever responds will get a compact vacuum cleaner just for trying the larger vacuum cleaner for 30 days.

I've been dry for 3 hours . . .
and I can prove it!

This headline is attributed to a happy little girl who is depicted in a photograph. The headline is for Pull-Ups training pants.

DECLARATIVE OR DIRECT These headlines typically present the selling proposition about the product or service in a straightforward manner. Usually, these headlines are matter-of-fact and void of any puns or words that may have more than one meaning. Look at the following headlines:

ELIMINATE SQUEAKS
WHEN YOU BUILD WITH THE SILENT FLOOR SYSTEM.

This headline is for a four-page advertisement for Trus Joist, a brand of I-beam that is used by contractors to support floors in houses.

Make cleaning a little easier
with the exclusive 8 rotating brush system from Hoover.

This headline is for the Hoover SteamVac Widepath, which scrubs away dirt and spills from carpets.

HUMOROUS These headlines may or may not mention the product, but in many instances the benefit is stated or implied. Look at the following examples:

Your dad wants you to have
things he never had.
Like hair.

This headline is for Rogaine Extra Strength for men. The product's benefit is understood. The headline is humorous, depending on the reader's perspective.

Wisk tablets
remove dirt like it
never happened.
If only they could
do the same for
your daughter's
new tattoo.

This headline is for Wisk Tablets. The benefit is stated and, to a certain extent, reinforced by the second sentence, even though it is humorous, depending on the reader's perspective.

DEMOGRAPHIC OR SELECTIVE These headlines target a certain consumer group by using such words as *dad*, *men*, *mom*, and *women* or by referring to the readers' chronological age. Usually, photographs of individuals who represent the target market are included in the advertisements. Look at the following headlines:

If you're over 60,
you should know
the warning signs
of osteoporosis.
Unfortunately,
there aren't any.

The body copy in this advertisement discusses osteoporosis as well as a Bone Density Test that can measure the health of bones. The advertisement is for Merck & Company.

We were there when you
were a child of the '60s
and when you became
a parent of the '90s.

This headline is for State Farm insurance and is targeting parents.

Other headlines can select a group of consumers by mentioning the product or physical condition of the intended target market. For instance, look at the following examples:

Menopause affects you in more ways than one.
That's why Caltrate Plus Soy does more.

This headline is for Caltrate 600+Soy, which is a dietary supplement for menopausal health.

You've tried
over and over again to
lose weight.
Maybe it's time to let
others give you
a hand.

This headline is for Weight Watchers, specifically the organization's meetings, which are for people who may need support from others in order to lose weight.

CURIOSITY OR PLAYFUL PHRASES These headlines contain unusual words, phrases, or clichés. These headlines do not necessarily work as well as other kinds of headlines at getting the reader's attention. Also, clichés or even parts of clichés should not be used in headlines or body copy.

Whenever an advertising copywriter uses a cliché it is a sign that he or she needs a break from work. Look at the following headlines:

CQ ON THE QT

This headline is for Clear Nicoderm CQ. Of course, part of the product's name is in the headline, but will the reader understand it without looking at some other element in the advertisement? Probably not. Will it capture the reader's attention? Perhaps, perhaps not.

The business of speed is now moving at the speed of business.

Readers may not understand this headline for UPS, even though part of it is the company's slogan. What does "The business of speed . . ." mean? The advertising copywriter should have written something less complicated.

There's more to this drop
than meets
the eye

This headline uses part of a cliché to advertise Refresh Tears eye drops, but it implies that the drop's ingredients do more than just soothe and relieve dry eyes. Indeed, according to the body copy, these drops protect eyes from dryness.

Pasta proof. Pizza proof. Passion proof.
It's more than a lipstick, it's Lipfinity.

This headline is for Lipfinity by Max Factor. It contains the benefit (stated in alliterative sentences) as well as the name of the product (the prefix comes from the word *lipstick*, and the suffix comes from the word *infinity*).

Of course, there may be other kinds of headlines, such as those that repeat a line or part of a line or those that appear to be nothing more than a title or label. But most headlines will be examples of the above.

Characteristics of Successful Headlines

Successful headlines capture the reader's attention. Then they arouse the reader's interest, causing the reader to read further and look at the artwork. Successful headlines share common characteristics; these characteristics include one or more of the following:

- appeals to the reader's interest
- arouses curiosity
- is believable
- is clearly stated
- is specific
- mentions the advertiser by name
- mentions the brand by name
- presents a strong sales message
- provides a benefit
- provides an easy solution to a problem
- provides news
- relates to the product or service
- selects the target market
- works well with the artwork and body copy

Characteristics of Unsuccessful Headlines

Headlines that fail do so for various reasons. However, many fail because they did one or more of the following:

- aroused curiosity and nothing else
- did not appeal to the reader's interest
- did not mention the advertiser by name
- did not mention the brand by name
- did not provide a benefit
- did not provide an easy solution to a problem
- did not provide news
- did not relate to the product or service
- did not select the target market
- did not work well with the artwork and body copy
- focused on the negative instead of the positive
- was not believable
- was not specific

What the Headline Should Say

A successful headline will most likely (1) appeal to the reader's interest; (2) arouse the reader's curiosity; (3) be specific and believable; (4) identify the target market, the product or service, or the advertiser; (5) provide a benefit or promise to the reader; and (6) provide news or an easy solution to a problem. For instance, look at the following headline:

BREAK GLASS
IN CASE OF
EMERGENCY
Introducing Curel Extreme Care.
Finally, there's a better way to relieve severely dry skin.

This headline contains the product's name, presents news, identifies the problem for which the product is manufactured, and provides a benefit or what the product will do for the reader. In addition, the first part of the headline, which is in capital letters, appears in black on the glass of a typical emergency box found in many buildings. Inside the box, behind the glass, are three different kinds of Curel Extreme Care products, so the reader will recognize the product when shopping. Even though there is a block of body copy and a slogan, the reader learns enough about the product from the headline.

How to Write Arresting Headlines

Writing a headline that will gain the reader's attention is not that difficult. Yet, even today, after numerous articles and books have discussed this topic as well as others relating to copy for advertisements, advertising copywriters still create headlines that fail. There are several formulas that can be used to write a winning headline. The first includes the following:

1. Identify the unique selling proposition for the product or service (what separates the product or service from its competition). The unique selling proposition is something that is different from or better than the competition.
2. Identify the major benefit (what the product or service will do for the reader). This major benefit should be used in the headline. Before writing the headline, however, think about how one or more of the following words can be used in the headline to get the reader's attention:

- *advice*
- *amazing*
- *announcing*
- *at last*
- *authentic*
- *bargain*
- *cash*
- *children*
- *discover*
- *easy*
- *facts*
- *family*
- *fast*
- *finally*
- *free*
- *genuine*
- *guaranteed*
- *health*
- *here*
- *how much*
- *how to*
- *how would*
- *imagine*
- *increase*
- *incredible*
- *love*
- *money*
- *new*
- *now*
- *protect*
- *proven*
- *safety*
- *save*
- *secrets of*
- *simple*
- *unique*
- *wanted*
- *why*
- *yes*
- *you*

3. These words—some of which were listed earlier in the discussion about Attention—have been used successfully by advertising copywriters for decades.

Let us recapitulate this formula for writing a successful headline:

1. include the unique selling proposition or
2. the major benefit and
3. try using one or more of the words listed above to attract the reader.

A second formula includes the following:

1. identify the target market;
2. provide the reasons for the product or service being important to the target market;
3. identify the most important benefit of the product or service (what the product or service will do for the target market);
4. write numerous declarative sentences about the benefit that has been identified—try including one or more words from the above list in these sentences;
5. examine the sentences—choose the one that appears to be the most powerful; and
6. see whether the sentence you have chosen may be the headline.

A third formula includes the following:

1. identify the unique selling proposition;
2. identify the selling features of the product or service (selling features are usually tangible characteristics of the product or service);
3. identify the benefits for these selling features (benefits are what these selling features provide for the target market);
4. use one or more words from the above list to attract the target market's interest;
5. write numerous headlines that include the unique selling proposition, one or more selling features, one or more benefits, and/or one of the words from the above list;
6. examine the numerous headlines that you have written and decide on the best two or three;
7. edit the headlines that you have considered the best; and
8. choose the best one.

A fourth formula includes:

1. Ask yourself, "What would make me buy this product?"
2. Write your response.
3. Express this reason in a sentence.
4. See whether this sentence may be enough for your headline.

This formula is perhaps the simplest; however, it should not be used often, primarily because you—the copywriter—may not represent the target market. In short, your answer (reason) to the question may not be the answer (reason) the target market would have provided if they had been asked. Also, a mere reason may not be enough to attract attention. Therefore, if this formula is used, the copywriter may wish to include the name of the product, service, or advertiser or include a word that identifies the target market.

The Long Headline

Headlines may be lengthy. In many cases, writing two or more sentences instead of one will shorten a lengthy headline. Another possibility is to shorten a lengthy headline by making part of it a subhead, which is usually an independent sentence in a smaller type size. Usually, a subhead completes or continues the thought presented in the headline. Look at the following examples:

Eucerin knows
sensitive skin
doesn't stop at your chin.
THAT'S WHY IT'S THE
#1 DERMATOLOGIST-RECOMMENDED
BRAND.

The second sentence is the subhead; it completes the thought presented in the first sentence or the headline.

Finally, lens wearers have a solution
for end-of-day dryness.
Only COMPLETE protects your lenses
all day with a cushion of moisture.

The subhead, the second sentence, explains what the headline, the first sentence, suggests. That is, Complete is the "solution for end-of-day dryness."

Capture the sleep you need
when you need it.
Discover Sonata
The first and only sleep aid that can help you fall asleep at bedtime or later.

In this instance, the subhead, the second sentence, introduces the product and continues the thought presented in the headline, the first sentence.

Sometimes the subhead may appear before the headline. Usually placed above the headline, this subhead is called a *kicker* or *overline* and is generally underlined. Of course, subheads may be used to break up lengthy blocks of body copy.

Suggestions for Writing Headlines and Subheads

1. Do not use all capital letters. Readers are not accustomed to reading anything in capital letters, except for the first letter of the first word in a sentence. If you think you need to capitalize every letter of the brand name, try it. However, if it appears too awkward—the brand name may contain too many letters—then you may decide to capitalize the first letter and use lowercase for the remaining letters.
2. Do not use excessive punctuation. One period, one exclamation mark, or one question mark is enough. If you use more than one, such as five exclamation marks, your headline or subhead will appear unprofessional.
3. Do not allow the artwork or body copy to overpower the headline or subhead. If attention is taken away from the headline and subhead, then the advertisement's message may not be read.
4. Do not rely on one kind of headline for every advertisement. Use different kinds. Try using a quotation or testimonial headline instead of a declarative sentence headline, for instance.
5. Try capitalizing the first letter of every word in the headline. If you do not have a lot of words or more than one lengthy sentence, this may work.
6. Try capitalizing only the first letter of the first word in the headline. As mentioned, this is what readers are used to reading.
7. Do not use a period at the end of a headline if the headline is not a complete sentence.
8. Use a larger typeface size for headlines and a smaller typeface size for subheads.
9. Do not use a humorous pun or a play on words in headlines or subheads. A sales message should be serious; after all, it is asking the reader to consider purchasing a product or service.
10. Use one of the formulas discussed earlier to write every headline and subhead. These formulas work.

"UNDER THE RADAR" ADVERTISING

In 1998, Jonathan Bond and Richard Kirshenbaum published the book *Under the Radar: Talking to Today's Cynical Consumer*, in which they claim that consumers, primarily because they are inundated with thousands of advertisements, have developed marketing radar, a defense mechanism that helps them screen out advertisements that they are exposed to every day. As a result, Bond and Kirshenbaum believe that advertising agencies need to create advertisements that slip in under the consumer's radar. They claim that honesty will help build trustworthiness and that humor will actually neutralize the consumer's defense mechanism. For instance, look at the following headline that was created by the authors' advertising agency for Positano, an Italian restaurant in New York City:

An
Authentic
Italian
Restaurant
Where
No
One's
Been Shot.
Yet.

The layout contained several bullet holes and smaller copy in the bottom right-hand corner that identified the advertiser and the advertiser's address and telephone number.[1]

SLOGANS

A slogan, also called a theme line or tag line, usually appears beneath a company's logo in a series of advertisements. Basically, a slogan is a phrase or a sentence that captures the heart of the advertisement's message or the heart of the advertiser.

Slogans may have started out as headlines in advertisements, or they may have been created specifically to reflect the theme of the advertising campaign. Unlike headlines and subheads, slogans usually last years, if not decades, and are memorable. For instance, look at the following slogans:

"Quality is job one." (Ford)

"We bring good things to life." (General Electric)

"The power to be your best." (Apple)

"It's everywhere you want to be." (Visa)

"We love to fly and it shows." (Delta Airlines)

"The seal outside means the best inside." (Chiquita bananas)

"It doesn't get any better than this." (Old Milwaukee beer)

"So nice to come home to." (Armstrong flooring)

"Have it your way." (Burger King)

"Better things for better living." (DuPont)

"Makin' it great." (Pizza Hut)

"The one beer to have when you're having more than one." (Schaefer Beer)

"So big, it eats like a meal." (Campbell's Chunky soup)

"When ordinary refreshment won't cut it." (Slice)

"The best a man can get." (Gillette)

"A powerful part of your life." (Westinghouse)

"A breed apart." (Merrill-Lynch)

"Lets the good times roll." (Kawasaki)

"We circle the world." (MasterCard)

"You deserve a break today." (McDonald's)

"Always the leader." (Mack Trucks)

"The closer you look, the better we look." (Ford)

"Think what we can do for you." (Bank of America)

"America's storyteller." (Eastman Kodak)

"Doing what we do best." (American Airlines)

"Getting people together." (Boeing)

"The softer side of Sears." (Sears, Roebuck, and Co.)

"Our people make the difference." (Wal-Mart)

"Expect more. Pay less." (Target)

"Now that's a great idea." (Best Buy)

"The arts and crafts store." (Michaels)

"That's more like it." (Kohl's)

"Pork. The other white meat." (Pork Producers Council)

"You're in good hands with Allstate." (Allstate insurance)

"An army of one." (U.S. Army)

"The world on time." (FedEx)

"Courage for your head." (Bell Helmets)

"Just do it." (Nike)

"Like a good neighbor, State Farm is there." (State Farm insurance)

"Does she or doesn't she? Only her hairdresser knows for sure." (Clairol)

"I'd walk a mile for a Camel." (Camel cigarettes)

"Soup is good food." (Campbell's)

"Get Met. It pays." (Metropolitan Life)

"This Bud's for you." (Budweiser beer)

Some of the above are older than the others. Some are no longer used, and some are. In fact, some have been used for numerous years; others, for only a few years. However, most, if not all, have something in common: they try to state in a few words the most important idea or theme about the product or advertiser. These few words help the reader remember the product or advertiser. In addition, these slogans, like all slogans, contain one or more of the following words:

> a, all, always, America, America's, an, and, are, as, at, be, beautiful, because, best, better, business, by, can, car, come, day, difference, do, don't, every, first, for, from, get, give, go, good, great, has, have, home, how, I, if, in, is, it, its, it's, just, keep, know, life, like, little, look, love, made, make, makes, more, most, name, need, never, new, no, not, now, of, on, one, only, our, out, people, quality, right, so, take, taste, than, that, the, they, things, this, time, to, up, us, want, way, we, we're, what, when, where, who, with, work, world, you, your, you're

How to Write Slogans

Writing slogans can be more difficult than writing headlines because headlines can be longer and consequently say more about the product and advertiser. In addition, a slogan's life cycle is much longer than that of a headline. At least, whoever has been assigned to create a slogan should try to write a slogan that will have memorability as well as a purpose, so that it will be used for years, if not decades, by the advertiser.

As mentioned, a good slogan will convey a product or advertiser's major characteristics to the target market. Look at the list of slogans again. Most, if not all, attempt to identify the product or advertiser's major strength. At the same time, these slogans try to respond to consumers' expectations. In short, these slogans attempt to present an image or personality of the product or advertiser.

When writing a slogan, keep in mind that it must be brief in order to be effective. Many slogans contain fewer than eight words. Xerox's slogan contains only three: "The document company."

A slogan should capture the nature of the product or advertiser. Of course, what is stated should be unique to the product or advertiser; it should not be similar to the slogans that have been created for other products or advertisers.

Suggestions for Writing Slogans

1. Separate the product or advertiser from the competition. One way of doing this is to focus on the major benefit of the product or on the nature of the advertiser.
2. Use words and phrases that the target market understands. Ambiguity will destroy a slogan's purpose.
3. State one compelling idea that grasps the product's major benefit or the advertiser's major reason for existence. Make sure that the idea has been stated in as few words as possible.
4. Be careful when using a pun, play on words, cliché, or rhyme; many have been used, and many are tiresome.
5. Include the product's or advertiser's name. Slogans that contain names usually have greater memorability.

In addition to the above, keep in mind that a slogan should not be adopted until it has been tested. Allow representative members of the target market to determine its worth. If they do not understand it or if they cannot remember it, then the slogan should be put aside, and another written and tested.

Also, if a slogan that has been written in English is translated into another language, it may not have the same meaning. For instance, the slogan for Kentucky Fried Chicken was translated into Chinese. "Finger-lickin' good" became "Eat your fingers off," which does not necessarily sound appetizing. Make sure whoever is responsible for the translation of the slogan does not make a similar blunder.

ILLUSTRATIONS

The artwork often works with the headline to identify the product, service, or advertiser. Advertising personnel have several choices. For instance, they may show the product by itself, in a setting, or even in use. They can show the product and the leading competitor's product. They can show a member of the target market before or after he or she has used the product. They may show just the package in which the product is sold.

No matter what is shown, advertising personnel must consider the following elements: headline, subhead (if applicable), body copy (if applicable), artwork (if applicable), logo (if applicable), and slogan (if applicable). In short, they must consider which element should come first, second, third, and so on in the advertisement. Usually, readers look at the artwork first, then at the headline, and then at the body copy. Readers' eyes move from left to right across the page and then down. Advertising personnel should think about placing the artwork at the top of the page (layout). The headline should be beneath the artwork; the body copy should be beneath the headline. The logo should be at the bottom of the page (layout), and the slogan should be below the logo. If a subhead is used, it should be beneath the headline.

Although the above describes the "ideal" layout of the elements, advertising personnel are arranging elements differently. However, no matter how the elements are arranged, make sure that the arrangement is based on logic. Otherwise, you may be asking a lot from the reader, particularly if you have a headline separated by several inches of artwork or space from the subhead or body copy. We will look at body copy in the next chapter.

EXERCISES

1. Look at a commercial on television and then think about how you would develop a print advertisement that plays up similar information. Try writing five headlines for the print advertisement.
2. Read the following blocks of copy and then write five headlines for each:
    - Chevrolet has made the Malibu just for you. An exciting, fun car for the entire family, and John Smith Chevrolet is proud to offer it. The Malibu, which is made in America, is a car worth looking at, especially since it costs considerably less than other models in its class. Just come in and test drive one; John Smith Chevrolet guarantees that you'll like it. In fact, John Smith Chevrolet will offer you a deal you can't refuse. Come in and see the various models. Malibu by Chevrolet.
    - Sears now offers Blue Jeans designed by Walter Taylor. Fashionable, exciting, and very comfortable, these jeans are made of cotton and Lycra. Made in America, these jeans are designed for women who know that Lycra helps whatever fabric it is mixed with to bend and stretch without losing shape. Lycra is the secret ingredient. Cotton is the fabric. The two together make an outstanding jean to wear. At $29.95, Blue Jeans by Walter Taylor are a steal, and they are only available at Sears!
    - Diamonds are a girl's best friend, especially if the diamonds are Jewels by Sadler's. Priced from $250 to $50,000, Jewel Diamonds sparkle like no other. And Sadler's Jewels are guaranteed not to lose their luster for as long as you own them. Diamonds . . . Jewel Diamonds by Sadler's. Guaranteed for life.
3. Examine the headline and body copy of a full-page ad in a magazine of your choice. Then try to write five headlines for another ad that continues the idea. Circle the headline that you think is the best.

NOTES

1. Jonathan Bond and Richard Kirshenbaum, *Under the Radar: Talking to Today's Cynical Consumer* (New York: John Wiley and Sons, Inc., 1998), p. xvii.

CHAPTER 4

Body Copy

In this chapter I will discuss the specifics of body copy and explain how it is written.

THE RIGHT ATTITUDE FOR WRITING BODY COPY

Now that the headline, subhead (if needed), and slogan (if needed) have been written, it is time to write the body copy of the advertisement. In order to do this, it is necessary to have the right attitude. This means that you must care about the product or service. If you do not care about the product or service, or if you would never have a need for the client's product or service, you must not let this fact be revealed in the headline, subhead, body copy, or slogan. One way to prevent this possible problem from occurring is to always put yourself in the position of a prospective consumer—that is, write the body copy from the consumer's perspective. Basically, answer the following question, "What is it about the product or service that is so attractive to the consumer?" For instance, will the product or service help the consumer to be appreciated or liked? Will it help the consumer to be healthy or feel secure? Will it help the consumer to have confidence? Will it help the consumer to be attractive or sexy? Will it help the consumer to feel important? Will it help the consumer to earn or save money? Will it help the consumer to be comfortable? Of course, there may be other reasons as to why consumers may purchase the product or service. What you must do is identify at least one or more reasons and address these in the advertisement. The answer(s) should be *selling features* and *benefits*, which have been discussed.

AN OUTLINE OF A TYPICAL ADVERTISEMENT

Most print advertisements will contain the following elements:

- Headline
- Introductory or Bridge Paragraph (which links the headline, subhead, and body copy)
- Supporting Paragraph(s) (which discuss additional selling features and benefits)

- Subhead (if needed)
- Call to Action Paragraph (which closes the sale)
- Slogan (if needed)
- Artwork (illustration or photograph)

The headline and subhead have been discussed in the previous chapter. The introductory or bridge paragraph usually continues the idea presented in the headline and subhead. In fact, it may continue the thought as if the copywriter had divided one paragraph into a headline and subhead and the body copy. Supporting paragraphs usually discuss selling points and benefits in descending order of importance. The call to action paragraph, which is usually the last paragraph, may be only a sentence in length. No matter how long it is, it has a major purpose: to cause the consumer to take action.

Generally, if the client has a slogan, it is included in the advertisement. The artwork, if needed, may be an illustration, a photograph, or a combination of the two. The artwork must relate to the headline and subhead and the body copy. If it does not, then it should not be included.

WHAT AN ADVERTISEMENT MUST HAVE

In addition to AIDA (attention, interest, desire, and action), which was addressed in a previous chapter and will be discussed later, there are other formulas that apply to advertisements. Russell H. Colley discussed ACCA (awareness, comprehension, conviction, and action) in his book *Defining Advertising Goals for Measured Advertising Results*, or DAGMAR, which was published in 1961. Colley claimed that consumers had to be made *aware* of a product or service's existence in the marketplace. Then these consumers had to *comprehend* or understand what the product or service would do for them. Next, consumers had to be *convinced* or persuaded to purchase the product or service. Finally, they had to take *action* and purchase the product or service.[1]

VIPS (visibility, identity, promise, and simplicity) was discussed by David Bernstein in his book *Creative Advertising: For This You Went to Oxford? A Personal Textbook of Advertising*, which was published in 1974. Bernstein claimed that an advertisement had to have *visibility* or something that made the advertisement stand out or capture attention. Second, it had to have *identity*—that is, it had to play up the brand name so consumers would not forget it. Third, it had to contain a *promise* or something that would cause consumers to choose the brand instead of one of its competitors. Fourth, it had to contain *simplicity* or, in other words, be simple. In short, the selling features and benefits needed to be stated clearly and logically—from the beginning to the end.

As you can surmise, these formulas are similar to AIDA, in the sense that they claim that advertisements must gain attention, be understood and persuasive, and cause action. How this is done usually depends on the type of advertisement that is created.

TYPES OF BODY COPY

"Reason Why" or Factual Copy

This type of body copy provides factual information about the product or service so that the consumer learns enough to make a purchasing decision. This type of body copy is used often, especially for expensive products and services.

Narrative Copy

This type of body copy weaves an emotional "story," primarily to draw consumers into the advertising message. Usually the "story" focuses on a problem that only the product or service can solve.

Testimonial or Monologue Copy

Testimonial copy is believable, particularly if consumers know and trust the person speaking about the product or service. However, in order for testimonials to work, the copy must be honest and, of course, delivered by a spokesperson whom consumers can identify. Testimonials can be by well-known experts who are known to use the product or service or by a celebrity whose "image" fits the "image" that consumers have of the product or service. An alternative to the expert or celebrity is the unknown spokesperson. In this instance, it is important that the unknown spokesperson represent the target market for the product or service; otherwise, consumers may not believe what the spokesperson says.

Another alternative is the nonperson character such as an animated figure. Generally, consumers remember such characters. Other factors for using an animated figure include the fact that such characters will not do something that embarrasses the company, they do not die, and they do not ask for more compensation.

Humorous or Offbeat Copy

Although this type of copy is used on occasion, it is important that the advertising copywriter understand that what is considered humorous by one person may not be considered humorous by another person; consequently, the copywriter must understand thoroughly the target market for the product or service before attempting to write this type of body copy. In fact, before this type of body copy is used, it should be tested to determine whether the sales message is understood and to determine whether the so-called humor is considered funny.

Descriptive Copy

This type of body copy discusses the various aspects of the product or service. Usually, it focuses on the selling points and benefits, much like "reason why" or factual copy. This type of copy may employ illustrations or photographs that depict the points the copy discusses.

Dialogue Copy

Similar to testimonial or monologue copy, dialogue copy employs two or more spokespersons who discuss the virtues of the product or service. If this type of body copy is used, it is important that the spokespersons represent the target market for the product or service. Generally, this type of body copy is best suited for broadcast commercials, not necessarily print, unless the copywriter is employing a comic strip or a continuity panel in which illustrations of spokespersons (characters) along with their comments are used.

Institutional Copy

This type of body copy is similar to the narrative type of body copy, but it focuses on the company or the company's perspective toward an issue, not on the company's product or service. Institutional copy can be one of the following: "corporate," "idea," "management," or "public relations." Institutional copy is used to enhance the image of the company, which, of course, should help the company sell more of its products or services to consumers or help to explain the company's perspective toward an issue, whether it is a company, political, or public issue.

HOW TO WRITE BODY COPY

Before we get into the specifics of how to write body copy, you must remember that you need to describe the product or service in terms of its benefits or what it will do for the consumer. In addition, you must remember to include enough information so that the consumer can make a logical decision to purchase the product or service. If you have a headline, a subhead, and several paragraphs of body copy that do not discuss selling features and, more important, benefits, then the advertisement will probably fail. Make sure that you focus on the positive, not the negative. Even if you are developing a comparative piece of body copy in which you compare the client's product to a competitor's product, you should not necessarily discuss the negative aspects of the competitor's product; rather, you should discuss the client's product, particularly its selling features and, more important, the benefits that make it better than the competitor's product.

Organization

Organizing the selling features and benefits in order of importance will help you develop body copy. In fact, each sentence or paragraph can discuss a selling feature and what that selling feature does for the consumer. As mentioned, what the selling feature does for the consumer is the benefit. Each selling feature may provide one or more benefits for the consumer.

Look at the following body copy for Stainmaster carpet:

The Next Level
of DuPont
Stainmaster
carpet.

The evolution of Stainmaster has become something of a revolution in carpets. You see, unlike any other carpet, a Stainmaster carpet is capable of keeping itself 40% cleaner.

That's because only Stainmaster has the DuPont Advanced Teflon repel system. This technology actually pushes away liquid, soil and stains from the carpet fiber.

Which means not only will DuPont Stainmaster virtually eliminate most soil and stain problems, it will also keep its true beauty longer. In fact, tests show that Stainmaster carpets stay 40% cleaner.

So the real beauty of a Stainmaster carpet may be just beneath the surface. For more information on DuPont Stainmaster carpets, visit your local retailer or call us at 1.800.4.DUPONT.

Remarkably keeps itself 40% cleaner.

[Stainmaster® carpet advertisement, DuPont Textiles and Interiors. Reprinted by permission.]

The major selling feature is the DuPont Advanced Teflon repel system. The benefits include a cleaner carpet (by 40 percent) and longer-lasting beauty.

Look at the following body copy for Egg Beaters:

> Ordinary eggs want to be
> as healthy as Egg Beaters.
> Fat chance.
>
> **Egg Beaters are delicious real eggs. But they have no fat, no cholesterol, and less than half the calories. That means you can eat healthy without having to give up favorite dishes like omelets and scrambled eggs. And they're available refrigerated or frozen. It's enough to turn ordinary shell eggs green with envy.**
>
> **Egg Beaters. We're Good Eggs!**
>
> *[Egg Beaters advertisement, ConAgra Foods, Inc. Reprinted by permission.]*

FIGURE 4.1 The Professional ColorPoint 2 by Seiko Instruments. *Courtesy of 3 Marketeers Advertising.*

Egg Beaters are not only "delicious real eggs"; they are healthy because they have no fat and no cholesterol. They also have fewer calories. Thus, the major selling feature is "real eggs," and the major benefit is healthiness.

Look at figure 4.1, which was created by personnel at 3 Marketeers Advertising. Notice the headline:

> **Get These in Under**
> **Three Minutes!**

The headline refers to the photographs above it, which are color printouts of shots apparently taken from space. The headline states that these photographs can be printed in less than three minutes.

The body copy is broken up into four paragraphs. Each paragraph is introduced by a subhead. The first paragraph discusses the time—four seconds—it takes to "capture renderings" and what these few seconds do for you, the user: "quick, high-quality color printouts" and "time to fine tune and review changes." The first paragraph also mentions that you can "print multiple views." Because of "16.7 million vivid colors, fine lines, call outs and crisp details are reflected precisely." In short, you will "get exactly what you see on screen."

The second paragraph mentions that you can print "from any monitor source" by pressing "a single button." The third paragraph discusses the various modes that you can use, such as the "thermal wax transfer mode for fast, low cost color drafts" and the "dye sublimation mode for photo realistic 24-bit continuous tone color prints." The fourth paragraph tells the reader to call for free information.

Look at figure 4.2, which was created by personnel at Colby & Partners. The headline reads:

FEAR NO MOUNTAIN, DESERT OR PARKING GARAGE.

The headline informs the reader that the Suzuki XL-7 SUV can go anywhere without any trouble or aggravation, including a parking garage that may cause claustrophobia.

FIGURE 4.2 Suzuki is introducing a new SUV. *Courtesy of American Suzuki Motor Corporation and*

The body copy reads:

> THE NEW SUZUKI XL-7. More cargo space than a Jeep Grand Cherokee, and more front seat headroom than a Lexus RX300. It's got all the size and power with none of the excess. Starting under $20,000.* To find out more call 1-877-MY-SUZUKI.

The body copy provides factual information such as "more cargo space than a Jeep Grand Cherokee" and "more front seat headroom than a Lexus RX300." The benefits of "spaciousness" and "roominess" are implied and understood. For those readers who are interested in learning more about the SUV, the body copy closes with a telephone number.

Box 4.1 is Colby & Partners' case study for the Suzuki XL-7. According to Colby & Partners, "We could have positioned Suzuki's new XL-7 against all the other SUVs in the market. Instead, we went up against the giant, gas-guzzlers and said the XL-7 gives you everything you need in an SUV. Without the excess. And that's a position we own."[2]

BOX 4.1 ***Suzuki XL-7 Case Study***

Problem: Suzuki, the smallest Japanese auto brand, was known for very small SUVs and passenger cars. Although Suzuki's all-new SUV was their largest model to date and designed to meet midsize SUV needs, it was still smaller than midsize and large SUV competitors. With a very low budget and little brand awareness, Suzuki needed to introduce the model with a relevant message that overcame consumers' preconceived brand perceptions and brought them into Suzuki dealerships to consider vehicles they would not have expected from Suzuki.

Creative Strategy: Tackle the subject of size head-on and position the XL-7 as reasonably sized and reasonably priced amid a sea of oversized, overpriced competitors.

Executional Element: Creative used huge SUVs as a foil for humor in a way that the viewer would both enjoy and identify with. Specifically, the real problem of huge SUVs were taken to absurd levels, making excessively large SUVs the butt of several jokes per spot. The XL-7 is then presented as a reasonably sized alternative.

Market Results: Following a year in which Suzuki was America's fastest-growing Japanese auto company, the XL-7 quickly became Suzuki's best-selling product. By the end of the calendar year, XL-7 accounted for almost 50 percent of Suzuki's monthly sales, leading the brand to its best annual sales in 15 years.

Key Insight: While the rest of the industry was trumpeting a "bigger is better" message, much of the target market was actually responding to a growing anti-huge SUV backlash, leading them to consider SUV size in terms not of "how much can I get" but, rather, "what is an appropriate size for my needs?"

Courtesy of American Suzuki Motor Corporation and Colby & Partners.

Now, you should understand the difference between a *selling feature* and a *benefit*. Remember, effective body copy emphasizes *benefits* primarily because benefits sell the product or service. *Selling features* do not.

If you were developing body copy for a casual leather shoe that laces, you may write the name of the product at the top of a piece of paper. On the left side of the piece of paper you may write "FEATURES."

On the right side of the piece of paper you may write "BENEFITS." Now, underline each word. List the product's features under "FEATURES." List the corresponding benefits under "BENEFITS." Your piece of paper should be similar to the following:

Leather Casual Shoes

FEATURES	BENEFITS
Leather construction	Cleans easily; durable
Laces	Fit comfortably; tie easily
Spongy rubber soles	Grips firmly, even on damp surfaces
Two colors: brown and black	Goes with any wardrobe

In order to write the advertising message, all you need to do is focus on the major selling features and, more important, the major benefits. Write a headline and then the body copy, or vice versa. Work the benefits into the body copy in order of importance. Although this is a simple formula for writing body copy, it may be used for practically any advertisement, no matter whether you are advertising a product or a service.

Elaboration

Most, if not all, advertisements are based on one of the previous formulas such as AIDA:

1. Attract the attention of the consumer.
2. Interest the consumer in the product or service.
3. Cause the consumer to desire the product or service.
4. Demand that the consumer take some sort of action.

Of course, the headline and artwork usually capture the consumer's attention. Generally, the headline will imply or contain a direct promise. In order for the headline to be successful, it must be specific and personal. In other words, it should sound as if the copywriter was writing to a particular individual. The headline may be stated as a question as long as it does not allow the consumer to respond with a simple yes or no.

After you have captured the consumer's attention, you must interest the consumer in the product or service. The easiest way to do this is by quickly explaining what the product or service will do for the consumer. Specifically, the consumer desires to learn how she or he is going to benefit from the product or service. Will the product or service improve the consumer's health? Will it help the consumer earn more money? Will it provide the consumer with more leisure time? Will it provide the consumer with greater comfort? Will it help the consumer become more popular? Will it help the consumer to be more physically attractive? No matter what the product or service will do for the consumer, no matter if these benefits have been stated or implied in the headline and subhead (if needed), these benefits must be discussed or reiterated.

In order to write successful body copy, you must appeal to the consumer's needs and emotional desires. One way of doing this is by putting yourself in the consumer's position. However, you will not be able to do this successfully if you do not understand who the consumer is. Hopefully, you will know who the consumer is based on primary and secondary research. In other words, you will know what the consumer's likes and dislikes are; you will know what the consumer desires. Only then will you be able to tell the consumer how the product or service will fulfill his or her wants or needs.

Also in the body copy, you need to discuss the facts of the product or service—that is, if these facts have corresponding benefits, which, of course, should be discussed. In other words, you must provide enough information—selling features and benefits—so that the consumer desires the product or service and can justify his or her action, which is making a purchase. These facts and benefits will make the product or service more credible to the consumer. If you can include facts about the product or service that are based on studies or tests, then the product or service will have greater credibility in the consumer's mind. You may even include endorsements from others who have used the product or service. In other words, such information will assure the consumer that she or he has made a wise decision in purchasing the product or service.

In a sentence or brief paragraph, summarize the benefits that you have promised. Allow the consumer to visualize owning the product or service or at least using the product or service and then close by asking or demanding the consumer to take action. You can actually induce the consumer to do this by offering a reward that relates to the product or service. However, if the advertiser is willing to offer a reward, make sure that it is offered for a limited time. Otherwise, the reward will lose its effectiveness. Also, do not discuss the reward too much; you do not wish to make the reward sound more important than the product or service.

To summarize the above, first, you need to understand the purpose or objective of the advertisement. For instance, are you trying to sell a product or service or to enhance the company's image? Are you trying to sell a new product or service or an old established product or service?

Second, let the purpose or objective guide the entire advertisement (headline, subhead [if needed], body copy, slogan, artwork). In short, every element must support the major selling proposition or the major idea.

Third, whatever idea is presented in the headline, it should be supported in the body copy. However, avoid outrageous claims that cannot be substantiated. Use figures or statistics, if possible, to document your statements. Such will help build credibility with the consumer. Make sure that you use words that are clear and easily understood by the consumer. Emphasize benefits, not selling features. Avoid using mere facts. The consumer is interested in knowing what the product or service will do for him or her, not necessarily what the product is made of or how it operates.

Fourth, ask or demand the consumer to take action. After all, you are trying to sell a product or service—or at least an idea that will help improve the consumer's life.

Writing Lengthy Body Copy

Whether you write short body copy or long body copy will depend largely on the product or service that needs to be advertised, specifically what needs to be discussed. For instance, if you are writing body copy about an expensive product such as a car or a technical product such as a computer, you will need several paragraphs in order to explain the selling features and, more important, the benefits.

In addition to the product or service, your decision to use short or long body copy will depend on the purpose or objective of the body copy and the target market. For instance, if you are writing body copy about a product that other firms should purchase, you may have to inform and persuade purchasing agents or engineers about the merits of the product. Think about the equipment that manufacturers need to manufacture products. How did their purchasing agents and engineers learn about the equipment? Usually, they learned from advertisements appearing in the form of flyers, brochures, sales information kits, or sales personnel.

Regarding lengthy body copy, David Ogilvy writes, "I believe . . . that advertisements with long copy convey the impression that you have *something important to say*, whether people read the copy or not."[3] In summary, lengthy body copy is usually desired for products that are purchased after much consideration. Generally, these products are more expensive than other products. In addition, they may be more mechanical or technical and perhaps require demonstration. They may be new products that need to be thoroughly explained to the prospective buyer.

Suggestions for Writing Body Copy

1. Organize the selling features and benefits in order of importance.
2. Avoid technical jargon or terms that consumers do not use or understand.
3. Use simple words that consumers understand.
4. Be specific and concise.
5. Use sentence fragments.
6. Vary sentence length, but have more short sentences than long sentences.
7. Use a personal conversational style of writing.
8. Use conjunctions, even at the beginning of sentences.
9. Use one-sentence paragraphs occasionally.
10. Use pronouns and contractions.
11. End a sentence with a preposition occasionally.
12. Use transitions to link sentences.
13. Use bullets or numbers to list specific features or other information.
14. Use certain techniques such as underlines, italics, or boldface type to emphasize words or phrases occasionally.
15. Use subheads to break up long body copy.
16. Use action verbs instead of passive verbs.
17. Write positive, not negative, body copy.
18. At the end of the body copy, urge the reader to act.
19. If relevant, offer an incentive so that the consumer will act.
20. If relevant, include a specific date or deadline so that the consumer will act.
21. If relevant, mention a guarantee, even in the headline or subhead.
22. Avoid sexist or offensive language.
23. Use the present tense.
24. Use singular nouns and verbs whenever possible.
25. Avoid clichés and abstract (vague) words.
26. Arouse the consumer's curiosity.
27. Be honest and sincere in what you claim.

Once you have written the headline, subhead (if needed), and body copy, ask the following questions:

1. Do the headline and subhead mention the most important benefit?
2. Do the headline and subhead mention news?
3. Do the headline and subhead promise a reward for reading the body copy?
4. Do the headline and subhead mention the target market?
5. Do the headline and subhead capture the consumer's attention?
6. Does the first (bridge) paragraph expand on the theme of the headline?
7. Is the body copy easy to understand?
8. Is the body copy believable? Concise? Interesting? Relevant?
9. Does the body copy present the sales features and benefits in order of importance?
10. Does the body copy provide enough information for the consumer to be convinced or persuaded to take action?
11. Does the body copy ask or demand that the consumer take action?

If the advertisement has illustrations or photographs, make sure that you write cutlines (captions) for each. Cutlines or captions should be sentences, not one or two words, that describe or identify what is in the illustration or photograph. In the next chapter I will discuss the principles of design.

EXERCISES

1. The following will reveal your creative ability. You should think about an advertising objective as well as a theme or concept before you attempt this exercise. The ad will appear in several mass-circulated magazines. An illustration of the collar and the device will be included in the ad. The copy will appear in the lower half of the ad. You do not have to worry about the illustration; just write 75 to 100 words (headline and body copy). You may wish to write the ad before you type it. Double-space!

   Product: Space-age Dog Collar.
   Distinctive Product Feature: The dog collar allows the owner to locate a dog without having to walk in all directions. All the owner has to do is press a button on a device kept in the home, and the dog collar sounds an alarm.
   Construction: The dog collar is leather; the attached alarm is metal.
   Description: The dog collar comes in two colors—black and brown. It has a link attached so that the dog can be fastened to a chain. The small metal alarm is silver.
   Prospect: Dog owners.
   Competition: There are various dog collars on the market, but none is like this one.
   Manufacturer: Space-age Dog Collars, Inc.

2. Look at a television commercial and then try to develop a headline and body copy for a print advertisement that plays up similar information.
3. Some people in the United States have grown concerned about litter and landfills. Certain companies have made their products biodegradable. They have also made their packages from recycled

paper. Let us say that Procter & Gamble has developed a package that is made from recycled paper for Tide and that the company has asked its agency, for which you work, to create a full-page magazine ad to announce the news. You will need to write a headline and body copy. If you desire to include a slogan, do so. The copy should relate to what has been termed "green marketing."

4. Examine a newspaper ad for a local retailer and then try to write a headline and body copy for another ad that continues the idea.

NOTES

1. Russell H. Colley, *Defining Advertising Goals for Measured Advertising Results* (New York: Association of National Advertisers, 1961), p. 38.
2. Colby & Partners, *Print Portfolio*, n.p.
3. David Ogilvy, *Ogilvy on Advertising* (New York: Vintage Books, 1985), p. 88.

↼ CHAPTER 5 ↼

An Introduction to Design

Advertising copywriters usually work with creative directors, graphics personnel, and layout artists. In fact, a copywriter and an artist may discuss the information and the product that have been given to them in an effort to formulate the big idea for the advertising. Because copywriters are involved in generating creative ideas, they need to know about design to understand what creative directors, graphics personnel, and layout artists do so that they can communicate with them.

LAYOUT ELEMENTS

The layout for an advertisement usually contains the following elements: illustration(s) or photograph(s), headline, body copy, price (if needed), logotype (logo), slogan (if needed), and white space. Some advertising personnel would add the elements typeface and color to this list. Let us examine each of these.

Illustration or Photograph

Most advertisements will have at least one illustration or photograph. It is important that this illustration or photograph help convey the image the advertiser desires. It is also essential that the illustration or photograph is appropriate for whatever is being advertised. It is imperative that this illustration or photograph is consistent in color, depiction, shape, and size with those that are used in the other advertisements in the campaign. It is also important for the person appearing in the illustration or photograph—that is, if a person appears—to represent the target market or audience. For instance, if you were designing an advertisement for baseball caps, you would not necessarily include an illustration or photograph of an elderly woman. Remember that larger illustrations or photographs attract more attention than smaller illustrations or photographs.

Headline

The headline should be relevant to the target market or audience as well as to the illustration or photograph. It should state what the product is or at least state the most important benefit. The headline should be in a typeface that helps convey the image the advertiser desires. The type size should be proportional to the other elements, especially to the illustration or photograph.

Body Copy

Body copy should expand on what is stated in the headline. It should focus on the selling features and, more important, the benefits. The typeface should be the same or similar to that used for the headline. The type size should be between 10 and 12 points.

Price (if Needed)

If you need to include the price (most retail advertisements do; most national advertisements do not), make sure that the typeface and type size are related and proportional to the typeface and type size used for the headline. The type size may change, depending on what type of retailer is advertising. For instance, the upscale retailer will usually desire a smaller size type for prices, whereas the discount retailer will usually desire a large type size for prices.

Logo

A logotype or logo is the name of the advertiser in a specific typeface or artwork. A logo will usually appear in this typeface or artwork in every advertisement in the campaign. In fact, an advertiser's logo may not change for years, if not decades.

Slogan (if Needed)

In order to be successful, slogans need to be easily remembered by consumers. Slogans should identify the advertiser. They should link advertisements in a campaign. Usually, they will tie campaigns together, primarily because they will remain the same for years, sometimes a decade or longer.

White Space

Most white space should be outside the other elements, not in between them. Of course, the amount of white space in an advertisement will depend on the number of other elements (and their sizes) as well as on the amount of information that needs to be conveyed to the reader. Proper use of white space can improve the design of any advertisement.

Typeface

The typeface selected should be appropriate for whatever is being advertised and for the image the advertiser desires. For most advertisements, one or two typefaces may be used. Variety can be obtained by using different type sizes; bold-, medium, or lightface; or italics. Whatever typeface is selected should be easy to read. For most advertisements, serif typefaces should be used.

Color

Spot color (one additional color to black and white) can help increase readership almost as much as full color (four color). Although color increases the cost of the advertisement, its value usually outweighs the extra expense. Also, certain products need to be advertised in color. For instance, carpet, hardwood flooring, blinds, draperies, and other products for the home should be depicted in color.

LAYOUT DESIGN

Successful advertisements are successful because they attract the reader's attention and they are easy to read—that is, the eyes move naturally from one element to another. There are several terms relating to design that need to be explained.

Flow (Eye Movement)

Normal eye movement is from left to right. Consequently, advertisements should encourage the reader to begin in the upper left section, then move to the upper right section, then look down to the lower left section, and then end at the lower right section. Creative directors, graphics personnel, and layout artists can achieve this by first attracting the reader's attention. Devices such as a bright color, an unusual shape, or a large illustration or photograph can attract attention. The advertising copywriter can achieve the same by writing an interesting headline.

Next, the reader has to be guided from one area of the advertisement to another. What is in the illustration or photograph can actually do this. For instance, if a person appears in the illustration or photograph, her or his eyes may direct the reader's eyes to a specific area of the advertisement. Of course, the same can be accomplished by having the person's head, fingers, arms, elbows, or feet pointing toward a specific area of the advertisement. Even tonal quality—say, dark to light—can achieve the same.

Dominance (Emphasis)

In advertisements, usually one element is emphasized more than the other elements. This element may attract the reader's attention to the advertisement. It is important that the emphasized element relates to the most important point of the advertising message. Generally, the emphasized element may be an illustration or photograph or the headline. Emphasis can be obtained by making the element unusual in shape or size, by making it bolder, by surrounding it with an abundant amount of white space, by putting it in the optical center of the advertisement (the optical center is slightly above the center of the advertisement and to the left), or by putting it in color and the other elements in black and white.

Balance

Balance may be formal (symmetrical) or informal (asymmetrical). Balance depends on the weight of the elements in the advertisement. For instance, dark elements are heavier than light elements. Big elements are heavier than small elements. Thick elements are heavier than thin elements. Illustrations or photographs are usually heavier than headlines, body copy, logos, or slogans. Headlines are usually heavier than body copy, logos, or slogans. Color is heavier than black and white. Unusual shapes are heavier than regular shapes.

Formal balance occurs when weight is evenly distributed at the top and bottom of the advertisement or on the right side and left side of the advertisement. For instance, if the illustration or photograph, headline, and body copy are centered in the advertisement, the advertisement has formal balance. Informal balance occurs when different weights appear in different areas of the advertisement. In other words, one part of the advertisement appears to have more weight than the other part because certain heavier elements have been positioned there.

Proportion

Proportion refers to the relationship of width to height or the size of one element to that of another. Usually, unequally sized elements are more attractive than equal-sized elements. For instance, rectangles are more interesting than squares. The size of each element in an advertisement should be proportionate to its significance or relevance. This includes every element: illustration or photograph, headline, body copy, logo, slogan, white space, color, and black and white. In layouts for advertisements, three units (uneven number) are preferred for proportion than two or four units (even numbers).

Unity

Unity refers to cohesiveness—that is, the elements within the advertisement appear to be related. Generally, the easiest way of achieving unity is by having an imaginary line or axis running through the advertisement from which two or more elements flare outward. For instance, the edge of an illustration or photograph may be even with the edge of a headline. When two or more elements use a common axis, they help hold all the elements together. Unity can be achieved by having elements of similar shapes, sizes, and color. Unity can come from using the same typeface for the headline and body copy. Unity also can be achieved by using borders or boxes.

LAYOUTS

Many creative directors, graphics personnel, and layout artists design advertisements in stages. These stages include thumbnails, roughs, and comprehensives:

Thumbnails: Thumbnails are sketches. They are miniature in size—generally about one-fourth the size of the actual advertisement. Thumbnails are used to generate a variety of approaches or possible advertisements. Only one or two, however, are chosen for roughs. See figure 5.1.

Roughs: Roughs depict the selected thumbnails in the exact size of the actual advertisement. Typically, these contain a lettered rendering of the headline and a drawn rendering of the illustration or photograph. See figure 5.2.

Comprehensives: A comprehensive is a detailed layout that is a perfect facsimile of the actual advertisement. Usually, it is used for the client's approval before the actual advertisement is produced. See figure 5.3.

The advent of the computer has altered the way thumbnails, roughs, and comprehensives are produced. Today, it is not uncommon to see creative personnel in advertising agencies producing final versions of advertisements on computers.

FREQUENTLY USED DESIGNS FOR ADVERTISEMENTS

Although there are numerous designs for advertisements, there are several that appear more often than others. These designs include the following: "Alphabet," "Editorial or Copy Filled," "Frame," "Mondrian," "Omnibus or Circus," "Picture Panel/Multipanel or Comic Strip," "Picture Window," "Scrapbook or Grid," "Silhouette," and "Typographical or Type Specimen."

FIGURE 5.1 This thumbnail is for a newspaper advertisement. *Courtesy of Metro Creative Graphics, Inc.*

FIGURE 5.2 This rough is for a newspaper advertisement. *Courtesy of Metro Creative Graphics, Inc.*

FIGURE 5.3 This comprehensive is for a newspaper advertisement. *Courtesy of Metro Creative Graphics, Inc.*

Alphabet

In this advertisement, the elements are positioned in such a way that together they resemble a letter of the alphabet, such as an "S" or a "Z" (See figures 5.1–5.3).

Editorial or Copy Filled

In this advertisement, the headline is centered. A second headline may follow it. The body copy may begin with a large initial letter. As the name implies, the advertisement contains an abundant amount of body copy, which usually occupies two or more columns. Subheads and illustrations or photographs may be used to break up the body copy.

Frame

In this advertisement, borders may be used to frame one or more elements or even the entire advertisement. Decorative devices, illustrations, or photographs may be used to frame the headline and body copy.

Mondrian

Various-sized rectangles of a headline, body copy, and illustrations or photographs are arranged in a Piet Mondrian–inspired geometric design in this advertisement. Lines may be used to separate the various elements. Typefaces may be bold, especially if lines have been used. Generally, a dark, thick sans serif typeface will be used for the headline and body copy.

Omnibus or Circus

Numerous products or items are featured in this advertisement. Typically, the advertisement contains large-size type, reverse blocks, or sunbursts to attract the reader's attention to specific areas. The elements are usually organized into units; the units are organized into a unified pattern. Variety is emphasized by the shape or size of the units within the advertisement.

Picture Panel/Multipanel or Comic Strip

Several rectangles of the same size are placed together and consequently form a panel in this advertisement. Usually, an illustration or photograph occupies each rectangle, and related copy appears directly beneath each rectangle. The panel or panels are larger than the space reserved for the headline, body copy, and logo. Generally, the panels present the selling message in a sequence of events or feature more than one product.

Picture Window

In this advertisement, the illustration or photograph occupies more than half of the space and generally bleeds off of the page. The headline is centered and placed below the illustration or photograph. Two or three brief columns of body copy immediately follow. The logo generally appears in the lower right corner of the advertisement. Occasionally, the headline is printed in reverse (white letters on black or some other dark color) on the illustration or photograph. Sometimes the headline is overprinted on the illustration or photograph.

Scrapbook or Grid

In this advertisement, the headline is generally placed at the top. Four rectangles featuring illustrations or photographs of a product usually follow. A cutline or caption appears directly beneath each illustration or photograph and identifies what is being depicted. The logo is usually centered at the bottom of the advertisement. Sometimes the headline is centered beneath the bottom row of illustrations or photographs. One or two columns of body copy immediately follow. Cutlines or captions may not be used if the body copy contains information that identifies what is being depicted in the illustrations or photographs.

Silhouette

The elements are arranged so as to form a silhouette in this advertisement. Generally, the headline is positioned at the top of the advertisement. White space is usually found outside, not in between, the elements. The illustration or photograph usually features foreground, not background, characters.

Typographical or Type Specimen

In this advertisement, the typeface and type size of the headline and the brief amount of body copy are enough to capture attention. In short, the typeface and the type size are more important than any illustration or photograph, which, of course, is not used in this advertisement. Generally, large and bold types as well as upper- and lowercase letters are used.

ILLUSTRATIONS OR PHOTOGRAPHS

Whether to use an illustration or photograph is a major decision. Of course, not every advertisement needs an illustration or photograph. For instance, small advertisements rarely have room for images. In fact, these advertisements typically have a headline that focuses on the most important benefit and some body copy. The name of the advertiser, the location of the advertiser (if needed), and the telephone number of the advertiser (if needed) follow. However, for advertisements that are a quarter page or larger, an illustration or photograph may help attract attention.

Before deciding on using an illustration or photograph, make sure that the image relates to the headline and body copy, that it communicates the major point of the selling message, and that it relates to the target market or audience. Of course, there are other variables such as shape, size, and color that need to be considered.

There are several reasons for using an illustration or photograph. In addition to probably attracting attention, which increases readership, an illustration or photograph can communicate the major point of the selling message quickly. Of course, each kind of artwork has its own advantages.

Illustrations

Illustrations can help establish a mood or provide an atmosphere for the advertisement. In addition, they can be prepared faster than photographs. Generally, outside professional photographers have to be hired for "shoots." Consequently, illustrations are usually less expensive. Illustrations can be obtained from clip art services, thus eliminating the need for a professional artist. In this case, the illustrations can be changed often, thus providing a variety of advertisements for the advertiser. In order to do this with photographs, a professional photographer would have to be hired to take a variety of shots. This, of course, would add to the cost of the advertisements. Illustrations are excellent when produced in newspapers, primarily because of the texture of the paper on which newspapers are printed.

Photographs

Photographs should be considered when realism is desired or when someone (a model) representing the target market or audience has been hired to help sell the product or service. Photographs should be considered when the advertisement is being placed in magazines, not newspapers. Generally, photographs do not produce well on newsprint. In fact, the reproduction may be so poor that the image of the advertiser is weakened. Photographs should be considered when the product is shown or its benefits are implied. They should be considered when certain types of merchandise are being advertised. For instance, food appears more appetizing in colored photographs than in illustrations.

Approaches to Visualization

There are several approaches to visualization that must be considered. These include showing the product by itself, showing the product in use, showing a major benefit as a result of using the product, showing a negative experience as a result of not using the product, or showing the product in its natural environment.

PRODUCT BY ITSELF In this illustration or photograph, the product is shown alone. Generally, there is nothing in the background (no people or environment), only the product. The purpose of this visualization is to bring attention to the product, nothing else. The headline and body copy typically discuss the product—that is, its features and its benefits.

PRODUCT IN USE In this illustration or photograph, a person is shown actually using the product. The background or setting is such that it does not attract attention. Although a headline and body copy will usually be present, the major feature and the benefit are occasionally shown or at least implied in the illustration or photograph.

PRODUCT BENEFIT FROM USE Similar to showing the product in use, this visualization shows the major benefit that the product provides when used properly. For instance, many household products such as tools, electric appliances, radios, televisions, computers, cleansers, and detergents as well as personal care products have been advertised in this manner.

NEGATIVE EXPERIENCE FROM NOT USING THE PRODUCT In this illustration or photograph, a person has a "bad" or negative experience because he or she did not use the product. This is occasionally used to advertise personal care products such as deodorants, toothpastes, and mouthwashes. It has been used to advertise various kinds of insurance as well as tires. It has also been used to advertise various cellular service providers as well as cars, trucks, and other vehicles.

PRODUCT IN NATURAL ENVIRONMENT In this illustration or photograph, the product is depicted in its natural or realistic environment such as a bathroom, kitchen, dining room, or garage. The realistic setting provides credibility and consequently enhances the product's image in the consumer's mind. It may even cause the consumer to desire the product more than she or he would have if it had been depicted by itself.

TYPOGRAPHY

The pica is used to measure column, illustration, or photograph widths and depths. The point is used to measure type sizes. There are 6 picas in an inch, and there are 72 points in an inch. There are 12 points in a pica.

Types vary in size. For instance, body copy type is available in 6, 7, 8, 9, 10, 11, and 12 points. Headline or display type is available in 14, 18, 24, 30, 36, 42, 48, 60, and 72 points. Of course, other sizes do exist for headline or display type, but these sizes are the most used.

Type Categories

Although there are thousands of different typefaces or fonts, most, if not all, can be grouped into one or more of the following categories: serifs, sans serifs, scripts, and miscellaneous.

SERIFS These fonts have strokes or feet at the tops and bottoms of letters. These strokes or feet actually enable the reader to read easier and faster. Serifs are generally referred to as Romans and may be considered old or modern in appearance. The following is an example of a serif typeface:

Times New Roman

SANS SERIFS Sans serifs are fonts that have strokes of even thickness. In short, these typefaces lack feet at the tops and bottoms of letters. Sans serifs are usually reserved for headlines and logotypes. The following is an example of a sans serif typeface:

Futura

SCRIPTS These fonts imitate written letters. The letters appear as if they are connected, thus giving the impression that someone actually wrote the letters with a pen. Scripts are not very effective when used in advertisements, however. In fact, they often distract, not attract, the reader. The following is an example of a script typeface:

BrushScript

MISCELLANEOUS Other fonts include Text as well as those that resemble what is produced by technological innovations such as computers or what has been designed for a science fiction film, comic book, or some other medium that has become part of popular culture. Most of these fonts are not suitable for most advertisements. The following are examples of miscellaneous typefaces:

Lucida

Wittenberger Fraktur

Italics

Some advertising professionals may consider italics as a separate category, but slanting characters are actually available for practically any typeface, no matter whether it is a serif or sans serif font.

What to Consider When Choosing Type

1. When you have to decide on a typeface, make sure that it is legible. For instance, you need to consider whether the typeface should be serif or sans serif. As mentioned, serif typefaces are easier to read than sans serif typefaces.
2. You also need to consider the type size. Although body copy can be as small as 6 points, you should use 10- or even 12-point type size. After all, you need to make it as easy on the reader as you possibly can, or he or she will not waste the time, especially if he or she has to strain.
3. You also need to consider using bolder, not lighter, type. Bolder type is easier to read than lighter type. Again, keep the reader in mind when making your selection. However, we are not suggesting that you use boldface. Indeed, boldface type should be used when you think something specific needs to be emphasized. If you use boldface type for the headline and the body copy, its purpose has been lost.
4. The headline should be legible as well—that is, it should be in a typeface and type size that are easy to read. Of course, your selections for the headline and body copy should relate well to the advertiser, the advertiser's product, and the target market or audience, as mentioned.
5. You also need to consider using uppercase and lowercase letters for the headline, subhead (if needed), and body copy. This is what the reader is used to reading.

6. You need to consider limiting the number of typefaces used in the advertisement to one or two. If you use two, make sure that they work well together. Otherwise, the contrast the typefaces present may distract the reader.
7. Although you may use italics to highlight or emphasize something specific in the headline or body copy, you should not use italics very often because, like too much boldface type, italics is not preferred by readers.
8. You should consider indenting paragraphs; you also should consider making most, if not all, of the paragraphs brief.
9. You should consider using subheads, illustrations, photographs, borders, or boxes to break up long blocks of body copy.
10. You should use caution when reversing print on a black or dark background. As mentioned, white letters on a black or dark background may be difficult to read. If you decide to do this, make sure that you use a sans serif typeface. In addition, make sure that the type size is larger than if it were printed in black on white.
11. You should consider using leading or white space between lines of type.
12. You should consider trying not to print any body copy on any artwork, no matter whether it is an illustration or photograph.
13. You should consider setting body copy flush left, primarily because this is what the reader is used to seeing.
14. You should consider setting type no wider than 40 characters, preferably fewer.
15. You should consider using normal punctuation, not unusual punctuation such as ellipses.
16. You should consider aligning all copy elements (headline, subhead, body copy) so that they do not appear jumbled or out of place.
17. You should consider using bullets or asterisks in front of copy that can be listed.
18. You should consider using numbers in front of copy that is not necessarily related but that can be listed.

THE USE OF COLOR

It is possible to attract attention in several different ways. One way is related to the ink that is used. For instance, you do not necessarily have to use black ink all the time. Red ink or some other warm-colored ink can attract attention, especially from women. Blue ink or some other cool-colored ink can attract attention, especially from men. Another way involves the paper stock on which the advertisement is printed. Less expensive paper stock such as newsprint, which is used primarily for printing newspapers, is not as attractive as, say, coated paper, which is used primarily for printing glossy magazines. Another way is related to the design that is used. Some of the designs that have been discussed have more appeal than others. For instance, the Picture Window design usually has more appeal than, say, the Editorial or Copy-Filled design. Still another way is the addition of color. As mentioned, even spot color can help increase readership. Full color or process color can help increase readership even more than spot color.

Although black is the best for reproducing type and ordinary illustrations and photographs, color adds realism to illustrations and photographs that feature the product, the product's natural environment, or the individuals who use the product. As mentioned, certain types of products such as food benefit from using colored photographs. Advertisements featuring fashions for women and men benefit from using colored photographs as well. Although color costs from 30 to 40 percent more than black and white, color is usually worth the extra expense. Of course, other processes that add color but not necessarily the extra expense may be used. For example, a duotone, for which a printer makes two negatives and two plates of a photograph, may be used. One plate is printed in a color, and the other plate is printed in black. The color adds to the black, yet the cost is not as much as it would be for full color or process color.

Primary and Secondary Colors

The primary colors include cyan (blue), magenta (red), and yellow. Secondary colors include green, orange, and violet. These are produced when two of the primary colors are mixed in equal amounts. For instance, green is made when yellow and blue are mixed; orange is made when yellow and red are mixed; and violet is made when blue and red are mixed.

What Colors Mean

Colors have different psychological definitions and effects. Consequently, colors should be called for when particular definitions or effects are desired. To most people born in the United States, colors have the following definitions:

- Blue: water, sky, fear, sobriety, aloofness
- Dark Blue: cold, depth, formal, dignity
- Light Blue: cool, youth, fragile, pure
- Red: passion, zealous, fire, heat, excitement, happy
- Yellow: cowardly, madness, warning, refresh, bright
- Green: freshness, disease, terror
- Dark Green: cheap, cold, unhealthy
- Light Green: cool, crisp, freshness
- Orange: energy, force, knowledge, warmth, power, action
- Violet: depression, royalty, stateliness, opulence
- White: pure, clean, truth, chastity
- Black: depression, gloom, death, elegance, mystery, cold, strong, heavy, sensual

If people have moved to the United States from other countries, definitions of colors may vary. For instance, white may mean death to a person from a country in Asia.

Colors That You Should Use

Women prefer red and other warm colors, whereas men prefer blue and other cool colors. However, some products, depending for which gender or which room of the house they are intended, should be advertised in warm environments, and some should be advertised in cool environments. Warm colors tend to stimulate the reader, whereas cool colors tend to calm the reader. Warm colors typically make environments (rooms, etc.) smaller in appearance, and cool colors make environments (rooms, etc.) larger in appearance. As noted, use of color should also be tied to the advertisement's medium. I will discuss newspaper advertising in the next chapter.

EXERCISES

1. Designing an ad is not difficult if you have read this chapter. For this exercise, do several thumbnails before you tackle the comprehensive. Depict a 12-ounce can of Diet Pepsi in a setting of your choice—that is, you may have a person drinking it, if you like. You will need to decide on how the product should be shown. Provide a headline and body copy; both should be positioned where you believe they work best. The typeface for the headline should be appropriate for the product. The illustration should be the dominant element, however. Include a logotype at the bottom of the ad. The outside border of the ad should be 7" wide × 10" high. You may use a computer.

CHAPTER 6

Newspaper Advertising

Advertisers are spending between $40 and $50 billion annually in newspapers.[1] The reasons for this high figure include the following: about 55 percent of the adult population read a daily newspaper, and about 64 percent of the adult population read a Sunday newspaper. Of course, more than two individuals read each copy of a daily and Sunday newspaper. As a result, more than 100 million people read daily and Sunday newspapers.

The typical daily and Sunday newspaper subscriber is a married woman or man who lives in a two-person household. The majority ranges in age from 35 to 65-plus. Most are parents with at least a high school education. A sizable minority has completed some college work, and another sizable minority has earned a bachelor's degree. Most are employed and hold a professional or managerial position. Most earn more than $40,000 a year and own the house in which they live. Most of these houses are worth more than $100,000, with a sizable minority worth more than $200,000. Most of these individuals have lived in their houses for more than 20 years. However, a sizable minority has lived between one and four years at their current address. Although most of these readers are white and live in the southern or north-central part of the country, a sizable minority are African Americans who live in the same regions.[2]

There are almost 1,500 daily newspapers published in the United States, with slightly more than 50 percent of these being delivered in the morning. These 1,500 newspapers enjoy being purchased by almost 56 million people.[3] In addition to daily and Sunday newspapers, there are almost 8,000 weekly newspapers. These weeklies have a total circulation of almost 71 million.[4] The majority of readers rate newspaper advertisements for job opportunities, real estate, cars or trucks, grocery stores, sporting events, entertainment activities, clothing stores, and other kinds of stores as excellent or very good.[5]

Newspapers, no matter whether they are published daily or weekly, will be either standard size or tabloid. A standard-size newspaper is about 13 inches wide and 22 inches high (deep); it usually has six columns, with a column approximately 2 inches wide. A tabloid newspaper is about 11 inches wide and 14 inches high (deep). Newspapers accept several different forms of advertising. Display advertisements, which vary in size and may appear in most sections, except on certain pages, contain illustrations or photographs, headlines, subheads (if needed), body copy, and usually logos. Sometimes these advertisements contain additional elements. Classified advertisements, which usually appear under subheads that categorize the goods or services the advertisements concern, may contain a brief headline. However, many merely contain a descriptive term and body copy. Advertisers' advertising departments or their advertising agencies create preprinted inserts that are delivered to the newspaper publishers for insertion. Usually, these colorful inserts appear in Sunday newspapers.

As mentioned, advertisers spend between $40 and $50 billion annually on advertising in newspapers. Of this amount, local advertisers spend more than $20 billion on retail advertising, and local advertisers and individuals spend more than $16 billion on classified advertising. National advertisers spend the remaining billions on national advertising.

Local advertisers place local or retail (display) advertisements that have been prepared by their advertising personnel or their advertising agencies or by the newspapers' advertising departments. In most instances, local advertisements do not necessarily resemble advertisements that are found in magazines, although many do contain illustrations or photographs, headlines, subheads, body copy, and logos. Local advertisements generally discuss more than one item, which is not the case for most advertisements that appear in magazines.

Local advertisers or individuals place classified advertisements that have been prepared by their advertising personnel or by the individuals, respectively, according to the newspapers' classified advertising section guidelines. Classified advertisements may contain an illustration or photograph, depending on the newspaper in which it is placed. For instance, a car dealership may place a classified advertisement that contains a photograph, headline, and body copy about a pre-owned car. This type of classified advertisement is called a *classified display advertisement* because it contains artwork as well as copy; yet it is positioned in the classified section of the newspaper. Of course, many newspapers do not necessarily accept classified display advertisements. Most, if not all, of the metropolitan newspapers do, however.

National advertisers place national (display) advertisements that have been prepared by their advertising departments or their advertising agencies. In most instances, national advertisements resemble advertisements that are found in magazines. In fact, some of these advertisements may be nothing more than a different size or variation of an advertisement that was prepared primarily for magazines.

ADVANTAGES OF NEWSPAPERS AS AN ADVERTISING MEDIUM

There are several advantages newspapers have that advertisers should consider. These include the following:

1. The typical daily newspaper has a history of high credibility with its readers, who generally are older and more affluent adults.
2. The typical daily newspaper has a short lead time that allows advertisers the opportunity to change their advertisements on a frequent basis.
3. The typical daily newspaper offers advertisers great flexibility, from placing black-and-white to four-color advertisements, from placing small- to large-space advertisements, and from inserting special advertisements with coupons to placing advertisements in specific sections.
4. The typical daily newspaper allows advertisers the opportunity to measure the effectiveness of their advertisements, especially those that contain coupons.

5. The typical daily newspaper attracts readers who live within a certain geographic area or market and who share common interests. These individuals appeal to local and regional advertisers primarily because they are customers or potential customers.
6. The typical daily newspaper offers advertisers the opportunity to reach potential consumers at a reasonable cost.

DISADVANTAGES OF NEWSPAPERS AS AN ADVERTISING MEDIUM

Newspapers have several disadvantages that advertisers need to be aware of. These include the following:

1. The typical daily newspaper is filled with advertisements. In fact, generally, advertising fills from 60 percent to almost 70 percent of the space, depending on which day of the week a paper is published. Thus, an advertiser may be competing with other advertisers, not just in the same issue but on the same page.
2. The typical daily newspaper is reaching fewer households and consequently readers, especially teens and young adults.
3. The typical daily newspaper has a very short life. If an advertisement is not seen when one reads a newspaper, the advertisement probably will not be seen.
4. The typical daily newspaper is published on newsprint. Because of the low quality of the paper, certain advertisements may not produce well.
5. The typical daily newspaper advertising staff will position advertisements on pages, in sections, unless advertisers pay more for preferred positions.

ADVERTISING RATES IN NEWSPAPERS

Local or retail advertising rates are usually lower than national or general advertising rates. The reasons for this include the fact that most national or general advertising is placed through advertising agencies, which typically receive a commission; most national or general advertising is solicited by newspaper representatives who are typically paid a percentage in addition to the advertising agency's commission; national or general advertising appeals to the newspaper's total circulation, whereas retail advertising usually appeals to only a portion of the newspaper's total circulation; and most national or general advertising appears in the newspaper on an infrequent basis, whereas retail advertising appears in the newspaper on a frequent basis. Consequently, newspapers offer retailers better deals primarily because they are better customers.

Newspapers generally offer advertisers an open rate or a flat rate. The open rate is actually a sliding scale that is based on the amount of space purchased over a certain period of time. The flat rate is the same amount charged for each column inch, regardless of the amount of space purchased or how often.

Most newspaper space is sold based on "run of paper." That is, the advertising director or another member of the newspaper's advertising staff will decide where an advertisement will be placed. Special rates may apply, however, if specific sections, such as the Business section or the Sports section, or if specific positions on a page are requested. This is termed the preferred-position rate.

Most newspapers have adopted the Standard Advertising Unit, which was developed to aid national or general advertisers and their advertising agencies to purchase space as well as produce advertisements for newspapers. In short, advertising agencies do not have to worry about designing advertisements based on column inches; they have dozens and dozens of different sizes from which to choose, no matter which newspaper page they desire.

RETAIL ADVERTISEMENTS

Organizing the Local or Retail Advertisement

The advertising copywriter and advertising graphics person or layout artist must first examine the number of items that are supposed to appear in the advertisement and organize these items in some logical fashion. For instance, if the advertiser is a men's store that desires an advertisement in which men's dress shirts, sports shirts, dress pants, sports pants, belts, shoes, and socks are featured, then the advertising copywriter must first think about which items should be featured. In short, the advertising copywriter realizes that at least one of these items should be larger than the others. However, two of these items may actually be put together in a large bordered area that is larger than the other items, even if two or more remaining items are put together. For instance, let us say that the store can earn more from selling dress pants and sports pants than from selling any other item. As a result, the advertising copywriter decides to feature these items together. She or he desires that an illustration or photograph of each kind of pair of pants will be placed close together in a bordered area that is near the optical center of the design or advertisement. Of course, she or he realizes that the headline should be near this large bordered area. Some of the other items may be featured together, as mentioned. For instance, the dress shirts and the sports shirts may appear in an area together. Or the belts and the shoes may appear in an area together. Of course, the socks may be featured with these items or separately.

In short, organizing an advertisement is determining what the major features of the advertisement are and grouping items that are related into subfeatures. Advertising personnel should not place or position items haphazardly anywhere on the design or advertisement.

Writing the Local or Retail Advertisement

Newspapers are filled with retail advertisements; most of these are well designed—that is, they have illustrations or photographs positioned in appropriate areas; they have attractive headlines and subheads that appeal to prospects; they have brief informative blocks of body copy; they play up the prices of the items that are on sale; and they have the advertiser's logo as well as the advertiser's address and telephone number. They also have the advertiser's hours of operation. Sometimes they have a small map showing where the advertiser is located. Usually, these maps contain two lines intersecting and a rectangle by one of the lines. The lines represent streets, and the rectangle represents the advertiser. Each, of course, is identified by a word or words in small, bold print.

These are the major elements that advertising copywriters and other advertising personnel must think about. The advertising copywriter must think about writing an attractive headline that relates well to what the advertiser is selling. In many instances, the headline may play up a sale. In addition, the advertising copywriter must have information about the item or items that will be advertised. For instance, using the previous example—men's dress shirts, sports shirts, dress pants, sports pants, belts, shoes, and socks—the advertising copywriter must know the brands, the fabric, the colors, the sizes, the styles, and, of course, the prices or range of prices. The body copy should present this information quickly and directly. In short, the advertising copywriter should briefly explain to prospective consumers what they receive for their money. In addition, the advertising copywriter should be enthusiastic. In other words, the advertising copywriter needs to express that these items have greater value than similar items that may be available at other retailers. The easiest means to express or imply a product's value is to use an involvement technique—that is, get the prospects to think about the product's benefits, not just its features. Benefits help sell products. Also, the advertising copywriter should play up the product's price. If the retailer sells a product for less, then the advertising copywriter should make certain that the prospects know this.

HEADLINES Writing a headline for a retail advertisement may seem easy, but it can be as difficult as writing a headline for an advertisement that will be placed in a magazine. However, there are several guidelines that may be useful. The first is capturing attention. Capturing the prospect's attention can be accomplished by using one or more of the following suggestions:

1. Address the prospect by name in the headline. For instance, "Runners" or something similar addresses those who are conscious about their health. Such a headline could be used in an advertisement for athletic shoes. "Overweight?" identifies prospects from all the readers and implies that the advertisement is for those who desire to lose excess pounds.
2. Use news in the headline. For instance, "Save $100 on the New Maytag Dynamo Washer" informs prospects that they can save $100 on a new washer that is manufactured by Maytag.
3. Show the product in use. An illustration or photograph of the product in use allows prospects to picture themselves using the product or wearing the product. In addition, if a female is depicted using the product, the advertising copywriter does not have to use *Women* in the headline to identify the prospects.
4. Use a conversational style of language. The advertising copywriter is trying to communicate with consumers. The best way to do this is to use words and phrases that prospects use to communicate. Generally, simple words and phrases are preferred.
5. Present the major benefit. A benefit, as mentioned, is what the product does for the consumer. Basically, benefits are the reasons individuals purchase goods and services. Advertising copywriters may have to examine the product from the consumer's perspective or read the manufacturer's literature about the product in order to determine the product's benefits to the prospective buyer.
6. Include the product's brand name in the headline. Well-known brand names have sales appeal.
7. If the product is manufactured near the advertiser, mention this in the headline. Certain advertisers even include "made in the U.S.A." in their headlines.

BODY COPY Generally, body copy in local or retail advertisements is brief and to the point. The following guidelines will help the advertising copywriter write more effective retail advertisements:

1. Provide complete and specific information. Make sure that you provide enough information about the product so that the consumer can pick up the telephone and order it with confidence.
2. Use benefits to describe the product. A benefit is what the product does for the buyer. Unfortunately, many retail advertisements focus on the product, the product's features, the store, or the store's features, not the product's benefits. You may mention the selling features but only if you include these features' benefits.

3. Use language that prospects understand. Use short, simple words as well as short, punchy phrases. After all, this is how most people talk.
4. Call to action. Tell the reader to purchase the product now, if appropriate. This call to action typically is near the end of the body copy. Sometimes it is a phrase printed in big, bold print such as "Call now" or "Come in today." Of course, if you use the former, make certain that you have included the advertiser's telephone number somewhere in the advertisement. It may also be a phrase such as "While supplies last" or "For one week only."

Many retail advertisements suffer from the following problems:

1. Headlines are similar to labels—that is, they identify the product and the retailer, but they do not necessarily cause the reader to read the body copy.
2. The body copy merely lists the product's selling features; it does not present the benefits.
3. The body copy does not involve the reader.
4. The body copy does not contain language that is imaginative and persuasive.
5. The design of the advertisement lacks a logical pattern that helps the reader move from one area of the advertisement to another.

Designing the Local or Retail Advertisement

Although advertising copywriters seldom are asked to design a retail advertisement, it is important that they understand certain principles about designing a retail ad. These principles include the following:

1. Make certain that the advertisement has a distinctive and recognizable design. If you are familiar with advertisements for Sears, J. C. Penny's, or some other major retailer, you realize that these advertisers' advertisements have a distinctive appearance. In short, the advertisements are consistent in design from one advertisement to another. The headlines and subheads are printed in the same typeface, if not the same size. The body copy is printed in the same typeface and usually the same size. The logo is printed in the same typeface and usually the same size; it is usually in the same position, too. In other words, the reader realizes that the advertisement is for Sears, J. C. Penny's, or some other major retailer without having to read the logo.
2. Make certain that the advertisement has a logo that can be easily recognized. This logo, plus the address, telephone number, hours of operation, credit information, website information, and so on, should appear in every advertisement, in the same typeface, and, if possible, in the same size.
3. Make certain that the advertisement is well organized. A well-organized design will help the consumer move from one element to another easily and quickly.
4. Make certain that the advertisement has an uncluttered appearance. An advertisement that appears clean and uncluttered presents a positive impression of the advertiser and the advertiser's merchandise.
5. Make certain that the illustration or photograph depicts the product in use or demonstrates a benefit. Of course, you may not have an illustration or photograph that accomplishes either, but if you do, use it. Such will help the prospects picture themselves using the product. For fashion advertisements, make certain that illustrations or photographs depict the articles of clothing being worn.

FIGURE 6.1
These are designs for one-item advertisements.
Courtesy of the Newspaper Association of America.

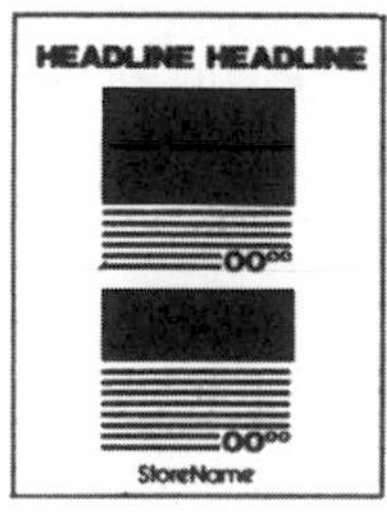

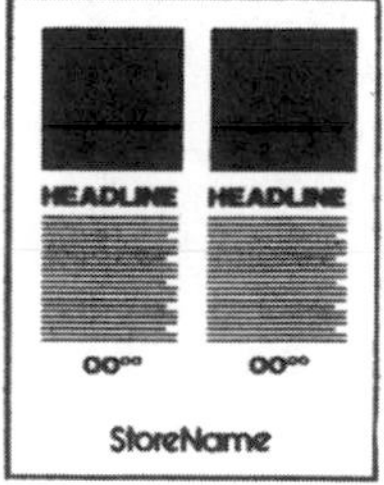

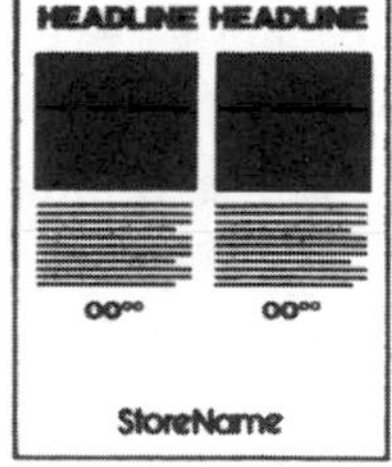

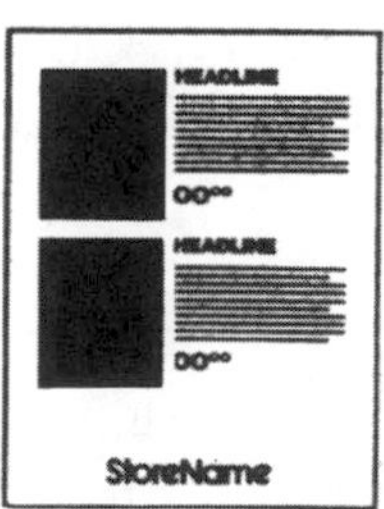

FIGURE 6.2
These are designs for two-item advertisements.
Courtesy of the Newspaper Association of America.

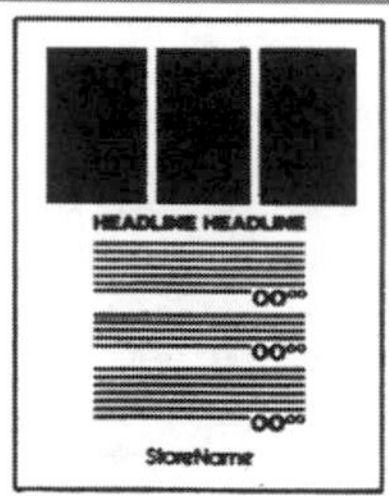

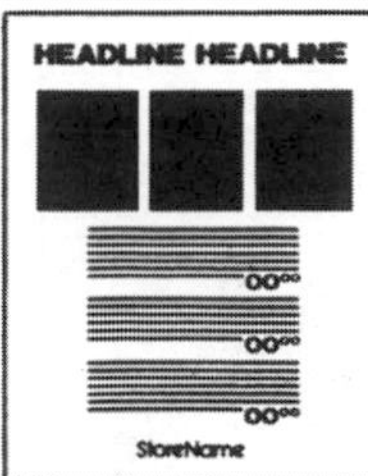

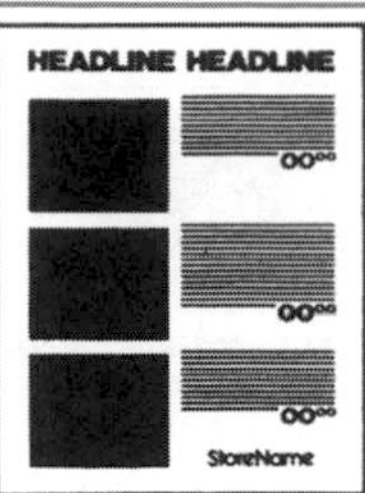

FIGURE 6.3 These are designs for three-item advertisements. *Courtesy of the Newspaper Association of America.*

6. Make certain that the illustration or photograph is large enough to attract attention. After all, prospects desire to actually *see* the merchandise, not just read about it.
7. Make certain that enough white space has been used. White space is important: it helps the advertisement attract attention. Do not underestimate its value.

The designs in figures 6.1–6.3 have been proven to be effective for retailers who advertise in newspapers. The one-item advertisements have only one item to sell (figure 6.1). The two-item advertisements have two items to sell (figure 6.2). If these items are related, a headline relating to both items should be used. On the other hand, if the items are not related, a headline, illustration or photograph, and body copy should be used for each. Finally, the three-item advertisements have three items to sell (figure 6.3). If these items are related, a headline relating to all three items should be used.

Positioning the Local or Retail Advertiser

Advertisers can position themselves in their market by the designs of their advertisements. Generally, the retailer with the leading reputation places advertisements that have abundant amounts of white space surrounding nicely drawn illustrations or nice, appealing photographs. Usually, the figures or models are wearing the latest fashions. The headlines are not necessarily large, but they are well tailored. The prices may be present, but they are not so pronounced that they scream at the prospect. Look at figure 6.4.

The retailer that has the reputation for having the best values on a regular basis places advertisements that have a crisper, more pronounced illustration or photograph and a more pronounced promotional headline that is printed in bigger, bolder type than the previous retailer's headline. Prices are more dominant as well. Look at figure 6.5.

The retailer that has the reputation for being the major discount retailer in the market places advertisements filled with elements that appear to be cluttered. The illustrations or photographs are more primitive in appearance; in fact, they may be big and bold. The headlines are big, bold, and usually printed in black. The prices, which play a major role, are also big, bold, and usually printed in black. Look at figure 6.6. Retailers, depending on how they wish to be perceived by prospects, will establish an advertising design and use it indefinitely.

Ethical Considerations in Retail Advertising

Retail advertising must be honest and certainly not deceptive. I suggest that anyone who aspires to become an advertising copywriter should become familiar with the Better Business Bureau's "Code of Advertising," which discusses numerous topics such as bait advertising, superlative claims, and contests.

There are terms that are used frequently in retail advertisements. These terms include *originally*, *regularly*, *comparable value*, and *special purchase*. Yet, in many instances, advertising copywriters do not use these terms correctly. For instance, take the latter. *Special purchase* should be used when a retailer does not normally offer an item but it has been stocked especially for a sale. When a "special purchase" is advertised, the term *regularly* followed by a price should not be used. Unfortunately, the term *regularly* followed by a price is often used. The correct phrase is "comparable value" or "compare at."

The terms *originally* and *regularly* are also misused often. *Originally* implies that the advertiser will never offer an item at its original high price. This informs the consumer that the price will remain low. Sometimes the price may be lowered over time. *Regularly* implies that the advertiser has reduced the price of an item but will actually reinstate the higher price once the sale ends.

When retail advertisers offer an item at a percentage off of its regular or original price, the complete range of markdown should be made clear, such as "10 percent to 25 percent off of the regular price." However, many retailers use the following phrase or something similar in their advertisements: "up to 50 percent off and more," which is deceptive. Also, prospective consumers may think that only one item has been reduced more than 50 percent and that only one item has been reduced 50 percent. Such defeats the purpose of the advertisement.

FIGURE 6.4 This advertisement's design is light and informal. *Courtesy of Metro Creative Graphics, Inc.*

FIGURE 6.5 This advertisement's design is moderate—that is, between light and informal and the hard sell. *Courtesy of Metro Creative Graphics, Inc.*

FIGURE 6.6 This advertisement's design is hard sell. *Courtesy of Metro Creative Graphics, Inc.*

Related to the above is the unqualified reduction, such as "save 50 percent" or "half-price sale." Such phrases should identify the basis of the reduction—half of what—and the extent of the items covered—complete stock or selected items.

Retailers' advertisements may be fully or partly paid for by a manufacturer whenever retailers agree to prominently display the manufacturer's products. This is called *cooperative advertising*, and many manufacturers offer cooperative advertising programs to retailers. In fact, many manufacturers provide the advertisements. Of course, these advertisements contain space for each participating retailer's logo.

SMALL-SPACE ADVERTISEMENTS

An advertiser must keep in mind that some products or services require large artwork or long blocks of copy. For these products or services, small advertisements should not be considered. Nonetheless, some retailers insist on using small advertisements, primarily because small advertisements do not cost as much as large advertisements.

Whenever a small advertisement has to be created, the copywriter must apply the same guidelines that apply to large advertisements. However, the copywriter must learn to condense the copy. One way of doing this is by writing a long advertisement first and then editing it until it has become a concise sales message. For instance, look at the following headline and piece of copy for a retailer's advertisement:

HURRY!
ONE DAY ONLY SALE!
THIS SATURDAY FROM 8 A.M. TO 8 P.M.!

McMurray's Men's Store is having a one-day sale this Saturday. Every suit, every sports jacket, every shirt, and every pair of pants will be reduced 25%! So come to McMurray's Men's Store this Saturday and Save!

The advertisement contained the store's logo—which was not necessary because the store's name was mentioned in the body copy—the store's address, and the store's telephone number. The headline contains more than 10 words; the body copy contains more than 35 words.

Now, look at how the above can be shortened:

ONE DAY ONLY SALE!
All men's suits, sports jackets, shirts, and pants will be reduced 25% this Saturday from 8 a.m. to 8 p.m.!

Of course, the store's logo, which is needed to identify the business, the store's address, and the store's telephone number should be included. The headline contains only 4 words; the body copy contains only 20 words.

Remember that the final version must fit the allotted space. This is true of the artwork—that is, if the advertisement has space for it.

SUBSCRIPTION SERVICE COMPANIES

If a copywriter works for a newspaper instead of an advertising agency or a client, then the newspaper may subscribe to an advertising service that provides the newspaper's advertising personnel with professionally

FIGURE 6.7 These advertisements vary in size and product; each allows an advertiser to drop in the product's brand name, price, the store name, and other information. *Courtesy of Metro Creative Graphics, Inc.*

designed advertisements. One of these firms is Metro Creative Graphics, Inc., New York, which was founded in 1910. Since that time Metro Creative Graphics, Inc., has purchased Stamps-Conhaim or SCW, Inc., another creative newspaper advertising service, and has experienced growth in its services. For instance, the company offers newspapers and other businesses, including advertising, public relations, and retail, ready-to-use layouts, graphic illustrations, photographs, speculative advertisements, and campaigns, among other items. The company offers the Metro Newspaper Service, the Metro Classified Dynamics, the Metro Sales Spectaculars, and the Metro Holiday Advertising Service, among other services. These services are available in print, CD-ROM, and online. Figure 6.7 contains only a few examples of advertisements that Metro Creative Graphics, Inc., offers its subscribers.

OTHER MEDIA FOR LOCAL OR RETAIL ADVERTISERS

In addition to newspapers, local or retail advertisers are also using radio and television. Radio, which is discussed in chapter 8, allows retail advertisers to make hourly or daily changes in their advertising copy. Television, which is examined in chapter 9, allows retail advertisers to make changes in their advertising copy but not as often as in radio. If local or retail advertisers intend to advertise successfully in a market, they should tie their radio and television advertising to their newspaper advertising. In

BOX 6.1 *A Typical Copy Sheet for a Local or Retail Advertisement*

FINE'S DEPARTMENT STORE

Full Page / Black and White

HEADLINE:	Autumn Allure
SUBHEADLINE:	At 10% to 50% off, these crisp, cool, back-to-school fashions fit you and the season!
SUBHEADLINE:	Step to the head of the class—and save 50%!
COPY A:	Whatever your style, we have the shoes for you! For men, try supple leather, comfortable and classy, in a variety of autumn colors. Choose from G. H. Bass and Co., J. Murphy, Rockport, and Sperry. Regularly $49 to $99, now $24.50 to $49.50. Women love our fabulous fall array of shoes from Ann Marino, Gloria Vanderbilt, and Naturalizer. Regularly $42 to $69, now $21 to $34.50. Athletic shoes for men and women include Adidas, Ecco, Fila, New Balance, Nike, Reebok, and Sketchers. Regularly $39 to $150, now $19.50 to $75. Sizes vary by brand and style. Men: 8–14M, 8–12W; women: 5–11M, 6.5–12W.
SUBHEADLINE:	Gold Toe men's socks, at 10% off, mean extra value!
COPY B:	Are you looking for athletic, casual or dress socks? We offer Gold Toe Metropolitan, Canterbury, Cambridge, and Microfiber Dress socks in 100% nylon, cotton/nylon, and acrylic/nylon. Black, brown, navy. One size 10–13. Popular three-pair packs, regularly $15 to $18, now $13.50 to $16.20.
SUBHEADLINE:	Easy-care men's slacks take you from campus to office to fun! Save 25%!
COPY C:	Men who know quality know Ivy Crew, Roundtree and Yorke, and Savane. With choices of pleated or flat front, cuffed or hemmed leg, and cotton twill or polyester/rayon blend, you'll want several pairs to suit your active lifestyle. Wrinkle- and fade-resistant, these slacks come in traditional black, khaki, navy, and taupe, as well as fantastic new fall colors. Waist, 30 to 42; inseam, 29 to 34. At 25% off the regular prices of $28 to $42, these slacks are now $21 to $31.50.
SUBHEADLINE:	For women on the go, the key words are "separates" and "save 25%"!
COPY D:	With our diverse selection of beautiful blouses and skirts, you'll find the perfect ensemble for school, career, or play. Choose from machine-washable, wrinkle-free cotton, linen, polyester, and rayon. Fashion-conscious women appreciate the style of Alfred Dunner, Koret, Norton McNaughton, and Sag Harbor. Available in a palette of autumn gold, orange, and red, as well as more traditional colors, these separates let you dress up or down, depending on the occasion. Misses and petites, 2–20; 14W–24W. Regularly $24 to $72, now $18 to $54.
SUBHEADLINE:	Fine's Department Store
COPY E:	Sale prices in effect September 2–8.
LOGOTYPE:	Fine's
SLOGAN:	THE FINEST IN FAMILY FASHION.
COPY F:	FINE'S 1234 Ryan Circle Phone 987-6543 Shop Monday–Saturday 10 a.m.–9 p.m., Sunday noon–6 p.m. Use your Fine's charge. We also welcome American Express, MasterCard, and Visa

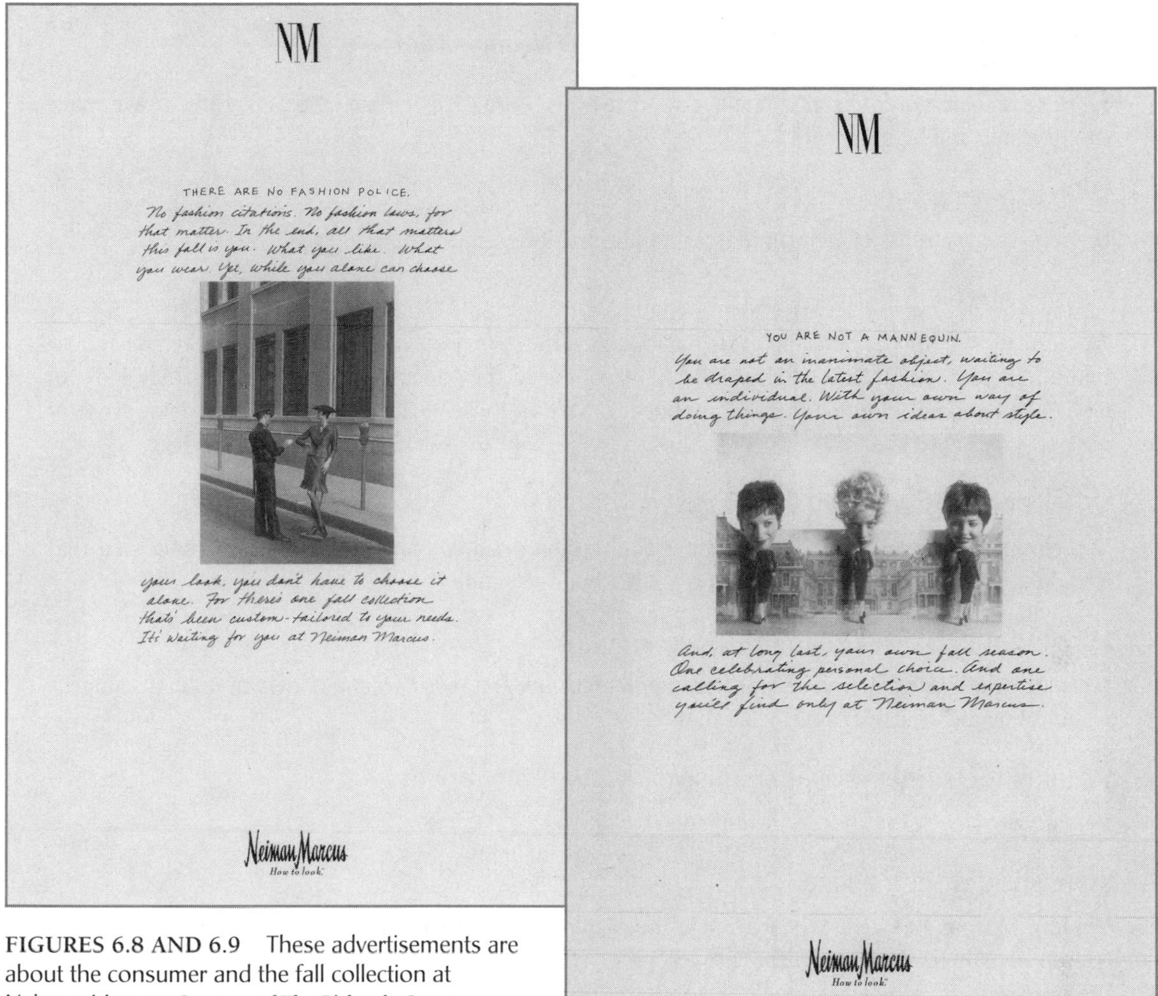

FIGURES 6.8 AND 6.9 These advertisements are about the consumer and the fall collection at Neiman Marcus. *Courtesy of The Richards Group.*

other words, they should use radio and television to remind prospects of the sale that was advertised in the morning or evening newspaper, so that the prospective consumers do not forget to take advantage of the reduced prices.

COPY SHEET FOR A LOCAL OR RETAIL ADVERTISEMENT THAT WILL RUN IN A NEWSPAPER

Many copy sheets for local or retail advertisements will include the following information in the upper left-hand corner: name of advertiser, name of newspaper, size of advertisement, and whether the advertisement is to be printed in color or black and white. The information about the various copy elements is identified by bold terms typed on the left-hand side. The actual copy is typed directly across from the bold terms. Each line starts at the same position, so that a nice column of white space separates the bold terms from the copy. Look at box 6.1.

BOX 6.2 *The Richards Group Creative Brief–Neiman Marcus*

Warning: People don't like ads. People don't trust ads. People don't remember ads. How do we make sure this one will be different?

Why are we advertising?

To increase awareness of Neiman Marcus' fall fashion offering.

Whom are we talking to?

Women, 35–44, who do not shop at Neiman Marcus. They are professionals with above average education and income of $75,000+. They have limited time so they appreciate good service. They look for high-quality career clothing. They're confident individuals who believe they have their own sense of style.

What do they currently think?

"I'm confused about the various directions top fashion designers are taking. I'm also concerned that Neiman Marcus is too expensive and too limited in its selection."

What would we like them to think?

"This year there is no definitive look. Neiman Marcus understands this and knows that I'm an individual with my own sense of style. I like that."

What is the single most persuasive idea we can convey?

Neiman Marcus clothes bring out the individual in you.

Why should they believe it?

Neiman Marcus has a huge selection of high-quality clothes ranging from the most outrageous fashion designers to more conservative couturiers, so customers can always find clothes to suit their styles.

Are there any creative guidelines?

Black-and-white newspaper.

Courtesy of The Richards Group.

Advertisements appearing in newspapers do not have to look like typical newspaper ads. Indeed, the Richards Group, Dallas, created the advertisements on p. 91 for Neiman Marcus. These advertisements, primarily because of their balanced design and simple elements, could have appeared in magazines (figures 6.8–6.9). The art director was Dennis Walker; the copywriter was Kevin Swisher. Box 6.2 is the "Creative Brief."

Sometimes, advertising agencies are hired to create public service–type advertisements, such as figure 6.10, prepared by BOHAN Advertising/ Marketing, Nashville, Tennessee. The message contains humor yet concerns a serious problem. Thus, newspaper advertisements come in various forms. Magazine advertising is discussed in the next chapter.

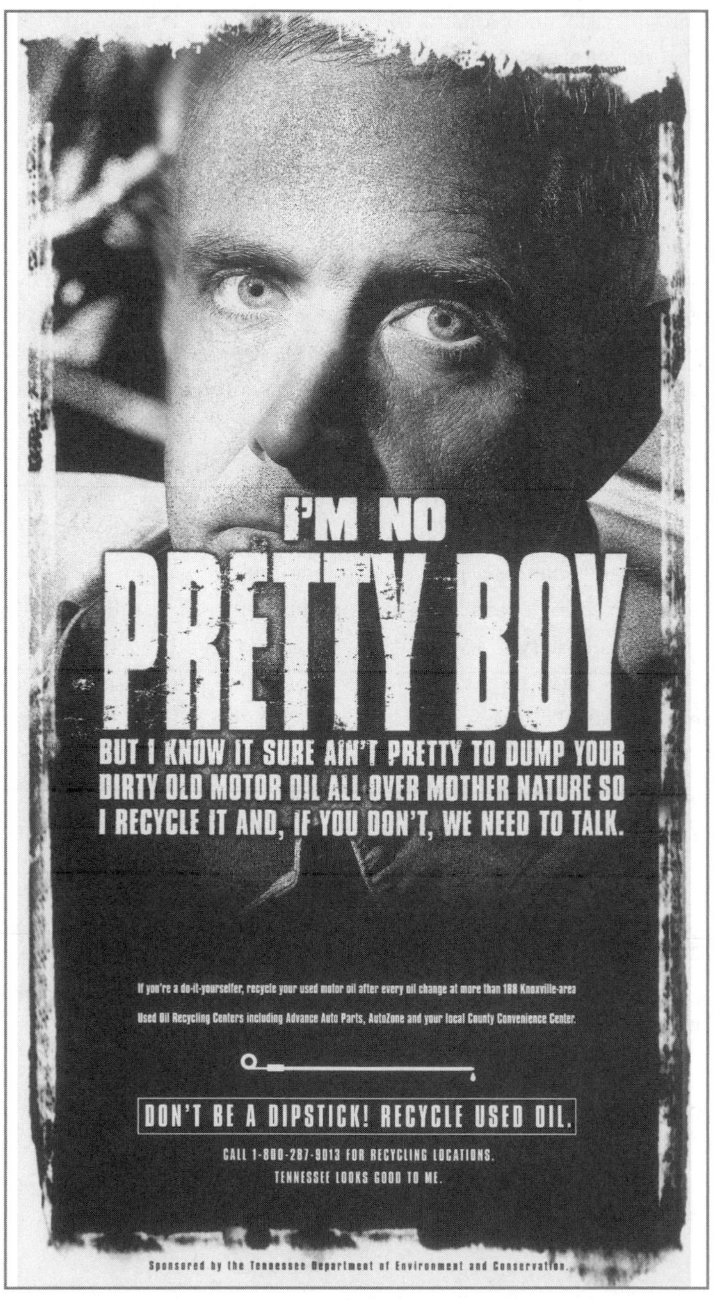

FIGURE 6.10 This advertisement tries to persuade people to recycle their dirty old motor oil. *Courtesy of BOHAN Advertising/Marketing.*

EXERCISES

1. Write the headline(s), subhead(s), and body copy for a newspaper ad for the M/W Store that features the following: men's sport shirts (long and short sleeves), $9.99 each; men's all-cotton jeans, $13.99 each; men's dress slacks, $25.99 each; women's all-cotton jeans, $15.99 each; women's blouses, $10.99 each; women's dresses, $24.99 each; and women's skirts, $12.99 each. The men's sport shirts come in various sizes and colors; the men's jeans come in various sizes and different shades of blue; and the men's dress slacks come in various sizes and colors. The women's jeans, blouses, dresses, and skirts come in various sizes and colors. All items are on sale. You may use specific brand names, if you desire.
2. Write the headline(s), subhead(s), and body copy for a newspaper ad for Only Males. The ad should feature the following: men's jeans—cotton, full-cut, four pockets; sizes—30 to 42 waist, 29 to 36 inseam; pair—$20.00, two pair—$35.00.
3. Write the headline(s), subhead(s), and body copy for a newspaper ad for Women's World. The ad will feature five pieces of women's clothing or accessories of your choice, such as dresses, skirts, sweaters, blouses, and shoes. Make sure that whatever is chosen is fully described, including the fabric, size, and so forth. Make sure you include a price for each piece advertised.
4. Write a retail ad for an upscale department store of your choice. Feature the following in the full-page ad: men's and women's shoes, various sizes and styles, 50 percent off; men's slacks, various sizes and lengths, 25 percent off; women's blouses and skirts, various sizes, 25 percent off; and men's socks, various colors, 10 percent off. You may use different brand names as well as additional copy that describes the merchandise. However, remember to focus on the information mentioned.
5. Write a retail ad for an upscale department store of your choice. The full-page ad will feature the following items: women's bulky acrylic sweaters (easy to launder and dry, in various sizes and colors, $15.99 each); an elegant sample of costume jewelry, including pins, earrings, necklaces, and bracelets (prices range from $10 to $50 each); women's roomy leather handbags (handsome, easy to clean, various colors, $14.99 each); women's shoes (various styles and colors, various sizes, $19.99 each); and women's scarves (various styles and colors, $10.99 each).

NOTES

1. Newspaper Association of America, "Trends and Numbers" (Vienna, VA: Newspaper Association of America, 2001; www.naa.org).
2. Newspaper Association of America, "Circulation and Readership" (Vienna, VA: Newspaper Association of America, 2001; www.naa.org).
3. Newspaper Association of America, "Trends and Numbers."
4. Newspaper Association of America, "Total U.S. Non-daily Newspapers," in *Facts about Newspapers 2001* (Vienna, VA: Newspaper Association of America, 2001; www.naa.org).
5. Newspaper Association of America, "How Single-Copy Buyers Rate Newspaper Advertising," in *Facts about Newspapers 2001* (Vienna, VA: Newspaper Association of America, 2001; www.naa.org).

CHAPTER 7

Magazine Advertising

There are almost 18,000 magazines published in the United States.[1] Magazines are usually classified as consumer, business, and agriculture or farm publications. There are more than 8,000 consumer magazines. These magazines, primarily because of their editorial content, appeal to specific groups of readers. For instance, these magazines target readers who are interested in learning about aviation, boating or yachting, camping or the outdoors, cars or trucks, computers, crafts or hobbies, fashion or beauty, health or fitness, marriage, motorcycles, music, pets, photography, religion, sports, and a host of other subjects and topics. And this does not include magazines that target readers who work in agriculture, business, industry, or a profession such as medicine.

Almost every American household receives at least one magazine that someone subscribes to or purchases at a newsstand every year. Almost six out of ten households both subscribe to and purchase magazines at a newsstand or other retail outlet.[2]

The typical reader of magazines is not necessarily average. Indeed, he or she has graduated from college; has a household income of more than $75,000 a year; has a house worth more than $150,000; works in a managerial, administrative, or professional position and makes managerial decisions; and reads at least five magazines a month.[3] Furthermore, the typical reader watches television less than other individuals. Consequently, in order to reach these well-educated, affluent individuals, advertisers must advertise in magazines.

Generally, readers of magazines are younger than 55 years of age. In fact, the heaviest readers of magazines are young adults, 18 to 24 years of age.[4] According to an analysis conducted by Foote, Cone & Belding, an advertising agency, "The top 25 broad-based magazines actually reach more consumers across a variety of targets than the top 25 prime-time television shows."[5] It is little wonder, then, that almost one out of every three dollars spent by advertisers in all national media is invested in magazines.[6]

According to one survey, readers trust and believe magazines more than they trust and believe what they see on television or the Internet. In addition, they are more inclined to pay attention to an advertisement that appears in a magazine instead of on television or the Internet.[7]

Magazine publishers trumpet the quality rather than the quantity of their readers, particularly when they attempt to attract advertisers. They continue to define their readers, sometimes too narrowly for their own economic welfare. Smaller groups of readers means fewer issues sold, which, in turn, usually means less interest on the part of advertisers. Nonetheless, magazine publishers introduce several new magazines each week with the hope that the editorial content will appeal to enough readers to attract advertisers and earn a profit.

Earning a profit can be difficult. For instance, most magazines are sold through subscription, not necessarily through newsstands. As a result, 83 percent of the total circulation is from magazine subscriptions; single-copy sales account for 17 percent.[8] Subscription rates, primarily to attract and keep readers for a long period, offer readers magazines at substantially reduced rates compared with single-copy prices. In addition, postage rates have increased several times during the last few years for magazine publishers. These increases have decreased some magazine publishers' profits. Furthermore, advertising rates have increased substantially during the past few years, forcing advertisers to pay more to potentially reach prospective consumers.

Most magazine publishers, no matter what their magazines' editorial content, accept advertising. In fact, most magazines have a ratio of about 50 percent editorial copy and about 50 percent advertising.[9]

Magazines come in different sizes, although most are considered standard-size or small-size publications. No matter what size a publication happens to be, advertising space is usually sold based on a full page or a partial page, such as a half page or a quarter page. Generally, magazine publishers will sell space based on columns, such as three columns or one column. In addition to these sizes, magazine publishers sell specific covers such as the inside front (second cover), inside back (third cover), and outside back (fourth cover). However, these highly favored positions are usually restricted to full-page, four-color advertisements, not partial-page black-and-white advertisements. Magazine publishers typically allow advertisers to purchase junior units; a junior unit is space in the middle for an advertisement that occupies 60 percent of a page. The advertisement is surrounded by editorial copy. Often, publishers offer island halves, which are surrounded by editorial copy. Of course, most magazine publishers will accept inserts, which are usually prepared by advertisers or their agencies and sent to the publishers. Generally, inserts are printed on heavier stock paper and are more dramatic in appearance. Some magazine publishers accept gatefolds, which are large inserts that have to be folded. Gatefolds are very expensive. An advertiser must weigh a gatefold's worth against the extra cost. Based on studies, table 7.1 shows recall scores with a four-color page as the base (100 percent).

Most magazine publishers offer advertisers discounts based on frequency (based on the number of pages) or volume (based on the total dollars spent for advertising during a certain period such as a year). Some magazine publishers offer other discounts. Various publishers allow advertisers to purchase less than the total circulation of their magazines, which is referred to as partial-run editions. This practice appeals to advertisers that wish to advertise in certain geographic areas.

In the early 2000s, companies spent almost $17 billion on advertising in magazines. Some of these companies included Philip Morris Companies Inc., General Motors Corporation, Procter & Gamble Company, DaimlerChrysler AG, AOL Time Warner Inc., Ford Motor Company, Toyota Motor Corporation, L'Oreal SA, Pfizer Inc., Johnson & Johnson, Unilever, Bristol-Myers Squibb Company, National Syndication Inc., Merck & Company Inc., Walt Disney Company, IBM Corporation, Nissan Motor Company, RJ Reynolds, Sony Corporation, and Honda Motor Corporation. Certain experts predict that these and other companies will spend more on advertising in magazines over the next few years.

TABLE 7.1 ***Impact of Magazine Advertising by Type of Unit***

AD TYPE	RECALL INDEX (%)	AD TYPE	RECALL INDEX (%)
Full-Page Four-Color (4C) Ad	100	Horizontal 1/3 Page (4C)	60
4th Cover (4C)	120	Vertical 2/3 Page (2C)	60
2d Cover (4C)	112	Vertical 2/3 Page (B&W)	60
3d Cover (4C)	90	Horizontal 1/2 Page (2C)	56
2d Cover Gatefold (4C)	145	Horizontal 1/2 Page (B&W)	56
Inside Spread (4C)	130	Horizontal 1/3 Page (2C)	47
Inside Spread (Two Color [2C])	110	Horizontal 1/3 Page (B&W)	47
Inside Spread (Black and White [B&W])	95	Vertical 1/3 Page (2C)	42
Vertical 2/3 Page (4C)	81	Vertical 1/3 Page (B&W)	42
Horizontal 1/2 Page (4C)	72	Full-Page 2C	78
Vertical 1/3 Page (4C)	60	Full-Page (B&W)	74

Source: Magazine Publishers of America, *The Magazine Handbook: 2001–2002* (New York: Magazine Publishers of America, 2002; www.magazine.org), p. 21.

TABLE 7.2 ***Top 25 Magazines Based on Circulation***

RANK	MAGAZINE	PAID CIRCULATION	RANK	MAGAZINE	PAID CIRCULATION
1	Modern Maturity*	17,780,127	14	Home & Away	3,307,217
2	Reader's Digest	12,565,779	15	Sports Illustrated	3,206,098
3	TV Guide	9,097,762	16	Playboy	3,157,540
4	National Geographic	7,664,658	17	Prevention	3,121,340
5	Better Homes & Gardens	7,601,377	18	Cosmopolitan	2,759,448
6	Family Circle	4,712,548	19	Guideposts	2,743,726
7	Good Housekeeping	4,527,447	20	VIA Magazine	2,624,929
8	Woman's Day	4,257,742	21	The American Legion Magazine	2,624,754
9	Time	4,189,981	22	Maxim	2,553,895
10	Ladies' Home Journal	4,100,675	23	Southern Living	2,549,601
11	People Weekly	3,723,848	24	O, The Oprah Magazine	2,530,712
12	Rosie	3,613,055	25	Martha Stewart Living	2,437,970
13	Newsweek	3,308,912			

*Decline caused by transfer of 3.1 million in circulation to sibling magazine *My Generation*.

Note: *Modern Maturity* is now *AARP The Magazine*; *Rosie* is no longer published; and *Martha Stewart Living*'s circulation may have been impacted by Martha Stewart's legal problems.

Source: *Advertising Age: FACTPACK: 2002 Edition: A Handy Guide to the Advertising Business*, *Advertising Age*, September 9, 2002, p. 24. Reprinted with permission. © 2002, Crain Communications Inc.

As mentioned, magazines vary in editorial content. They also vary as to when they are published. Most magazines are published using one of the following schedules: every month, every week, every two months, every two weeks, or every three months. The top 25 magazines based on circulation, for instance, are published weekly, monthly, or every two months (table 7.2). Although these magazines have the largest circulations, they do not necessarily publish the most advertisements. However, their advertising rates are typically higher than those of other magazines, primarily because of their circulation.

ADVANTAGES OF MAGAZINES AS AN ADVERTISING MEDIUM

Magazines have several advantages that advertisers need to consider. These include the following:

1. Magazines enjoy a high readership among adults, especially young adults, which, of course, tends to interest advertisers because this group spends a significant portion of its income.
2. Magazines, particularly specialty magazines, are aimed at specific groups of readers. As a result, advertisers can aim their advertising to specific groups of consumers. Generally, these groups have similar demographics, psychographics, and lifestyles.
3. Magazines offer advertisers the opportunity to display ads that are very creative. Indeed, advertisers may use artistic photographs, unusual graphics, beautiful color, and stylistic typefaces.
4. Partial editions of certain magazines allow local or regional advertisers the opportunity to reach potential consumers with aesthetically appealing advertisements.
5. Based on studies, advertisements in magazines help build brand awareness for various products and services.
6. Magazines enjoy a long life among readers. Not only do readers keep magazines longer than, say, newspapers, they pass magazines along to other readers. In addition, magazines are read almost everywhere.

DISADVANTAGES OF MAGAZINES AS AN ADVERTISING MEDIUM

Magazines do have several disadvantages, at least from an advertising perspective:

1. Generally, magazines have high advertising rates, especially when one calculates the cost to reach potentially 1,000 readers.
2. There are numerous magazines in every category. Because of this fact, it may be difficult for advertisers to choose the most effective magazine or magazines that will reach the consumers they desire.
3. Magazines, like other media, have advertising clutter in the sense that most have about a 50/50 ratio of advertising and editorial matter. Advertisers that advertise in magazines will in all likelihood be competing against other advertisers.
4. Generally, magazines have a long closing date, primarily because of the printing process. As a result, advertisements for magazines have to be prepared weeks, if not months, ahead of publication. Such prevents advertisers from reacting to societal or market changes.

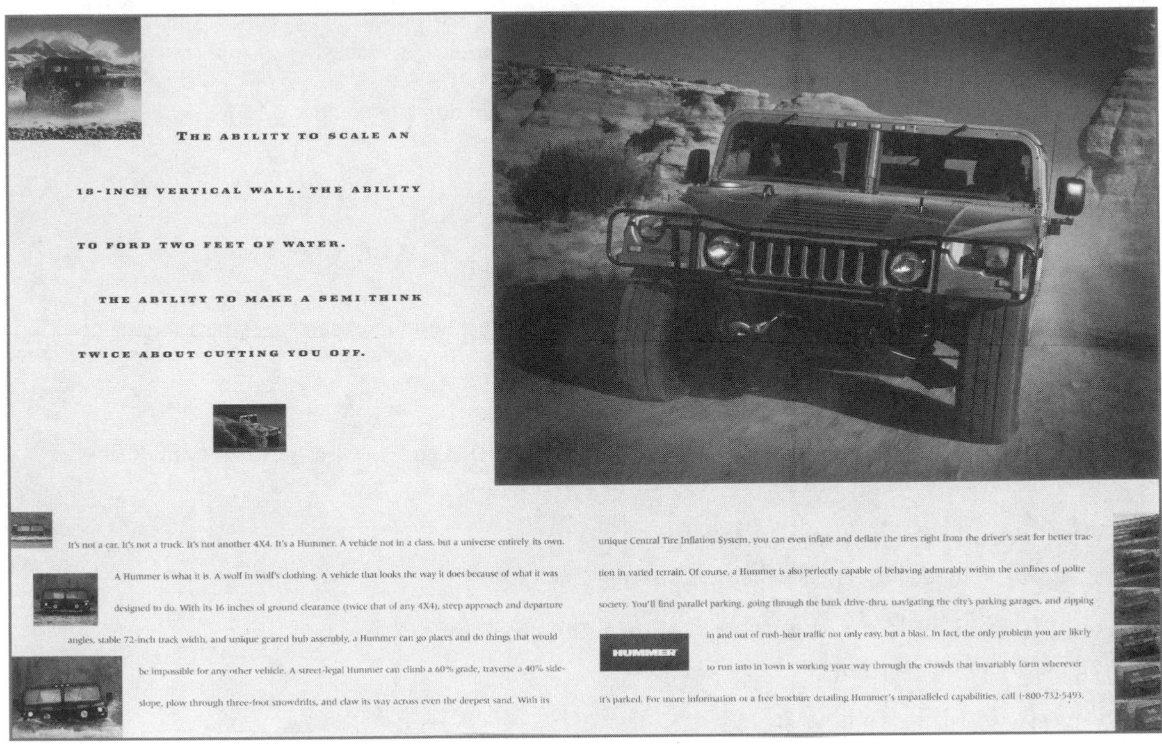

FIGURE 7.1 Two-page magazine advertisement for the Hummer. *Courtesy of The Richards Group.*

HOW TO WRITE ADVERTISEMENTS FOR CONSUMER MAGAZINES

As discussed in chapter 4, most advertisements created for print, including consumer magazines, will contain the following elements:

- Headline
- Subhead (if needed)
- Introductory or Bridge Paragraph (which links the headline, subhead, and body copy)
- Supporting Paragraph(s) (which discuss additional selling features and benefits)
- Call to Action Paragraph (which closes the sale)
- Slogan (if needed)
- Artwork (illustration or photograph)

Of course, whether a copywriter uses all of the above will depend on what is being advertised—that is, what the product or service is. After all, some products or services require more elements than others.

Figure 7.1 is a two-page spread advertisement for the Hummer, which was created by Terence Reynolds (creative director and art director) and Todd Tilford (creative director and copywriter) of the Richards Group, Dallas. Look at the headline:

> **THE ABILITY TO SCALE AN 18-INCH VERTICAL WALL.**
> **THE ABILITY TO FORD TWO FEET OF WATER.**
> **THE ABILITY TO MAKE A SEMI THINK TWICE ABOUT CUTTING YOU OFF.**

BOX 7.1 *The Richards Group Creative Brief–Hummer*

Warning: People don't like ads. People don't trust ads. People don't remember ads. How do we make sure this one will be different?

Why are we advertising?
To generate qualified leads.

Whom are we talking to?
Affluent ($200K+) men who use discretionary income to seek unique experiences as a means of self-expression. They are thrill-seekers who find exhilaration in winning.

What do they currently think?
"I'm successful and have overcome a lot of obstacles to get where I am. Now I want to enjoy my success. Hummer? I've never considered one."

What would we like them to think?
"Hummer is a unique experience that lets me enjoy my success."

What is the single most persuasive idea we can convey?
Nothing stands in your way.

Why should they believe it?
- Empowerment. You can go places others can't.
- Adventure. You'll be able to explore the unknown.
- Individualism. The Hummer is as unique as you are.

Are there any creative guidelines?
Copy should reinforce that the Hummer is also practical for everyday use.

Courtesy of The Richards Group.

It identifies the product's benefits to the prospective consumer. These benefits are, of course, a result of what the headline hints at: the Hummer's capabilities and large size, which are its major selling features.

The body copy reads:

> It's not a car. It's not a truck. It's not another 4×4. It's a Hummer.
> A vehicle not in a class, but a universe entirely its own. A Hummer is what it is. A wolf in wolf's clothing. A vehicle that looks the way it does because of what it was designed to do. With its 16 inches of ground clearance (twice that of any 4×4), steep approach and departure angles, stable 72-inch track width, and unique geared hub assembly, a Hummer can go places and do things that would be impossible for any other vehicle. A street-legal Hummer can climb a 60% grade, traverse a 40% side-slope, plow through three-foot snowdrifts, and claw its way across even the deepest sand. With its unique Central Tire Inflation System, you can even inflate and deflate the tires right from the driver's seat for better traction in varied terrain.

> Of course, a Hummer is also perfectly capable of behaving admirably within the confines of polite society. You'll find parallel parking, going through the bank drive-thru, navigating the city's parking garages, and zipping in and out of rush-hour traffic not only easy, but a blast. In fact, the only problem you are likely to run into in town is working your way through the crowds that invariably form wherever it's parked. For more information or a free brochure detailing Hummer's unparalleled capabilities, call 1-800-732-5493.

The copy addresses the product's selling points: "16 inches of ground clearance," "stable 72-inch track width," and "unique geared hub assembly." Then it presents the benefits of these selling features to the consumer: "go places and do things that would be impossible for any other vehicle," "climb a 60% grade," "traverse a 40% side-slope," "plow through three-foot snowdrifts," and "claw [your] way across . . . the deepest sand." Then the copy shifts gears; instead of describing what the Hummer can do on rough terrain, it focuses on the Hummer's ability to perform in everyday situations such as "rush-hour traffic." Finally, the copy summarizes what has come before with "unparalleled capabilities" and ends with almost a direct action message: "call 1-800-732-5493."

The advertisement employs photographs of different sizes, including a dominant one, of the product as it performs on snow, in water, and on sand. The dominant photograph has the Hummer facing the body copy, thus drawing the reader's eyes into the advertisement's message.

In chapter 4, several types of body copy were discussed. Which type is the copywriter using in the above? Box 7.1 is the creative brief for the Hummer, which was prepared by personnel at the Richards Group.

Figure 7.2 shows an advertisement for the Ebonite's Big Mouth bag, which was created by personnel at BOHAN Advertising/Marketing, Nashville, Tennessee. Look at the headline, which is directly on the photograph of a man or a contortionist who has put himself into a bag:

> **Finally, there's a bag that's easier to get into.**

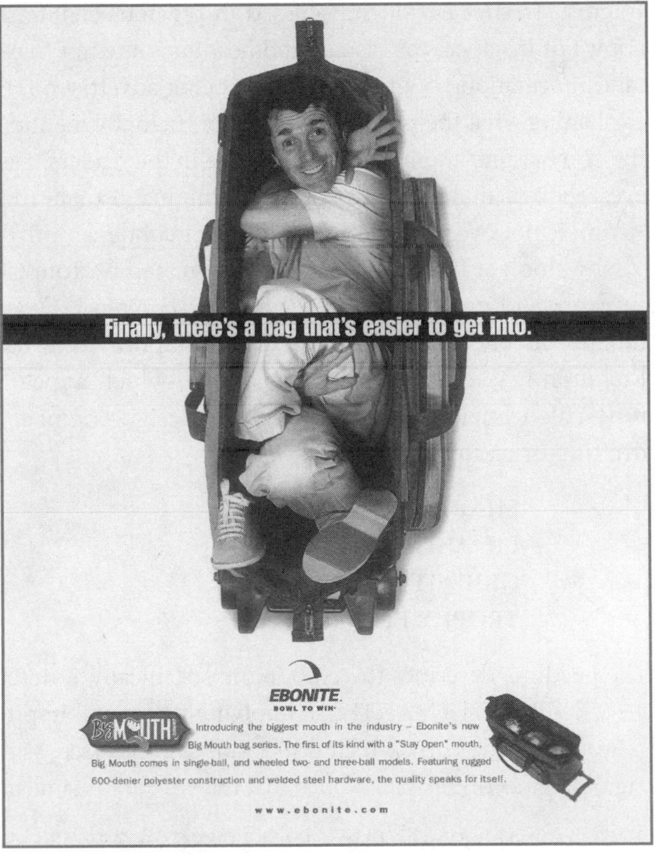

FIGURE 7.2 One-page magazine advertisement for Ebonite's Big Mouth bag. *Courtesy of BOHAN Advertising/Marketing.*

This headline works well with the photograph. It also emphasizes a major benefit:

"easier to get into." Most, if not all, serious bowlers have owned bowling ball bags that were difficult to handle. Usually, these bags do not open wide enough for bowlers to easily retrieve their bowling ball or balls.

The body copy reads:

> Introducing the biggest mouth in the industry—Ebonite's new Big Mouth bag series. The first of its kind with a "Stay Open" mouth, Big Mouth comes in single-ball, and wheeled two- and three-ball models. Featuring rugged 600-denier polyester construction and welded steel hardware, the quality speaks for itself.

The copy emphasizes the bag's "Stay Open" mouth, which is certainly important to the prospective consumer. The body copy also mentions that the bag "comes in single-ball, and wheeled two- and three-ball models," which is important to the consumer. Serious bowlers typically have more than one bowling ball and may use several when they bowl. Finally, the copy mentions the bag's physical characteristics: "rugged 600-denier polyester construction and welded steel hardware." This information implies that the bag is durable and consequently will last a very long time. So, which type of body copy is the copywriter using in the above?

In these examples, the copywriters remembered to use one of the formulas, such as AIDA (Attention, Interest, Desire, Action), discussed in previous chapters, when they created the headlines and body copy. For instance, the visuals and headlines attempt to capture readers' attention by conveying important information about the products being advertised. Then the copywriters try to interest readers by explaining what the products will do for them. By mentioning features and benefits about the products, the copywriters attempt to create desire in the readers. Last, they try to persuade readers to take action, even though they do not necessarily command them to "buy a Hummer" or "buy a Big Mouth bag." Action is not overt but, rather, indirect or subtle.

Now, look at figure 7.3, which was created by Tom Gibson (art director), Joe Alexander (creative director and copywriter), Joe Lawson (copywriter), Paul Martin (print producer), Julie Ahlman (art producer), Bruce Peterson (photographer), and Ben Eley (studio artist) at the Martin Agency, Richmond, Virginia. Read the headline, which appears to have been produced by hand on carefully ruled lines, as if a draftsman or design engineer had created it (and the advertisement) on drafting or engineering paper:

> **SHAFT FITS SWING.**
> **LIE ANGLE FITS HEIGHT.**
> **GRIP FITS HAND.**
> **TROPHY FITS MANTEL.**

The headline describes the club; more specifically, it describes how it will benefit the person who uses it ("TROPHY FITS MANTEL"), implying that it will improve any golfer's game.

Read the body copy, which is in a sans serif typeface, as if it had been produced especially for the drafting or engineering paper. Notice that the typeface is similar to the typeface used for the company's logo:

> ALL PING CLUBS, INCLUDING OUR IRONS, WOODS AND PUTTERS, CAN BE CUSTOM-FIT—A PROCESS THAT IS BOTH FUN AND REWARDING. YOU DON'T HAVE TO WAIT ANY LONGER OR PAY MORE FOR YOUR CUSTOM-

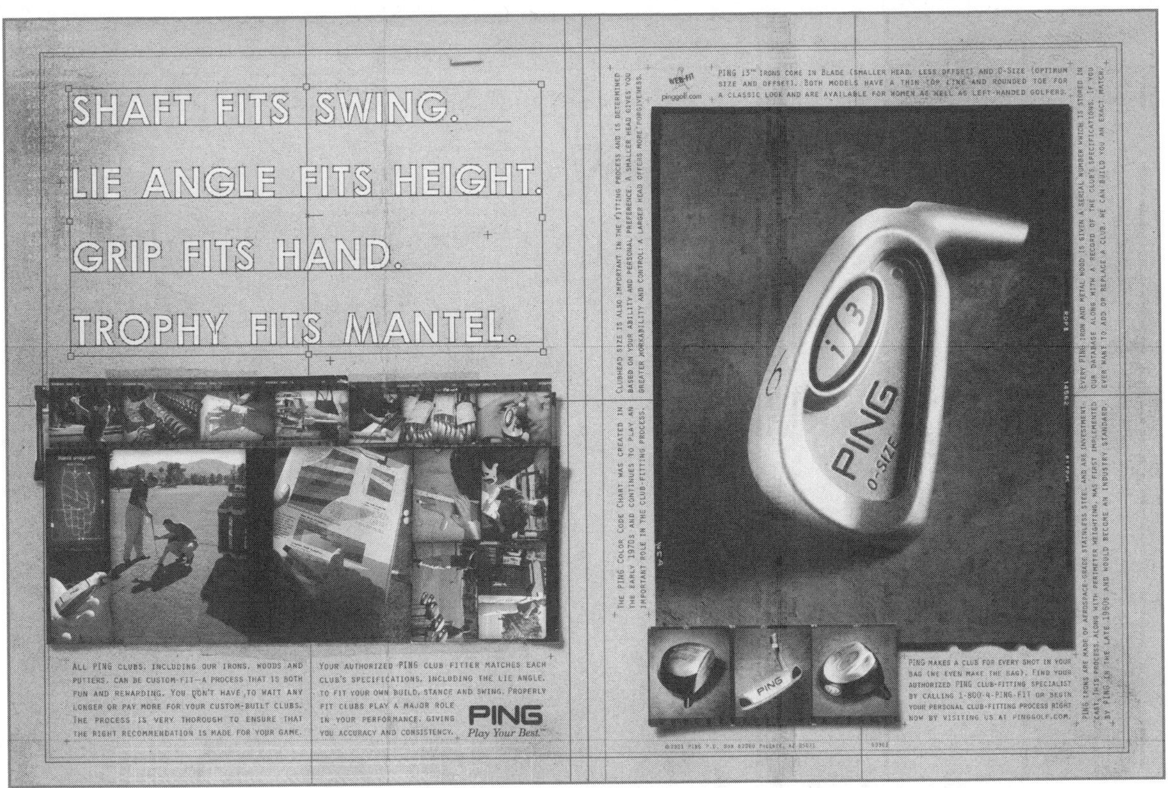

FIGURE 7.3 Two-page magazine advertisement for Ping clubs. *Courtesy of The Martin Agency.*

> BUILT CLUBS. THE PROCESS IS VERY THOROUGH TO ENSURE THAT THE RIGHT RECOMMENDATION IS MADE FOR YOUR GAME.
>
> YOUR AUTHORIZED PING CLUB FITTER MATCHES EACH CLUB'S SPECIFICATIONS, INCLUDING THE LIE ANGLE, TO FIT YOUR OWN BUILD, STANCE AND SWING. PROPERLY FIT CLUBS PLAY A MAJOR ROLE IN YOUR PERFORMANCE, GIVING YOU ACCURACY AND CONSISTENCY.
>
> PING MAKES A CLUB FOR EVERY SHOT IN YOUR BAG (WE EVEN MAKE THE BAG). FIND YOUR AUTHORIZED PING CLUB-FITTING SPECIALIST BY CALLING 1-800-4-PING-FIT OR BEGIN YOUR PERSONAL CLUB-FITTING PROCESS RIGHT NOW BY VISITING US AT PINGGOLF.COM.

The body copy elaborates on the major features and benefits mentioned in the headline, especially "LIE ANGLE FITS HEIGHT." The copy emphasizes that "PING CLUBS . . . CAN BE CUSTOM-FIT . . . TO ENSURE THAT THE RIGHT RECOMMENDATION IS MADE FOR YOUR GAME." The body copy also mentions that "PROPERLY FIT CLUBS" provide "ACCURACY AND CONSISTENCY." Finally, it informs readers how they can locate an "AUTHORIZED PING CLUB-FITTING SPECIALIST" or begin their "PERSONAL CLUB-FITTING PROCESS" by going on the Internet.

FIGURE 7.4 Two-page magazine advertisement for Suzuki motorcycles. *Courtesy of American Suzuki Motor Corporation and Colby & Partners.*

The body copy surrounding the large visual of the club's head contains the following:

> THE PING COLOR CODE CHART WAS CREATED IN THE EARLY 1970S AND CONTINUES TO PLAY AN IMPORTANT ROLE IN THE CLUB-FITTING PROCESS.
>
> CLUBHEAD SIZE IS ALSO IMPORTANT IN THE FITTING PROCESS AND IS DETERMINED BASED ON YOUR ABILITY AND PERSONAL PREFERENCE. A SMALLER HEAD GIVES YOU GREATER WORKABILITY AND CONTROL; A LARGER HEAD OFFERS MORE FORGIVENESS.
>
> PING 13 IRONS COME IN BLADE (SMALLER HEAD, LESS OFFSET) AND O-SIZE (OPTIMISM SIZE AND OFFSET). BOTH MODELS HAVE A THIN TOP LINE AND ROUNDED TOE FOR A CLASSIC LOOK AND ARE AVAILABLE FOR WOMEN AS WELL AS LFET-HANDED GOLFERS.
>
> PING IRONS ARE MADE OF AEROSPACE-GRADE STAINLESS STEEL AND ARE INVESTMENT-CAST. THIS PROCESS, ALONG WITH PERIMETER WEIGHTING, WAS FIRST IMPLEMENTED BY PING IN THE LATE 1960S AND WOULD BECOME AN INDUSTRY STANDARD.

> EVERY PING IRON AND METAL WOOD IS GIVEN A SERIAL NUMBER WHICH IS STORED IN OUR DATABASE ALONG WITH A RECORD OF THE CLUB'S SPECIFICATIONS. IF YOU EVER WANT TO ADD OR REPLACE A CLUB, WE CAN BUILD YOU AN EXACT MATCH.

These blocks of copy provide readers with additional information about PING and its products, including some history.

Figure 7.4 contains a two-page spread advertisement that was created by personnel at Colby & Partners. Look at the headline:

> **THAT'S NOT A PERIOD AT THE END OF THIS SENTENCE, THAT'S THE COMPETITION.**

The headline implies that this motorcycle will leave other motorcycles behind.

Now, look at the body copy:

> No other race-replica even comes close to the GSX-R750 and 600. The 750 won back-to-back AMA 750cc Supersport Championships. The 600 won more AMA 600cc Supersport races in '97 than any other bike. Yet we still weren't satisfied. For 1998, we gave the GSX-R750 electronic fuel injection. And we made over 20 major improvements to the GSX-R600 to give it superior handling, mid-range power and overall performance. The new Suzuki GSX-Rs. The competition is starting to look pretty small.

BOX 7.2 *Suzuki GSX-R600 Case Study*

Problem: Suzuki lacked a viable model in the key 600cc sportbike arena. Suzuki's last 600cc new model introduction (five years ago) was a disaster due to an underdeveloped and overpriced product.

Creative Strategy: Leverage Suzuki's racing success with National Championships in other categories to position their new GSX-R600 as the motorcycle of choice in this very competitive segment.

Executional Elements: We used print and television to communicate the strength of Suzuki's winning heritage and to present the GSX-R as the assumptive leader of the segment the moment it was introduced.

Market Result: The GSX-R600 rocketed Suzuki's share of the midsize sportbike segment to 42%, scavenging share from Honda and Kawasaki.

Key Insight: Motorcycle buyers are knowledgeable and skeptical. We were able to own the sportbike segment by positioning Suzuki as the innovator through key product introductions and consistent race victory advertising. This strategy was accepted by consumers as believable rather than unsubstantiated boasting.

Courtesy of American Suzuki Motor Corporation and Colby & Partners.

The body copy emphasizes the performance of the GSX-Rs in competition as well as the improvements that have been made, thus assuring the prospective buyer that even though the GSX-Rs have been very good in the past, they will be even better in the future. The copy closes with a reference to the headline. Colby & Partners' case study for the Suzuki GSX-R600 is presented in box 7.2.

FIGURE 7.5 One-page magazine advertisement for the beaches of South Walton. *Courtesy of BOHAN Advertising/Marketing.*

Advertisements appearing in magazines concern other companies and organizations, not just manufacturers of products. For instance, figure 7.5, which was created by personnel at BOHAN Advertising/Marketing, Nashville, is for the beaches of South Walton, Florida. The headline, "If I could be anywhere," which is printed on the blurred visual, suggests that the reader dream about where she or he would like to be. The body copy, "it'd be a place where the morning tide brings a flood of memories," completes the dream and actually refers to the beach in the blurred photograph.

The advertisement in figure 7.6 was created by Joe Alexander (creative director and copywriter), Cliff Sorah (creative director and art director), Mike Hughes (creative director), Tom Gibson (art director), Jacques Lowe (photographer), Cindy Hicks (art producer), Matt Wieringo (studio artist), Ben Eley (studio artist), and Daniel Leimberger (studio artist) at the Martin Agency, Richmond, Virginia. Read the headline:

EAT. SLEEP. HOFFA.

The headline works well with the large visual of Robert Kennedy, who served as attorney general when his brother John F. Kennedy served as president of the United States, as well as with the body copy:

> 1957 to 1964. Bobby Kennedy pursues Jimmy Hoffa because the Teamsters boss is abusing his power over union workers. Proving again how RFK never backed down from a chance to defend the little guy. To learn more, visit Boston today.

The advertisement, which was one in a series for the Museum at the John F. Kennedy Library, was created to inform readers about the close relationship between Robert and John F. Kennedy as well as their impact on important issues at the time. The advertisement was a finalist in the Magazine Publishers of America Kelly Awards competition in 2000. The campaign helped maintain the museum's status as the most-visited presidential library.

Guidelines for Writing the Consumer Magazine Advertisement

Writing advertisements for consumer magazines is usually easier when one adheres to the following guidelines. Indeed, these guidelines will help any copywriter create a much more effective advertisement.

HEADLINES

1. Attract the reader's attention in the headline.
2. Appeal to the reader's self-interest in the headline.
3. Arouse the reader's curiosity in the headline.
4. Write simply, clearly, and believably in the headline.
5. Identify the prospective consumers in the headline.
6. Identify the product or service in the headline.
7. Identify the advertiser in the headline.
8. Present a benefit or promise in the headline.
9. Present news or an easy solution to a problem in the headline.
10. State the unique selling proposition in the headline.

FIGURE 7.6 Two-page magazine advertisement for the Museum at the John F. Kennedy Library. *Courtesy of The Martin Agency.*

BODY COPY

1. Write to the prospect in his or her language.
2. Put news into the first paragraph of the body copy.
3. Use concrete terms, not abstract terms, in the body copy.
4. Use more short sentences than long sentences in the body copy.
5. Use short paragraphs.
6. Do not use too many adjectives and adverbs in the body copy.
7. Try not to talk down to the consumer in the body copy.
8. Set the product or service apart from its competition by making it different or unique.
9. Try not to stray from the major points or benefits in the body copy.
10. Present the most important points and benefits in order of their importance to the prospect.
11. Try not to use a negative tone in the body copy.
12. Use subheads whenever long body copy exists.
13. Use active verbs in the body copy.
14. Avoid exaggerated claims or superlatives in the body copy.

Of course, you may not be able to use all of the above in either the headline or the body copy, but you should try to use as many as are relevant.

BUSINESS-TO-BUSINESS ADVERTISING

There are several thousand publications that are classified as business magazines. These publications can be divided into several categories based on readership. Indeed, readers of these magazines usually are experts when it comes to purchasing products that they or their businesses need.

In addition to targeting specific audiences based on profession or type of business, publishers of business publications typically attempt to reach those who make major business decisions. Consequently, advertisers and their advertising agencies realize the importance of these magazines.

However, there is a major difference between advertisements that are created for business publications and advertisements that are created for consumer magazines. Advertisements that are created for business publications are more serious in tone. After all, these advertisements are sandwiched in between articles that are read by people who desire to learn about how they can improve their productivity, their department's productivity, and their company's productivity. In short, business publications generally contain features that inform readers about their profession, industry, and competition, among other helpful subjects.

Who reads specialized business magazines? According to a study, subscribers to specialized business magazines "are high-income, educated managers and professionals who are buyers and specifiers of products and services used in their industries and by their companies."[10] The average age of a reader of a specialized business magazine is 46. Furthermore, 67 percent of the readers have completed 16 to 20 years of formal education. More than 30 percent work for companies that have more than 1,000 employees. More than 90 percent are in professional, managerial, and technical occupations. Almost 90 percent are involved in purchases for their company. The average personal income of a reader is $77,000.[11]

How well do these readers read specialized business magazines? According to a study, more than 70 percent of the subscribers read at least 75 percent of the issues on a regular basis. More than 90 percent read at least 75 percent of the issues on an occasional basis.[12]

Do these readers read specialized business magazines more often than they read general business magazines? According to a study, specialized business magazines are read more often than general business magazines. Indeed, almost 80 percent read at least 75 percent of the issues "of a specialized business magazine in their field." Only 58 percent read at least 75 percent of the issues of any 10 leading general business magazines.[13] Although business publications continue to be popular among advertisers that desire to reach professionals, other media such as direct mail and the Internet are growing in popularity.

Types of Business-to-Business Publications

Business-to-business publications can be categorized as industrial, professional, and trade. Employees of manufacturing firms typically read industrial publications. These readers include controllers, engineers, managers, and purchasing agents, among others. These manufacturing firms typically manufacture products that other manufacturing firms need in order to manufacture products. For instance, a manufacturer of machines, parts, or tools may advertise in these publications primarily because most, if not all, of the firm's sales are to other manufacturers. Although the manufacturer typically will have a competent sales staff, the company's advertising will aid members of the sales force as well as enlighten executives at prospective manufacturing firms who are charged with purchasing decisions.

Professional publications are addressed to accountants, architects, dentists, lawyers, physicians, surgeons, and other professionals who desire to learn about the latest trends or discoveries. In short, these readers desire to stay abreast of their professions. Consequently, these publications feature articles that inform readers about managing offices more efficiently, solving clients' problems faster and better, and using new technological equipment, as well as a host of other topics. Primarily because these individuals are highly educated and work in professions that allow them to have an influence on others, advertisers usually place advertisements that are of a scientific or technical nature, generally filled with factual information.

Trade publications are directed to those who purchase products for resale. These include wholesalers and retailers, among others. Trade publications exist primarily to help wholesalers and retailers learn about the products, prices, and promotions of manufacturers. Consequently, manufacturers advertise in these publications primarily to inform prospective wholesalers and retailers about their brands or their marketing efforts.

Business-to-Business Advertisements

Look at figure 7.7, which was created by personnel at 3 Marketeers Advertising, San Jose, California. The advertisement concerns Shoreline Robust IP Phone Systems. The headline reads:

> **"Shoreline's**
> **IP Phone**
> **System Saves**
> **BKF**
> **$631,250 . . .**
> ***(and counting)*.**"

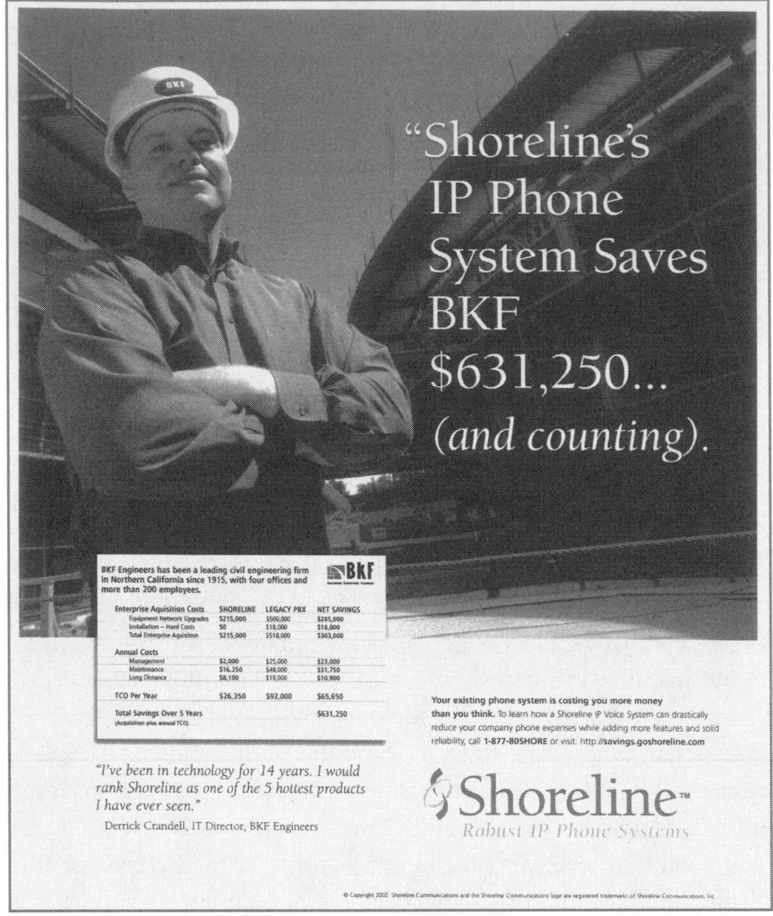

FIGURE 7.7 One-page magazine advertisement for Shoreline. *Courtesy of 3 Marketeers Advertising.*

The body copy continues with testimony from Derrick Crandell, IT Director, BKF Engineers:

> **"I've been in technology for 14 years. I would rank Shoreline as one of the 5 hottest products I have ever seen."**

The body copy ends with a brief paragraph that calls for the reader to take action by calling a toll-free number or visiting the company online:

> **Your existing phone system is costing you more money than you think. To learn how a Shoreline IP Voice System can drastically reduce your company phone expenses while adding more features and solid reliability, call 1-877-80SHORE or visit: http://savings.goshoreline.com**

The advertisement also contains information about BKF's savings for five years. So, this advertisement would appear in which type of business publication?

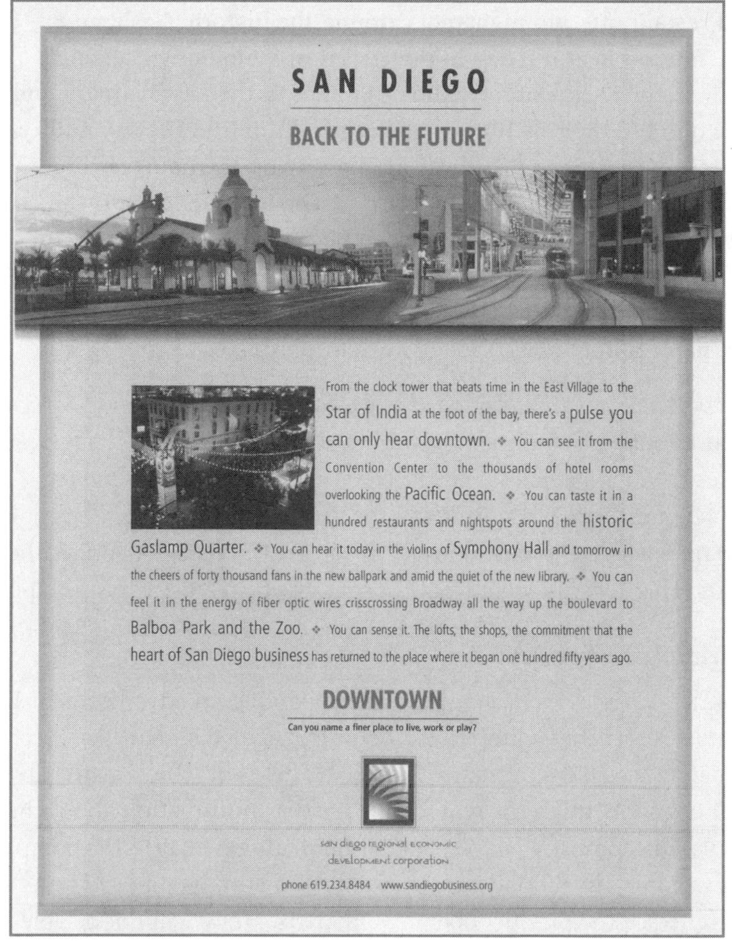

FIGURE 7.8 One-page magazine advertisement for San Diego.
Courtesy of Gavin & Gavin Advertising, Inc.

Figure 7.8, which was created by Sally P. Gavin (art director) and Robert A. Gavin (copywriter) of Gavin & Gavin Advertising, Inc., San Diego, California, features a business-to-business advertisement that targets CEOs who are considering moving their businesses to a different city. The headline reads:

SAN DIEGO
BACK TO THE FUTURE

The headline suggests what will be discussed in the body copy.

Now, read the body copy:

> **From the clock tower that beats time in the East Village to the Star of India at the foot of the bay, there's a pulse you can only hear downtown. You can see it from the Convention Center to the thousands of hotel rooms overlooking the Pacific Ocean. You can taste it in a**

hundred restaurants and nightspots around the historic Gaslamp Quarter. You can hear it today in the violins of Symphony Hall and tomorrow in the cheers of forty thousand fans in the new ballpark and amid the quiet of the new library. You can feel it in the energy of fiber optic wires crisscrossing Broadway all the way up the boulevard to Balboa Park and the Zoo. You can sense it. The lofts, the shops, the commitment that the heart of San Diego business has returned to the place where it began one hundred fifty years ago.
DOWNTOWN
Can you name a finer place to live, work or play?

The body copy attempts to allow the reader to *feel* as well as *visualize* the heart of San Diego: "a pulse . . . see it . . . taste it . . . hear it today . . . and tomorrow . . . feel it . . . sense it. . . . Star of India . . . Convention Center . . . Pacific Ocean . . . restaurants . . . nightspots . . . historic Gaslamp Quarter . . . Symphony Hall . . . new ballpark . . . new library . . . Balboa Park and the Zoo." In other words, the copywriter tries to allow prospective CEOs to have a sense of what downtown San Diego offers. Of course, the visual elements aid the copywriter's words. This advertisement would appear in which type of business publication?

Writing the Industrial Advertisement

Writing the industrial advertisement may be difficult. Unlike an advertisement for consumer magazines, an industrial advertisement is directed to chemists, engineers, managers, technicians, and others who have been formally educated and trained in specific fields of which many advertising copywriters have no knowledge. Consequently, copywriters must gather information about the products from the company's salespeople, the company's advertising or marketing manager, the company's engineers, and others. Copywriters will in all likelihood have to examine the product as well as its specifications sheet. Copywriters will have to see the product operate. Otherwise, they will not be able to write an effective advertisement about the product.

Copywriters must make certain that they stay away from an informal conversational style of writing when they write an industrial advertisement. Indeed, every word should be examined to determine if it is the most appropriate word to use. A call to action is also out of place. Usually, more than one individual, if not a committee, is responsible for purchasing a product for industrial use because of the product's use and price.

HEADLINES

1. Make certain that the headline is specific. Specifics attract attention.
2. Try to use news in the headline. Individuals are interested in learning about something new.
3. Try offering the product as a solution to a problem in the headline. Individuals are interested in learning about how a product can solve their problems.

BODY COPY

1. Body copy should focus on how much the product will save the prospective buyer, not on how much the product will cost the prospective buyer.

2. Body copy should focus on an individual reader, not on several readers, even though several readers may be responsible for making a decision to purchase the product. In other words, direct the sales message to a particular professional such as an engineer, not to an engineer, a manager, and others all at the same time. Remember that the words used in the sales message should be words that the intended readers understand as a result of their formal education and training.
3. Body copy should provide enough information about the product, its construction, its qualities, its purpose, and its performance, as well as the manufacturer's services for the product after the sale.
4. Body copy should include a case history of the product. A case history is merely information about the successful use of the product by another company. However, in order for a case history to work, it should be about a company that is similar to those where the intended readers work.

It may not be possible to include all of the above suggestions in every advertisement. However, most, if not all, of the above may be included in many industrial advertisements.

Writing the Trade Advertisement

Trade advertisements are usually filled with factual information about products that are purchased by wholesalers and retailers for resale. However, this does not mean that trade advertisements cannot be dramatic or at least contain an appeal for action. Sometimes trade advertisements inform wholesalers and retailers about current advertising campaigns, primarily to let wholesalers and retailers know that the manufacturer is advertising its product to consumers, which, of course, should help wholesalers and retailers sell more of the manufacturer's product. Usually, these advertisements explain the purpose of the advertising campaigns targeting consumers.

Trade advertisements typically explain to the wholesaler and retailer how they can earn money by purchasing the manufacturer's product. In addition, these advertisements suggest how the manufacturer's product can be displayed in stores. In other words, trade advertisements must often perform a complete sales job, much like an effective salesperson. Consequently, the product being advertised needs to be emphasized with factual, even statistical, information. Sometimes trade advertisements explain the manufacturer's various national, regional, and local advertising programs that may offer wholesalers and retailers assistance with their advertising programs. In short, these advertisements may inform wholesalers and retailers about the various promotional materials that the manufacturer has produced for their benefit.

HEADLINES

1. The headline should make clear what is being sold.
2. The headline should attract attention by being interesting.
3. The headline should promote the product or the advertising for the product.
4. The headline should focus attention on how much profit the dealer will earn from selling the product.
5. The headline should offer a major benefit.
6. The headline should be printed in large, bold letters.

BODY COPY

1. The body copy should sell the product. That is, it should provide thorough details about the product.
2. The body copy should explain the manufacturer's national, regional, and local advertising programs (if relevant).
3. The body copy should provide information about display or promotional materials that are provided by the manufacturer.
4. The body copy should explain the product's sales appeal. If the product's overall sales figures exist, include these, especially if these figures are high comparatively speaking.
5. The body copy should contain interesting subheads that break up the copy and relate well to the copy that immediately follows.

Of course, it may not be possible to include all of the above suggestions in every advertisement. After all, the purposes of trade advertisements differ. However, most, if not all, of the above may be included in many trade advertisements.

General Guidelines for Writing Business-to-Business Advertisements

1. Remember the prospective buyer. You need to know what the buyer's problems are. Perhaps the product you are advertising will help the prospective buyer solve one of these problems.
2. Remember to use specific information, not generalities, in the advertisement. In addition to informing business executives, the advertisement may serve as an aid to the company's sales staff.
3. Remember to put the most important point (feature or benefit) first. Then put the remaining points in order of their significance to the buyer.
4. Remember to emphasize benefits, not features, in the headline and body copy.
5. Remember to use active voice; it is more emphatic.
6. Remember to write from the prospective consumer's perspective. In short, use a natural personal style to communicate.
7. Remember to use declarative sentences whenever possible. These kinds of sentences help move the reader through the copy easier and faster.
8. Remember to use action verbs, not adjectives or adverbs, whenever possible.
9. Remember that your prospective buyer is an educated professional who expects to read factual information about the product. Diagrams, charts, graphs, lists of specifications, and case histories of the product should be included whenever appropriate.

AGRICULTURAL OR FARM PUBLICATIONS

These magazines have had to change in the past 50 years, primarily because farming has changed—from individual families owning and operating farms to companies or cooperatives hiring managers to operate farms. In fact, the number of individuals working on farms has decreased dramatically. As a result, companies that advertise in agricultural or farm publications have changed their messages. No longer are they addressing the single family who lives on a farm. Instead, they are addressing managers who are well educated, much like other professional people who oversee businesses. Consequently, their advertisements are similar to other advertisements that are directed to professionals.

Agricultural publications usually are classified as general, regional, and vocational farm publications. General farm publications attempt to address all aspects of living on and running a farm, with an emphasis on the latter. Regional farm publications are directed to those who live on or manage a farm in a specific geographic area. Usually, the content focuses on crops and livestock that are grown or bred on farms in the region. Sometimes relevant government legislation is discussed. Vocational farm publications concern specific types of farming or livestock breeding.

Advertising copywriters should use the general guidelines listed above whenever they have to write an advertisement for an agricultural publication. These guidelines shift somewhat in other media. The next chapter discusses radio advertising.

EXERCISES

1. The publisher of *Newsweek* is having its advertising agency launch a campaign that will include four full-page, four-color magazine ads. All ads will emphasize the following: 26 issues of *Newsweek* for 50 cents an issue or $13; the cost is more than 50 percent off the regular price; and the subscriber will receive a 20-minute video about how and where to invest. The deadline for ordering at this price is December 31 of the current year. You are to do one of the ads. In addition to doing the copy sheet that includes the headline, subhead(s) (if desired), body copy, slogan (if desired), and logo, you will need to do at least a rough to show how the ad will be designed.
2. Using a current television commercial, create a full-page ad that will be placed in a popular magazine. The ad should be comprehensive—that is, all the elements—headline, subhead(s), body copy, illustration, slogan, and logo—should be in the ad. Make sure that your typeface and point size are appropriate for the product or service and message.
3. Develop a copy sheet that contains a headline, subhead(s) (if needed), body copy, and slogan (if needed) for Zest bath soap. The ad, which will appear in a popular magazine, should target women 18 to 35 years of age.
4. Develop a copy sheet for an ad that will be addressed to advertisers to try to persuade them to advertise in *Fortune*. In other words, the ad will be addressed to prospective advertisers for *Fortune*. Think about the following before you try to write the ad: *Fortune* provides in-depth articles that appeal to upper management; the magazine never rehashes what can be found in newspapers; the magazine is published twice a month; the magazine is one of the leading business magazines; the magazine's average reader has graduated from college, earns more than $200,000 a year, and is employed in business, industry, or one of the professions; and the magazine accepts full-page, two-third-page, half-page, and one-third-page ads. Ads can be purchased for the following covers: Cover 2, Cover 3, and Cover 4. The magazine's circulation is about 900,000.

NOTES

1. Magazine Publishers of America, *The Magazine Handbook*: 2001–2002 (New York: Magazine Publishers of America, 2002; www.magazine.org), p. 6.

2. Magazine Publishers of America, *The Magazine Handbook*, p. 14.
3. Magazine Publishers of America, *The Magazine Handbook*, p. 22.
4. Magazine Publishers of America, *The Magazine Handbook*, p. 33.
5. Magazine Publishers of America, *The Magazine Handbook*, p. 20.
6. Magazine Publishers of America, *The Magazine Handbook*, p. 23.
7. Magazine Publishers of America, *The Magazine Handbook*, p. 40.
8. Magazine Publishers of America, *The Magazine Handbook*, p. 13.
9. Magazine Publishers of America, *The Magazine Handbook*, p. 9.
10. "Profile of Readers of Specialized Business Magazines," *Cahners Advertising Research Report*, No. 500.1C.
11. "Profile of Readers of Specialized Business Magazines."
12. "How Well Are Specialized Business Publications Read?" *Cahners Advertising Research Report*, No. 411.1C.
13. "Are Specialized Business Magazines Read More Often than General Business/Interest Magazines?" *Cahners Advertising Research Report*, No. 442.2C.

CHAPTER 8

Radio Advertising

Radio stations earn more than $19 billion from advertising annually, which is about 8 percent of the total amount spent by advertisers in the various media.[1] The reasons advertisers are interested in advertising on radio stations include the facts that radio reaches more than 96 percent of people aged 12 and older every week, radio reaches 78 percent of people aged 12 and older every day, and radio reaches more than 51 percent of people aged 12 and older from 6 A.M. to 10 A.M. every day.[2] Of course, 6 A.M. to 10 A.M. is considered prime time for radio, which means that more people listen to radio during this period than during any other period of the day or night. The number of listeners also increases from 3 P.M. to 7 P.M.; however, this number is not as high as the number of listeners during prime time.

Radio also reaches practically everyone, unlike newspapers and other media. Indeed, teenagers as well as adult women and men listen to radio. Every week, individuals who are aged 12 and older listen to their favorite stations for more than 20 hours. For instance, 96 percent of African Americans aged 12 and older listen to their favorite stations more than 24 hours each week, and 95 percent of Hispanic Americans aged 12 and older listen to their favorite stations more than 23 hours each week.[3] Radio also reaches affluent listeners. For instance, almost 99 percent of adults who earn more than $50,000 a year listen to radio; most of these individuals have college educations and hold managerial or professional positions.[4]

Where do listeners listen to radio? They listen practically everywhere, including at home, in cars and trucks, at work, at the beach, and even while shopping. Unlike television, which experiences fewer viewers during certain periods of the year, radio is consistent. Listeners listen throughout the year, and, unlike with television and other media, more than 60 percent of the adults have listened to their favorite radio stations within one hour of making their largest purchase of the day.[5]

As mentioned, radio stations earn more than $19 billion from advertising annually. Local spot advertising accounts for more than $15 billion, national spot advertising accounts for more than $3 billion, and network advertising accounts for $1 billion.[6] Various advertisers—from national corporations to local businesses—advertise on radio stations throughout the United States. A reason so many advertisers use radio is because radio works well to reinforce advertisers' advertisements and

TABLE 8.1 ***Most Popular Formats for Listeners***

FORMAT	INDIVIDUALS 12 AND OLDER	FORMAT	INDIVIDUALS 12 AND OLDER
News/Talk	16.9%	Album Rock	4.8%
Adult Contemporary	15.3%	Classic Rock	4.2%
Contemporary Hits Radio	11.4%	Adult Standards	3.0%
Country	9.0%	Smooth Jazz	2.7%
Oldies	8.1%	Religious	2.5%
Urban	8.0%	Classical	1.7%
Hispanic	6.9%	Other Formats	0.5%
Alternative	5.0%		

Source: Radio Advertising Bureau, *Radio Marketing Guide and Fact Book for Advertisers 2001–2002 Edition* (Irving, TX: Radio Advertising Bureau, 2002; www.rab.com), p. 43.

commercials that appear in newspapers and magazines or have been broadcast on television stations or television networks.

One reason for radio's popularity among listeners is the numerous formats or kinds of programming that are available. For instance, radio stations generally specialize in one kind of format such as news and talk, which is the most popular format among listeners aged 12 and older. The most popular formats among listeners are listed in table 8.1.[7] Of course, the above percentages differ when age ranges, such as 12 to 17 or 18 to 24 and so on, are used to segment listeners.

Today, there are more than 10,500 commercial radio stations in the United States. Table 8.2 lists the numerous formats as well as the number of stations that have adopted them.[8] Radio stations may be small or large in power, independently owned and operated, or owned and operated by media companies or corporations.

TYPES OF RADIO ADVERTISING

Advertisers may actually purchase network radio, spot radio, or local radio airtime. Networks may be national or regional in size. National networks enable advertisers to have their commercial messages broadcast nationally through stations that are subscribers to the networks' programs. Regional networks enable advertisers to have their commercial messages broadcast regionally or in specific geographic areas through stations that are subscribers to the networks' programs. National and regional networks provide affiliate stations with news, sports, entertainment features, and other kinds of programs. Advertisers are encouraged to associate their commercial messages with these programs.

Spot radio enables national and regional advertisers more flexibility in their selection of markets or stations and even airtime. Such enables advertisers to reach their intended target markets with greater impact and immediacy for fewer dollars. Local radio enables local advertisers to reach their intended target markets with immediacy.

TABLE 8.2 ***Formats of Radio Stations***

RANK / FORMAT		NUMBER OF STATIONS	RANK / FORMAT		NUMBER OF STATIONS
1	Country	2,195	17	R & B	183
2	News/Talk	1,133	18	Contemporary Christian	163
3	Oldies	784	19	Modern Rock	139
4	Adult Contemporary	713	20	Urban Adult Contemporary	118
5	Hispanic	574	21	R & B Adult/Oldies	113
6	Adult Standards	572	22	Alternative Rock	94
7	Top 40	469	23	Ethnic	91
8	Soft Adult Contemporary	381	24	Jazz	78
9	Hot Adult Contemporary	360	25	Modern Adult Contemporary	64
10	Religious	354	26	Pre-teen	55
11	Classic Rock	336	27	Gospel	40
12	Sports	332	28	Variety	40
13	Rock	282	29	Classical	34
14	Classic Hits	264	30	Easy Listening	29
15	Black Gospel	261	31	Other	23
16	Southern Gospel	251			

Source: Radio Advertising Bureau, *Radio Marketing Guide and Fact Book for Advertisers 2001–2002 Edition* (Irving, TX: Radio Advertising Bureau, 2002; www.rab.com), p. 46.

IMAGERY TRANSFER

Radio stations allow advertisers the opportunity to actually strengthen their commercials that have been broadcast on television stations or networks. Such is known as "imagery transfer." For instance, if a radio station broadcasts the audio portion of a previously broadcast television commercial, the listener's mind actually visualizes the images observed in the television commercial. This practice extends the television commercial's reach and increases message frequency; it also increases awareness.[9]

ADVANTAGES OF RADIO AS AN ADVERTISING MEDIUM

There are several advantages that radio offers advertisers. In addition to reaching everyone just about everywhere, other advantages include the following:

1. Radio offers timeliness, just like daily newspapers. Advertisers may write and produce commercials an hour or two before they are to be broadcast by radio stations. Other media are not this timely.
2. Radio allows advertisers to select their target markets based on format, geography, and time of day. Format refers to the station's programming such as news/talk or rock. Geography refers to the strength of the station's broadcast signal. Time of day refers to the different audiences that stations attract throughout the day and night.

3. Radio is considered a local medium; consequently, advertisers can tie their commercials to local events.
4. Airtime on radio is usually cost-efficient for advertisers.
5. Radio reaches listeners when they are in their cars or trucks; therefore, they may be close to the advertiser.
6. Radio reaches young listeners as well as adults.
7. Radio stations usually have well-known personalities who can actually help sell products and services.
8. Radio is a very personal medium.

DISADVANTAGES OF RADIO AS AN ADVERTISING MEDIUM

Of course, radio has a few disadvantages as an advertising medium:

1. It is nonvisual, even though it is considered "the theater of the mind" medium. In other words, radio commercials should cause listeners to visualize in their minds what is being discussed because they cannot actually see it.
2. Once a commercial is broadcast on radio it is gone; the listener has no way of bringing it back, unlike an advertisement that appears in a newspaper or magazine.

TYPES OF RADIO COMMERCIALS

There are several types of radio commercials. These include the following:

1. Musical copy
2. Testimonial copy
3. Straight copy or Straight Announcer copy
4. Dialogue or Conversational copy or Man-on-the-Street copy
5. Dramatized copy or Vignette copy

The first type, Musical copy, may be nothing more than a jingle. Typically, a jingle is four or more lines of copy set to music. If the lines are easy to remember, and the music lends itself to the memorability of the lines, then the musical commercial may succeed. However, the jingle should be about the most important benefit that the product or service provides to the consumer or at least evoke a mood that relates well to the product or service. For instance, Coca-Cola has been advertised successfully periodically via musical commercials that evoke a mood. Generally, advertising agencies contract with specialty firms such as "jingle houses" to develop musical commercials.

Testimonial copy is the type of commercial that has at least one individual saying positive points about the product or service. Although celebrities may be used, they should be believable. In short, listeners have to believe what the celebrity is saying in order for the commercial to work. This means that the listener needs to believe that the celebrity has used the product or service. Thus, the copy must employ words and phrases that listeners understand and believe. The copy must not sound artificial; it must sound realistic and reflect the individual speaking. Look at box 8.1, which was created for Motel

BOX 8.1 ***Script of a Radio Commercial Featuring a Spokesperson for Motel 6***

CLIENT:	MOTEL 6
JOB:	:60 Radio
TITLE:	"DEFICIT REDUCTION"
JOB #:	MTL-0593
DATE:	06/24/02

TOM: *Hi. Tom Bodett for Motel 6 with an open letter to the president. Well, Sir, you asked us all to contribute to help shrinking up the deficit. And since what's good for the goose is good for the gander, I've got a painless way for you to contribute along with the rest of us—Motel 6. Instead of staying at those big, fancy places when you go out on business, you could stay at the Six. You'd get a clean, comfortable room for the lowest prices of any national chain and a good night's sleep to go along with it. Those guys in the suits and dark glasses that follow you around could stay in the room with you for just a few extra dollars. Heck, maybe you could all watch a free in-room movie or make a few free local phone calls or something. It'd be a blast. Oh, sure, you'd have to do without a shower cap and that fancy guava-gel conditioning shampoo but, all in all, Mr. President, I'd say you've probably spent enough money on your hair anyway. I'm Tom Bodett for Motel 6, and we'll leave the light on for you . . . Sir.*

ANNCR: *Motel 6 is an Accor hotel.*

For the above radio commercial, Mike Renfro and Jim Baldwin were the creative directors; Mike Renfro was the copywriter, too.
Courtesy of The Richards Group.

6 by personnel at the Richards Group, Dallas, and features Tom Bodett, who has a pleasant voice and sounds sincere.

The third type is the commercial that has one voice speaking about the features and benefits of the product or service. The major problem with this Straight or Straight Announcer type of commercial is finding a spokesperson who sounds interesting *and* authentic. The advertising copywriter must use language that arrests as well as informs listeners. In addition, the copywriter must use words and phrases that do not cause the spokesperson problems, such as mispronunciation or awkward pacing. Indeed, the spokesperson must be able to pronounce each word naturally, as if the word is part of the spokesperson's vocabulary. The pace must be natural as well. In other words, the phrasing must be natural, so that the spokesperson does not necessarily have to slow down or speed up to the point that the listener grows bored with the message or cannot understand what the spokesperson is saying. Look at box 8.2, which was created for United Way by personnel at BOHAN Advertising/Marketing, Nashville, Tennessee.

The fourth type is usually easier to write than the previous types, primarily because in a dialogue or conversation there is more than one spokesperson. However, the advertising copywriter must use caution when writing about the features and benefits of the product or service, or these points will sound as if they were written by the advertiser and put into the spokespersons' mouths. In short, the features and benefits

BOX 8.2 ***Script of a Radio Commercial Featuring an Announcer Talking about United Way***

CLIENT: United Way
JOB TITLE: 6481UW/Metro Radio Copy
DATE/VERS: August 1, 2001 / v4 / ds
UNITED WAY
:60 RADIO

"THANKS TO YOU" (UW6260-01)

MUSIC: UP AND UNDER

ANNCR: *Thanks to you, more than 2,000 children receive quality childcare where they can learn more and laugh more. . . . Thanks to you, more than 12,000 young people are being tutored, counseled, and encouraged to dream big dreams. . . . Thanks to you, more than 6,000 senior citizens enjoy hot meals and other services that allow them to live safely in their own homes. . . . United Way of Metropolitan Nashville would like to thank you on behalf of your neighbors who are helped each year through our Community Solutions Fund. . . . The Community Solutions Fund partners United Way with public schools, corporations and over 120 health and human service agencies shown to have the greatest impact on Nashville's most urgent needs. . . . And thanks to you, more people are being helped than ever before, but there are many more dreams to fulfill. . . . To see how your generosity is helping people throughout Nashville, log onto unitedwaynashville.org. United Way. Help us. Help others.*

Courtesy of BOHAN Advertising/Marketing.

must be introduced naturally, in words and phrases the spokespersons would actually use in everyday speech, not in terms or jargon that would be used by a typical advertiser. Look at box 8.3, which was created for Pigeon Forge (Tennessee) by personnel at BOHAN Advertising/Marketing, Nashville.

The fifth type, Dramatized or Vignette copy, is similar to a brief play or short story in that the commercial has a beginning, a middle, and an end. Generally, one spokesperson introduces a problem that he or she has; then a second spokesperson or an announcer introduces a solution to the problem. Of course, the product or service serves as the solution to the problem.

Although music is required for the first type of radio commercial, music can be used for the other types of commercials as well, especially to evoke a mood or establish an atmosphere. Sound effects may also be employed or even take the place of music, depending on the commercial's premise. In fact, some commercials can be developed around specific sound effects. For instance, if you are trying to sell an additive that is typically added to gasoline tanks, you may call for an engine that sounds as if one or more spark plugs are not firing properly. You may desire to have the listener hear the engine more than once. In this case, it is important for the sound effect to be placed in the appropriate spots in the commercial. You may even desire to have the listener hear the engine running smoothly after the additive has been put into the gas tank. Such may prove to the listener that the product actually does what the spokesperson claims.

BOX 8.3 ***Script of a Radio Commercial Featuring More Than One Person Talking about Pigeon Forge***

PIGEON FORGE

:60 RADIO w/:38 DONUT

"SUMMER 2002–DOLLY"

MUSIC: (JINGLE UP AND UNDER)

DOLLY: *Are you ready for some fun in the Smokies this summer? Well, here in Pigeon Forge, the rides are running, the music's playing, and there are smiles all around. You can hear the laughter all the way to the top of the Tennessee Tornado roller coaster at Dollywood, because there's more to see and do in Pigeon Forge than ever before, like my Splash Country Adventure Water Park. Summer's here and so is the fun, right here in Pigeon Forge.*

ANNCR: *For a free Pigeon Forge Travel Planner and info on coupon books filled with discounts, call 1-800-333-4FUN or go online to mypigeonforge.com.*

MUSIC: (JINGLE UP AND OUT)

Courtesy of BOHAN Advertising/Marketing.

FORMS OF RADIO COMMERCIALS

There are several forms of radio commercials. These include the following:

1. Produced Commercial
2. Combination Live/Taped Commercial
3. Fact Sheet Commercial
4. Live Script Commercial

The first form is the professionally produced commercial that arrives at the radio station on tape or disk. National advertisers and their advertising agencies prefer to send professionally produced commercials to radio stations because they have control over the commercial's presentation. Local advertisers should consider having commercials produced by professionals when music, numerous voices, and sound effects are desired.

The combination form is also known as the donut commercial, which usually has music professionally produced on tape or disk. The music is audible at the beginning and at the end of the commercial. It fades under or is less audible in the middle of the commercial. Sometimes the music fades out in the middle of the commercial. This action allows copy, which is supplied by the advertiser or the advertiser's advertising agency, to be read by someone at the radio station. This someone may be a particular radio station personality. This form is popular among national and local advertisers that desire copy to be read by popular radio station personalities. (Look at box 8.3 again and notice the music before and after what is spoken.)

The third form is a sheet that lists the facts or features and benefits of the product or service that is sent to radio stations. Generally, advertisers use this form when they desire to have radio station personalities discuss the product or service in positive terms.

The fourth form is a script that has been prepared by an advertiser or the advertiser's advertising agency. The script is then sent to radio stations, where it is read on the air or is recorded by someone at the radio station to be broadcast later. Although advertisers or their advertising agencies do not necessarily have control over how the commercial will be presented, many radio stations attempt to have their station personalities read or record this form of commercial.

EVOKING PICTURES IN RADIO COMMERCIALS

Radio commercials should help listeners to actually visualize who is speaking, how he or she is dressed, and where he or she is supposed to be. You can do this by giving the spokesperson an accent or suggesting that she or he speak in a particular way such as "quickly," "slowly," like an elderly woman or man, and so forth. You can even have one spokesperson describe how another spokesperson is dressed. Of course, this should only be done if it is relevant to what is being advertised, such as an article or articles of clothing. Identifying where the commercial is occurring is easy as well. For instance, sound effects such as horns blowing can be used to identify traffic in cities. Such is used for on-the-street interviews or similar types of commercials. Sound effects such as people talking in the background and music playing can be used for depicting malls or stores. Of course, a spokesperson can identify where he or she is located by saying, for example, "I'm standing on the corner of Madison and Forty-second Street in . . ." near the beginning of the commercial.

In order to advertise a product in a radio commercial, you should mention the product by name several times—at least three times in a 30-second commercial and five or six times in a 60-second commercial. However, the name should not be repeated so often that it interferes with the natural flow of the commercial or bothers the listener. You should also describe the product or at least the package in which it is sold. This will help the listener to look for the product when shopping.

MUSIC, VOICES, AND SOUND EFFECTS

Music in radio commercials, especially at the beginning, can establish an atmosphere or evoke a mood. In fact, an all-music radio commercial, especially broadcast on an all-talk radio station, may gain the listener's attention because he or she is not used to hearing music broadcast by this station. Of course, music does not have to be used. For instance, if the commercial will be broadcast on an all-music radio station, you may desire to produce a radio commercial with no music. Such a commercial may gain the attention of the listener because he or she is not used to hearing someone speak for 30 or 60 seconds on this station. Of course, if music is desired, you may use music that is readily available for no or a small fee, or you may use an original composition that has been produced exclusively for the commercials in the advertising campaign.

Voices may reflect young, old, female, male, English, French, Italian, and so on. You should call for a voice that is relevant to the commercial's premise as well as to the product or service that is being advertised. Remember, you will need to describe what kind of voice you desire. The spokesperson will not necessarily know unless he or she has been informed. In addition, you will need to inform the spokesperson as to how you wish a statement to be said, such as "angrily," "exasperated," and so forth. See box 8.4, which was created for Pigeon Forge (Tennessee) by personnel at BOHAN Advertising/Marketing, Nashville.

BOX 8.4 ***Script of a Radio Commercial Featuring Music and More Than One Person Talking about Pigeon Forge***

PIGEON FORGE

:60 RADIO w/:38 DONUT

"SUMMER BOY"

MUSIC: (JINGLE UP)

BOY 8–10 Y. O.—ANIMATED: When we got to Pigeon Forge, Tennessee, I was . . . (LOUDLY) so excited, but I had to be cool . . . because, well, I am cool. . . . And so is Pigeon Forge. . . . They have this whole town full of fun stuff to do . . . go-carts, water parks, miniature golf, the Dixie Stampede . . . and that's even before you get to (YELLING) Dollywood! . . . Pigeon Forge is just so cool. And if you can leave your sister at home . . . now that is very cool.

ANNCR: Family Fun *magazine readers name Pigeon Forge one of the top Tourist Towns in the Southeast year after year. For a free Travel Planner and info on coupon books filled with discounts, call 1-800-333-4FUN or visit mypigeonforge.com.*

MUSIC: (JINGLE UP AND OUT)

Courtesy of BOHAN Advertising/Marketing.

Sound effects should be used when such are warranted. For instance, if you need to imply that someone is at the door, you will need to have a doorbell sound. If you need to imply that someone dropped a dish, you will need to have the sound of a dish breaking on a floor. Remember, sounds take the place of a spokesperson describing an activity; sounds may also provide visual images in the listener's mind. Look at box 8.5 (next page), which was created for Chick-fil-A by personnel at the Richards Group, Dallas. This radio commercial uses sound effects effectively and is humorous.

HOW MANY WORDS SHOULD YOU USE IN RADIO COMMERCIALS

Basically, you can have about two words for each second in a radio commercial. Of course, these words should be no more than one or two syllables and should be easy to pronounce. You do not want to include alliterative phrases such as "comprehensive collision coverage" or words or phrases that can cause the spokesperson's tongue to become twisted. The following list provides the estimated number of words in particular amounts of time:

10 seconds = 20–25 words
20 seconds = 40–45 words
30 seconds = 60–65 words
60 seconds = 120–125 words
90 seconds = 180–190 words

When you have written a radio commercial, make certain that you check for alliterative and awkward phrases as well as tongue twisters and words that do not sound natural when spoken. Also, use a stopwatch to time the commercial. If it is too short or too long, you will have to edit. If you can, record the commercial as it is supposed to be and then check it for the above problems. Generally, it is easier to identify what needs to be edited in a radio commercial by listening to it.

BOX 8.5 ***Script of a Radio Commercial Featuring Sound Effects and an Announcer Talking about Chick-fil-A***

CLIENT:	CHICK-FIL-A
JOB:	:60 Radio
TITLE:	"Calling All Cows"
JOB #:	CFA-187
DATE:	04/25/96
SFX:	(Open on SFX of dial tone. Then we hear numbers being dialed, but the tone is slightly off as if the numbers aren't being pressed properly. This goes on for a few seconds and is followed by an off the hook SFX.)
ANNCR:	*The cows are calling . . .*
SFX:	(We hear a sort of cow grumbling/moo, and then more effort misdialing the phone.)
ANNCR:	*The cows are trying to call you on the phone.*
SFX:	(Disgruntled moo)
ANNCR:	*The cows are trying to call you on the phone to tell you to eat more chicken.*
SFX:	(Disgruntled moo. Misdial, misdial, misdial)
ANNCR:	*Unfortunately, cows have hooves. So not only is the receiver hard to pick up, but the little numbers are nearly impossible to dial.*
SFX:	(Poorly dialed numbers and cow SFX continue under.)
ANNCR:	*Oh, how stubborn cows can be. You see, they want to tell you about Chick-fil-A. They invented the chicken sandwich over 30 years ago. Made a special way, it's more tender, juicier, better. The cows want to tell you, "Please, oh please, don't eat burgers." Eat Chick-fil-A chicken sandwiches.*
SFX:	(Dial tone)

For the above radio commercial, Doug Rucker was the creative director, and Bill Cochran was the copywriter. Courtesy of The Richards Group.

HUMOR IN RADIO COMMERCIALS

Should you use humor in radio commercials? You can when the humor relates to the commercial's premise and to the product or service that is being advertised. Otherwise, forget using humor. Before you consider using humor in radio commercials, ask yourself the following questions:

1. Is the commercial really humorous? What is humorous to one person may not be humorous to another.
2. Does the humor actually help sell the product or service? If not, then you should not use it.
3. Does the humor respect or disrespect the product or service? If it does not respect the product, then you should not use it.
4. Does the humor relate to human experience? If it does not, then you should not use it.
5. Does the humor have appeal, especially to the target market or audience? If it does not, then you should not use it.

In addition to the questions above, try the humor out on your coworkers to determine whether it is humorous and whether it relates well to the product or service that you are advertising, before you decide to use it in a commercial. (Look at box 8.5 again and notice the humorous approach.)

TERMS AN ADVERTISING COPYWRITER NEEDS TO KNOW BEFORE WRITING A RADIO COMMERCIAL

There are certain terms that are used in radio commercials. These terms refer to the position of the sound and to change. Consequently, you need to understand what these terms mean:

Off mike and *on mike* concern the sound in relation to the microphone. The former means that the sound is away from the microphone; the latter means that the sound is near or next to the microphone. Behind and under also mean that the sound is either in the background or away from the microphone.

Fade refers to the volume. *Fade in* and *fade up* mean to gradually increase a sound's volume. *Fade on* means to begin with silence and gradually increase the sound's volume. *Fade down* means to gradually decrease a sound's volume. *Fade under* means to gradually decrease a sound's volume and hold it while some other sound can be heard or while a spokesperson speaks. *Fade out* means to gradually decrease a sound's volume until it cannot be heard.

Segue means that two sounds are fading at the same time. One sound increases in volume as the other sound decreases in volume. *Cross fade* is similar to *segue*, except that the sounds overlap as they dissolve from one to the other. *Blending* means that the overlap is held so that two or more sounds occur at the same time.

Cutting and *switching* refer to a sudden change from one microphone to another.

RADIO SCRIPT FORMAT

A radio script should contain some, if not all, of the following at the top of the sheet of paper, preferably on the left-hand side: the client, the product, the title of the commercial, the length of the commercial, and the name of the advertising copywriter. Some advertising agencies merely include the client, the length of the commercial, and the title.

A radio script should be double-spaced so that the spokesperson(s) can read the copy without difficulty and so that notations may be made at the last minute, if necessary. On the left-hand side of the sheet of paper are typed the source and the audio effects, in capital letters. Such includes ANNOUNCER (ANNCR), MAN, WOMAN, NAMES (of characters), MUSIC, and SOUND EFFECTS (SFX). These are typed directly across from the copy that is to be read or the description of the music or sounds.

On the right-hand side of the sheet of paper are typed the copy that is spoken, including the directions concerning how the words or phrases are to be spoken, and the music and sound effects. Spoken copy is typed in upper- and lowercase. Directions are typed in all capital letters and placed in parentheses. If you wish to emphasize spoken copy, underline the word or words being spoken or use capital letters.

If your commercial needs a second page, type "more" at the bottom of the first page and "page 2 of ___" at the top of the second page, as well as the name of the advertising copywriter and the title of the commercial. If your commercial continues to a third page, type "more" at the bottom of the second page and "page 3 of ___" at the top of the third page, as well as the name of the copywriter and the title. If the third page is the last page, the above should be "page 3 of 3." You would type "end" at the bottom of the page.

You should make certain that you have reasons for what you do or do not do in a commercial. Usually, these reasons are expressed as decisions in an accompanying creative strategy or copy platform. Of

BOX 8.6 ***Example of a Copy Sheet (Script) for a Radio Commercial***

CLIENT: Sears
PRODUCT: Car batteries
TIME: :60
TITLE: "BATTERIES ON SALE AT SEARS"
COPYWRITER:

SFX: CAR STARTING . . . IN FAST AND FULL . . . FADE OUT (5 SECONDS).
CHARLEY: *Ralph, this makes the fifth time this week that I've had to jump-start your car. Why don't you buy a new battery?*
RALPH: *I would, but money's tight right now.*
CHARLEY: *But Sears is having their annual sale on batteries.*
RALPH: *Really?*
CHARLEY: *Really. And they are guaranteed. And you can use a credit card, or make monthly payments.*
RALPH: *Huh, I didn't know that. Thanks, Charley.*
CHARLEY: *Where're you goin'?*
RALPH: *To Sears, before the sale ends.*
SFX: TIRES SQUEALING . . . IN FAST AND FULL . . . FADE OUT (5 SECONDS).
ANNCR: *Don't be like Ralph . . . don't wait until your battery has to be jumped before you buy a new one. Get to Sears today and take advantage of their annual sale on batteries, before it's too late.*

course, as mentioned, a creative strategy or copy platform should accompany any advertisement, no matter what medium it is going in. Some advertising agencies merely use an abbreviated version of a creative strategy and refer to it as a "copy rationale" or "creative rationale."

Look at box 8.6, which contains an example copy sheet for a radio commercial. Note that the sound effects are underlined. Some copywriters do this for all sound effects, including music, primarily to inform the production staff about the sound effect and its location in the script. Also note that, in addition to the sound effects and two characters speaking, an announcer calls for action at the end of the commercial. Basically, he is directing the listener to go to Sears today to take advantage of the annual sale on batteries, "before it's too late." Most, if not all, radio commercials that are written for retailers' sales will end similarly to this example.

GUIDELINES FOR WRITING RADIO COMMERCIALS

1. Use easy-to-read (and -understand) one- or two-syllable words. You should not use words that are not familiar or are difficult to pronounce.
2. Use short sentences. People use short sentences and even sentence fragments when they speak.
3. Use contractions when relevant. Contractions are more natural than speaking two words in many instances.

4. Punctuate when needed. Help the spokesperson present the copy the way you intend it to be presented.
5. Do not use alliterative phrases or words that twist the tongue.
6. Try not to use words that have a "k," "s," or "z" sound. These words tend to cause problems when pronounced and consequently can be misinterpreted by the listener.
7. Make certain that you repeat the most important information, such as the product name, several times. If the commercial is about a business such as a retailer, repeat the name of the business several times.
8. Promise a benefit, if relevant, and repeat it several times. The listener will appreciate it.
9. If you know beforehand the radio station that will broadcast the commercial, make the commercial relate to it. For instance, you do not wish to have a loud, hard-sell commercial broadcast on a classical music formatted station.
10. Remember, music or another sound effect can attract the listener's attention. However, such should be used only if it is relevant to the advertising message.
11. Remember, prime time for radio is in the morning. This means that more people listen to radio at this time than at any other time.
12. Remember, a radio station, primarily because of its format, has a distinct audience. Make certain that the station that reaches your intended target market broadcasts your commercial.
13. If you use a celebrity sound-alike, use a disclaimer that informs listeners that a sound-alike is being used.
14. Do not make disparaging statements about your client's competition or their products or services. You may face a lawsuit.
15. Use conversational language, not stilted formal language, or your commercial will not be well received.
16. If you include an address, make certain that you use landmarks or noncompeting businesses that are well known by the listener. Do not use numerals.
17. Do not include a telephone number. Refer to it by informing the listener that it is listed in the local *Yellow Pages*.
18. Remember, you must capture the listener's attention immediately.
19. If relevant, make certain that the ending contains a call to action, so that the listener will respond.

Many of these aural cues are also important when writing for television. We examine television advertising in the next chapter.

EXERCISES

1. Write a 30-second radio commercial promoting a new CD by the artist of your choice. Make sure that the commercial is oriented toward the stations that air the artist you chose. For instance, a commercial promoting a new compilation by Elvis Presley would not air on stations that play jazz. Also, think about the potential consumers. What will make them purchase your product? The artist's name, the music, what? Once you have made your decision you should incorporate whatever you deem necessary. If you think that parts of one or two selections should be mixed with copy, include the selections. Remember, a

30-second commercial will have about 60 to 75 words—that is, if the commercial is all talk.

2. Write a 60-second radio commercial for Oceanview, using only an announcer. Oceanview, a seafood restaurant, will open in Nashville next Saturday. Oceanview, part of a chain, will feature fish on its menu. Fish of all kinds will be fresh, guaranteed. Flown in daily, offerings will include shrimp, scallops, haddock, shark, lobster, crab, clams, oysters, and perch, to name a few. Drinks (nonalcoholic) and desserts are free on opening day. The first 100 customers will receive coupons worth $10.00 off on their second meal. Remember, a 60-second commercial will have from 120 to 150 words—that is, if the commercial is all talk.
3. Write a 30-second radio commercial about STP Gas Treatment, which is a liquid additive that, when added to the fuel in one's car, removes water in the gas line, cleans the carburetor, inhibits rust in the fuel system, and may save gas. Water in gas lines can freeze, causing cars to stall. Rust can clog fuel filters or block carburetor jets, causing hard starting, stalling, and sputtering. A dirty carburetor can waste gas. This commercial is to run during the winter months in cold climates and should position the product against less expensive brands. "STP Gas Treatment costs more, but it does more" should be your approach. The audience will be men, aged 21 to 50, who know little about cars but desire to keep them running well.
4. Write a 60-second radio commercial using any technique you wish. The commercial should use the theme "It doesn't pay to steal" and should be directed toward teenagers. You may mention that stealing results in higher prices and that thieves face criminal charges, if caught. You may wish to include that shoplifting is a criminal offense. Remember, a 60-second commercial will have from 120 to 150 words, if the commercial is all talk.
5. Write a radio commercial about Pigeon Forge, Tennessee, which is close to the Great Smoky Mountains and home of Dollywood. Pigeon Forge is known for its numerous discount shops, rides, and shows. The commercial should be one of the types discussed in this chapter.

NOTES

1. Newspaper Association of America, "U.S. Advertising Expenditures—All Media," in *Facts about Newspapers 2001* (Vienna, VA: Newspaper Association of America, 2002; www.naa.org).
2. Radio Advertising Bureau, *Radio Marketing Guide and Fact Book for Advertisers 2001–2002 Edition* (Irving, TX: Radio Advertising Bureau, 2002; www.rab.com).
3. Radio Advertising Bureau, *Radio Marketing Guide and Fact Book for Advertisers 2001–2002 Edition.*
4. Radio Advertising Bureau, *Radio Marketing Guide and Fact Book for Advertisers 2001–2002 Edition.*
5. Radio Advertising Bureau, *Radio Marketing Guide and Fact Book for Advertisers 2001–2002 Edition.*
6. Radio Advertising Bureau, *Radio Marketing Guide and Fact Book for Advertisers 2001–2002 Edition.*
7. Radio Advertising Bureau, *Radio Marketing Guide and Fact Book for Advertisers 2001–2002 Edition.*
8. Radio Advertising Bureau, *Radio Marketing Guide and Fact Book for Advertisers 2001–2002 Edition.*
9. Radio Advertising Bureau, "Media Facts: A Guide to Competitive Media" (Irving, TX: Radio Advertising Bureau, 2002; www.rab.com).

CHAPTER 9

Television Advertising

Advertising on television accounts for more than 29 percent of the advertising dollars spent in the major media (television, newspapers, direct mail, radio, *Yellow Pages*, and magazines) annually in the United States. Broadcast television accounts for more than 19 percent, and cable television accounts for almost 10 percent.[1] Advertisers spend more than $54 billion on advertising in this medium. Without question, television is the preferred medium, especially by national advertisers. Local stations earn more than $21 billion annually, broadcast networks earn more than $14 billion, cable networks earn more than $15 billion, and syndicated television earns more than $3 billion.[2]

Advertisers such as DaimlerChrysler AG, General Motors Corporation, Ford Motor Company, Honda Motor Company Limited, Nissan Motor Company Limited, and Toyota Motor Corporation spend millions of dollars annually on advertising in this medium. In addition to manufacturers of cars and trucks, other advertisers, including General Mills Incorporated, McDonald's Corporation, AT&T, Philip Morris Companies Incorporated, Walt Disney Company, Wal-Mart Stores Incorporated, Proctor & Gamble Company, and others spend millions of dollars annually on advertising in this medium as well.

Advertisers that purchase the most national and local spot advertising are members of various categories. The top 20 categories are listed in table 9.1.[3] Advertisers that purchase the most time on the over-the-air broadcast networks are members of various categories. The top 20 categories are listed in table 9.2 (p.133).[4]

Advertising on television will increase, primarily because television is an influential and persuasive medium. Indeed, television sets are in more than 98 percent of the homes in the United States. In fact, two or more television sets are in more than 75 percent of the homes in the United States. Almost 70 percent of U.S. homes have cable.[5]

Today, there are almost 1,300 commercial television stations. Of these, more than 700 are UHF (ultra-high frequency) stations, and almost 600 are VHF (very high frequency) stations.[6] Americans are averaging more than seven hours a day watching television. Men average more than four hours a day, whereas women average almost five hours a day. Children and teenagers average more than three hours a day.[7]

Although the over-the-air broadcast networks have seen a decrease in viewership as a result of more cable networks offering programs, the over-the-air networks still reach more viewers. In fact, almost

TABLE 9.1 ***Top 20 Spot Categories***

RANK	CATEGORY	ADVERTISING EXPENDITURES FOR 2000
1	Automotive	$3.8+ billion
2	Restaurants	$1.4+ billion
3	Telecommunications	$947+ million
4	Government and Organizations	$913+ million
5	Food and Food Products	$762+ million
6	Car and Truck Dealers	$619+ million
7	Furniture Stores	$522+ million
8	Financial	$508+ million
9	Travel, Hotels, and Resorts	$487+ million
10	Media and Advertising	$442+ million
11	Medicines and Remedies	$432+ million
12	Motion Pictures	$407+ million
13	Insurance and Real Estate	$403+ million
14	Leisure Time Activities and Events	$364+ million
15	Food Stores and Supermarkets	$330+ million
16	Department Stores	$321+ million
17	Soft Drinks, Candy and Snacks	$288+ million
18	Schools, Colleges, and Camps	$265+ million
19	Home Electronics and Video Stores	$263+ million
20	Discount Department Stores	$244+ million

Source: Television Bureau of Advertising, Inc., "Top 25 Spot TV Categories," in *TV Basics* (New York: Television Bureau of Advertising, Inc., 2001; www.tvb.org).

twice as many viewers watch ABC, CBS, and NBC as any of the cable networks in a typical week. Fox, another over-the-air broadcast network, is close behind the previous three.[8]

The 60-second commercial was the standard for television for decades. Today, however, the 30-second commercial is the standard, followed by the 15-second commercial. Some commercials are 10 seconds, 20 seconds, 45 seconds, or 60 seconds long. Some networks even broadcast 90-second commercials.[9]

Although goods and services are advertised on television, political organizations and their candidates are also advertised. In 2000, for instance, more than $600 million was spent on advertising national and state politicians.[10]

ADVANTAGES OF TELEVISION AS AN ADVERTISING MEDIUM

As an advertising medium, television has several advantages that advertisers should consider. These include the following:

1. The most important advantage of television as an advertising medium is that it offers action or motion, color as well as black and white, sight, and sound.
2. Television is intrusive or pervasive. The viewer does not have to be actively involved to receive the message.

3. When it comes to trying to reach a target audience, television offers an advertiser several choices: by market, network, program, and time of day. For instance, if the advertiser wishes to advertise to those who live in Miami, the advertising agency may select a particular station in that city. Or if the advertiser wishes to reach those who watch a particular network such as ESPN, then the advertising agency may select that network, which, of course, enjoys a much larger audience. Of course, an advertiser may choose a particular program on a station or a network because those who make up the target market view the program. Or the advertiser may choose to advertise at different times of the day because members of a target audience do not watch television at the same time.
4. Television enjoys a certain amount of prestige that may enhance the advertiser's message.
5. Television engages the viewer's emotions. Even television commercials can arouse the viewer's emotions.
6. Television can help create an image for the advertiser and the advertiser's product or service.

DISADVANTAGES OF TELEVISION AS AN ADVERTISING MEDIUM

There are several disadvantages that advertisers should consider. These include the following:

1. Television commercials can be expensive to produce and to broadcast, especially to broadcast on over-the-air networks. A typical 30-second commercial may cost several hundred thousand dollars to produce. If a celebrity is involved, this cost may increase substantially, depending on the celebrity.

TABLE 9.2 ***Top 20 Network Categories***

RANK	CATEGORY	ADVERTISING EXPENDITURES FOR 2000
1	Automotive	$2.6+ billion
2	Medicines and Remedies	$1.9+ billion
3	Financial	$1.3+ billion
4	Toiletries and Cosmetics	$1.3+ billion
5	Restaurants	$1.2+ billion
6	Food and Food Products	$1.1+ billion
7	Computers and Software	$1+ billion
8	Soft Drinks, Candy, and Snacks	$961+ million
9	Motion Pictures	$934+ million
10	Telecommunications	$879+ million
11	Beer and Wine	$501+ million
12	Insurance and Real Estate	$374+ million
13	Government and Organizations	$358+ million
14	Household Supplies	$338+ million
15	Apparel, Footwear, and Accessories	$314+ million
16	Toys, Games, and Hobby/craft	$310+ million
17	Discount Department Stores	$299+ million
18	Department Stores	$297+ million
19	Soaps, Cleaners, Polishes	$277+ million
20	Audio and Video Equipment	$273+ million

Source: Television Bureau of Advertising, Inc., "Top 25 Network TV Categories," in *TV Basics* (New York: Television Bureau of Advertising, Inc., 2001; www.tvb.org).

2. Viewers can avoid television commercials through the use of technology. For instance, commercials are "zipped" and "zapped" by viewers all the time.
3. Over-the-air broadcast network television reaches broad groups of people and may not reach enough members of a target audience for it to be cost-effective for an advertiser. Cable network television reaches more defined groups of people and consequently may be cost-effective for an advertiser. However, cable network television does not reach as many viewers as the typical over-the-air broadcast network. Thus, an advertiser's advertising agency must make some difficult decisions when considering television as an advertising medium.
4. Television audiences have become more fragmented because of additional networks and stations being offered to viewers. As a result, an advertiser's message is actually seen by fewer people today than it would have been 10, 20, or 30 years ago.
5. Commercial breaks in television have increased in length and number. As a result, an advertiser's message may be sandwiched among several others and consequently lost and not paid any attention to by viewers.
6. People who are less educated and who are less affluent view television more often than those who are well educated and who are more affluent. In fact, many of these individuals are considered light viewers.
7. Most households own a VCR; about one-third of households own a DVD player. Whenever these are used, television commercials are not seen. Also, as if these technical devices are not enough to cause problems for advertisers, television is being used for other purposes such as to play games or to get online.

WHAT A GOOD TELEVISION COMMERCIAL MUST HAVE

1. A good television commercial must have a major selling feature or benefit, just as in print advertising and radio advertising.
2. The selling proposition must be relevant to the intended consumers. In short, they must be provided with a reason for needing the product or service. Of course, relevancy can be determined by secondary or primary research of the intended consumers.
3. The television commercial must open strong—that is, it should capture attention so that viewers do not zap to another channel. Indeed, the first three to five seconds of a television commercial must offer viewers something such as information that is important to them.
4. An appropriate presentation, such as the problem/solution, the demonstration, the spokesperson, and so on, should be used.
5. Do not overlook the opportunity to show the product. After all, the product is the heart of the commercial. Furthermore, a good television commercial should close on the product, if possible.
6. Make certain that the audio works in tandem with what is being shown. Even sound effects such as music should work in tandem with what is being shown.
7. Try to involve the viewer with the product or service. This may be difficult; however, if you have seen television commercials that depict body building equipment or diet remedies, most, if not all, of these attempt to connect the viewers with the products by showing people who have been successful at improving their physiques or losing excess weight by using

the equipment or taking the diet remedies. Such helps viewers to put themselves in these people's shoes or at least say to themselves, "Hey, if they can do it, I can too."

TAPE OR FILM: WHICH SHOULD BE USED?

If you work for an advertising agency, you will desire that your clients use film for television commercials. Most television commercials that are produced for regional and national dissemination are shot on 16-mm or 35-mm film. There are several reasons for this: first, film does not present a grainy image of settings, products, and actors. Unlike the image on videotape, the image on film is truer and softer, just like the image in films that are made by studios in Hollywood. Second, film may be less expensive than videotape when numerous prints are needed. Third, editing film can be more precise; thus, the quality of the end product is greater than that from videotape. Fourth, directors prefer using film when special effects are part of a television commercial.

However, cable companies and local television stations are competing with advertising agencies and are producing commercials for local businesses. These commercials, which are broadcast for a specific period of time on cable channels or local stations, are produced on videotape and are consequently inexpensive. Often, these commercials feature spokespersons who manage or work in these local businesses. Some of these spokespersons are convincing, but many are not. The reason videotape is used is because it is fast. Indeed, videotape does not require processing; such allows directors and advertisers to immediately view what has been shot and to immediately do retakes, if needed. However, as mentioned, videotape produces a grainy image. Local businesses must remember that many of these commercials appear "cheap." Usually, this is not the image local businesses wish to convey.

PRODUCTION TECHNIQUES

Live Action

Unquestionably, this is the most believable technique because it is realistic in the sense that viewers can relate the television commercial's message to their experiences. Basically, live action refers to products, settings, and people being filmed or videotaped and recorded. A live action commercial may be narrative or dialogue—that is, having the spokesperson(s) offscreen in the first instance and having the spokesperson(s) on-screen in the second instance.

Animation or Cartoon

These television commercials may not have as much credibility as live action, particularly if the intended consumers are adults. However, these commercials may be appropriate and believable when the intended consumers are children. Basically, drawing pictures and exposing them, one frame at a time, on film or videotape creates animation or cartoon commercials. As a result, this technique is less expensive than other techniques.

Stop Action or Motion

This technique refers to the manipulated movement of a lifeless three-dimensional object. The object is changed or moved slightly and then exposed to one or two frames of film. Stop action or motion has been used by advertisers and advertising agencies for decades. The Pillsbury Doughboy, a star in its own right, has appeared in numerous Pillsbury television commercials. The California Raisins, although popular in the past, have not been around as long. In addition to these examples, other stop-action or -motion commercials have shown packages or products coming to life and having personalities. These commercials are expensive to produce, primarily because they take so much time. For instance, for each second of picture, 24 shots are required.

Timing

Television commercials must be timed for the number of seconds that advertisers have purchased, which is usually 30 seconds. Other commercial lengths are 15 seconds, 10 seconds, 20 seconds, 45 seconds, and 60 seconds, although the latter two are not as popular as the former. When film is used, the sound track is 24 frames ahead of the visual or picture; thus, the audio portion of the commercial should be limited to at least two seconds less than the length of the commercial.

Camera Shots

Advertising copywriters must know the different camera shots that are used in television commercials. These shots refer to the distance between the lens of the camera and the objects, people, and settings that are shown to viewers:

Extreme Close-up or Tight Close-up: This is a bigger-than-life, detailed shot that brings the object very close to the viewer. Usually, it is used to show part of the product or its package, such as the product's name.

Close-up: This shot is used frequently in television commercials to show an object such as a package or a person's face. It does not allow objects in the background to distract the viewer.

Medium Close-up: In this shot, the viewer is allowed to see an object such as a package as well as what it is resting on. In short, this shot shows relationships between objects.

Medium Shot: This shot allows the viewer to see more objects or even an object in relation to a person as well as the background or setting.

Long Shot: Also known as an establishing shot, a long shot reveals the location or setting as well as the objects and people of the commercial.

Medium Long Shot: This shot reveals not only the people and the objects but part of the background or setting as well.

Extreme Long Shot: Similar to the establishing shot, this shot is usually reserved for a panoramic vista such as a mountain range, a river, a lake, or a desert. People may be shown as a group but not individually.

Camera Movements

A copywriter must understand the various terms that refer to the movement of the camera alone and the movement of the camera and its base. These terms include the following:

Dolly (in or out): The camera and its base move toward or away from whatever is being shot. As a result, the object becomes larger or smaller. A similar effect can be accomplished by using a zoom lens (see below).

Pan (right or left): The camera swivels to one side or the other, but the base does not; it remains in one place. Usually, a pan follows an object as it moves.

Tilt (up or down): The camera swivels up or down; the base remains in one place.

Truck (right or left): The camera and camera base move parallel to what is being shot. Trucks take more time than a pan. However, a pan may not accomplish what is called for in a commercial.

Zoom (in or out): The lens of the camera is adjusted toward or away from what is being shot. Close-ups to long shots can be done with a zoom lens; the camera and the camera base do not have to move toward or away from what is being shot.

Transitions

Changing scenes require transitions, and copywriters must know what transitions are available and their definitions. If a copywriter forgets to include a transition, the director will have to guess as to what type of change between scenes is desired. The following are the most commonly used transitions:

Cut or Take: The simplest and most popular transition, the cut or take refers to an immediate change from one scene to another.

Dissolve: The dissolve is used for a slow, softer change between scenes. It refers to an image overlapping another—that is, one image fades out as a second image fades in.

Fade (in or out): Fade refers to the intensity of an image—from brightness (in) to darkness (out), or vice versa. Fades are usually employed at the beginnings and endings of television commercials.

Wipe: A wipe can be horizontal, vertical, or diagonal. It refers to an image being "wiped off" as a second image is "wiped on." A straight horizontal or vertical black line usually separates the two images. If a wipe stops halfway on the screen, it is referred to as a split screen (see below), allowing the two images to appear simultaneously.

Special Effects

Special effects, which usually are a combination of images or at least a manipulation of images, should not be used unless they actually help "sell" the product or service, primarily because they tend to increase the cost of the commercial. A copywriter should understand the following terms:

Chromakey: Refers to combining or matting individuals or products with another scene or background. For instance, if a commercial calls for the owner of a business to be in a store, the owner can be in a studio but appear as if she or he is in a store. A film of the interior of a store is merely blended in behind the owner.

Freeze Frame: Refers to keeping a scene on the screen for a certain period of time. Usually, this is done at the end of a commercial.

Key Insert: Refers to inserting an image onto another image. Usually, this is the act of keying in numbers or letters such as a phone number or an address on another image or keying in the product on another image, which occurs often, especially in the final scenes of particular commercials.

Matte: Similar to chromakey, this term refers to placing a certain background scene behind another image such as a spokesperson. However, the area around the spokesperson may not be visible on screen. For instance, the spokesperson may appear to be in a silhouette.

Split Screen: Refers to two or more images appearing on screen simultaneously. Usually, this is used when the advertiser's brand is compared with a competitor's brand or when a product needs to be demonstrated, as in a "before" image and an "after" image.

Super: Refers to superimpose or superimposition, which means that one image such as an object, individual, or character (e.g., a numeral or a letter) is superimposed over another image. Usually, a super is a strong means for expressing a major selling point or benefit. For instance, if a spokesperson states the major selling point or benefit while she or he demonstrates a product's purpose, the major selling point or benefit can be presented in letters that are superimposed over the spokesperson's demonstration. As a result, the superimposed letters match the spokesperson's words and demonstration.

SHOWING THE PRODUCT

A copywriter must remember to show the product. Indeed, if a product is being sold, it should be the "star" of the commercial in the sense that it should be the most important element in the commercial. Therefore, a copywriter should show the product often and long enough for it to register in the consumer's mind. In a typical 30-second commercial, the product not only will be shown several times but quite possibly will be referred to by a spokesperson several times. The last scene will in all likelihood close on the product.

TELEVISION COMMERCIAL FORMATS

There are several types of television commercials that present sales messages to viewers. These include the problem/solution format, the demonstration format, the slice-of-life format, the testimonial or endorsement format, the spokesperson or presenter format, and the musical or jingle format. Of course, there may be others, but these formats are the most popular.

The Problem/Solution Format

This is a popular format; it has been used to help sell all kinds of products—from automobile batteries to vacuum cleaners. Basically, it works best when a product can be demonstrated to solve a problem that has been introduced. For instance, if a television commercial presents a problem such as a filthy carpet, a vacuum cleaner may be used to clean the carpet. A copywriter must think about the following when writing a problem/solution television commercial:

1. The problem must be realistic—that is, one that the intended consumer can relate to based on his or her experience.
2. The introduction of the product as the solution to the problem must be realistic—that is, the product must be demonstrated to prove that it is the "right" product to solve the problem. The demonstration should be dramatic.
3. The person demonstrating the product should exhibit satisfaction from using the product. Usually, the benefits from using the product are mentioned and are shown in the television commercial. Of course, the intended consumer should understand the importance of these benefits. In addition to solving a problem, other benefits may include saving time, saving money, performing a task easier, or enhancing one's self-image, among others.
4. Make certain that the product's name is mentioned several times.

The Demonstration Format

A demonstration, which may be used in a problem/solution format as well as other formats, is one of the most popular formats used in television commercials primarily because a product can be shown as it is intended—that is, being used. A demonstration must be realistic, however, in order to be effective and must provide reasons for the prospective consumer to consider purchasing the product. A copywriter needs to think about the following when writing a demonstration television commercial:

1. Be concise and precise. A copywriter must not present a lengthy demonstration. Most commercials are 30 seconds long or less.
2. Make certain that the demonstration is easy to understand, particularly by the intended consumer, and honest. Trickery should not be considered.
3. Make certain that the product's name is mentioned and shown several times to the intended consumer. A copywriter should use extreme close-up and close-up shots, particularly of the product as it is demonstrated.
4. Try to show the demonstration in its entirety. If this is not possible, a copywriter needs to explain to the intended consumer what has been done. For instance, if a cut has been used, the copywriter must provide an explanation for the cut's existence or representation.
5. Make certain that the demonstration presents benefits—that is, what the product will do for the intended consumer.

The Slice-of-Life Format

The slice-of-life format is based on the oldest dramatic technique: a story or vignette. Usually, the story involves at least two characters and the product, with the product playing an important role. Sometimes, however, a slice-of-life television commercial does not work, primarily because the intended consumer's attention is pulled away from the product and to one of the characters or some other element in the story, such as a dog or cat. In short, a slice-of-life design will only work if the consumer's attention is on the product and sales message. A copywriter must think about the following when writing a slice-of-life television commercial:

1. The story or vignette must be realistic and easy to understand, particularly by the intended consumer. In addition, if a character or characters are used, a copywriter should make certain that the character(s) relates well to the intended consumer. In short, a character should be believable.
2. Make certain that the intended consumer's attention is captured in the first few seconds.
3. Make certain that the product becomes central to the plot of the story. The product's name should be mentioned several times so that it registers in the consumer's mind.
4. Make certain that the product's major benefit to the consumer is conveyed.
5. Make certain that the intended consumer's attention focuses on the product, not on something else.

The Testimonial or Endorsement Format

The testimonial or endorsement format allows an individual to deliver a sales message to an intended audience. The individual may be a celebrity such as a sports figure or a television or film personality. The individual may be a qualified expert such as an engineer or an average person with high credibility. Usually, this format allows the person to explain his or her experience with the product and, of course, present his or her recommendation to purchase the product; or it allows the celebrity to merely be linked to the product without him or her saying anything about the product or its benefit to the consumer.

Regardless of which type of individual is used, it is important to remember that the individual must relate well to the product. For instance, a sports personality may not necessarily be an appropriate celebrity to advertise vacuum cleaners or ice cream. The following rules should help a copywriter write a testimonial or endorsement television commercial:

1. Make certain that the celebrity selected is thought about during the writing of the commercial. The celebrity's words should sound natural, as if the celebrity had written the words instead of a copywriter.
2. Make certain that the product is mentioned by name and shown several times throughout the commercial.
3. Make certain that the celebrity selected appears and sounds believable and sincere. The celebrity selected should not have appeared in too many commercials; overexposure may diminish the celebrity's testimonial or endorsement. In addition, the celebrity selected should be someone who would use the product.
4. Make certain that the celebrity selected brings value to the commercial's sales message; otherwise, the added cost (celebrity's fee) will be for naught.

The Presenter or Spokesperson Format

This format is similar to the testimonial or endorsement format. Usually, this format has a spokesperson standing in front of a camera; the product may be in the spokesperson's hands or beside the spokesperson as he or she discusses the product and its benefits to the intended consumer. Sometimes the presenter or spokesperson is off camera. In these instances, the announcer discusses the product and its benefits to the viewer. There are several guidelines that will help the copywriter write a television commercial featuring a presenter or spokesperson:

1. Make certain that the presenter or spokesperson is thought about when writing this type of commercial. In short, what is said should sound natural and authentic. The style should be conversational, not formal.
2. Make certain that the product is mentioned and shown several times throughout the commercial.
3. Make certain that the spokesperson's image relates well to the product's image—that is, to the image that the intended consumer has of the product. The decision to use a man or a woman as a spokesperson usually depends on the product being advertised.

The Musical or Jingle Format

In this television commercial format, the entire message must be presented in lyrics set to music. Only a copywriter who knows something about rhyme and music will be able to employ this format successfully. In many instances, advertising agencies hire music production houses or specialty firms whenever this format is desired. There are several rules that a copywriter should adhere to when attempting this type of television commercial:

1. Make certain that the lyrics correspond to the visuals that will be depicted in the commercial.
2. Make certain that the music is appropriate for the lyrics, visuals, and, of course, the intended consumer. For instance, a bluegrass tune would not necessarily work if the target consumer happens to be an affluent city dweller.

HUMOR IN TELEVISION COMMERCIALS

Although many people would assume that humor in television commercials helps sell products, sales are not necessarily related to humor in commercials. For instance, humor does not have to be in commercials whatsoever in order for the product to appeal to the intended consumer. On the other hand, humor can be used successfully to capture the consumer's attention. But capturing the consumer's attention is not enough. Humor, if it is to be considered successful, must be linked to the product and its personality in order for the intended consumer to "associate it with the brand."[11] In other words, humor must be integral to the sales message; otherwise, it may be considered merely a joke that has nothing to do with the product.

Finally, as David Ogilvy mentions, "very few writers can write funny commercials which *are* funny."[12] However, if a copywriter thinks that he or she can write humorous commercials, he or she should test humorous copy by having others read it before it is used. What a copywriter thinks is humorous may not be to someone else. More important, a copywriter must ask, Does the humor relate well to the product? Or does it attract attention to itself? Does it make light of or insult the product or its value to the intended consumer? If the answers to the last two questions are yes, then the humor should not be used.

SEX IN TELEVISION COMMERCIALS

It seems that sex or sex appeal is used in numerous television commercials. Yet sex or sex appeal should be used only in commercials in which a sexy product such as perfume, cologne, cosmetics, or undergarments, among others, is being advertised. Victoria's Secret, for instance, employs sex or sex appeal in its commercials primarily because of the products being advertised.

Recently, Coca-Cola and Calvin Klein, among other advertisers, have used sex or sex appeal in commercials. Yet is sex or sex appeal appropriate when selling Diet Coke? Or jeans? What about a cruise line? Ogilvy has suggested that the test for using sex or sex appeal in an advertisement is *relevance*—that is, one needs to ask if sex or sex appeal is appropriate for advertising the product.[13]

THE SCRIPT

A copywriter must realize that a script for a television commercial must be clear to everyone who has been given the task of transforming the script into a commercial. This is especially true today, when advertising agencies may not necessarily ask for storyboards, which typically contain cells or frames filled with cartoon-like drawings that represent what will be shown in the commercials. Relevant copy usually is positioned beneath the cells or frames.

The typical script for a television commercial is divided into two columns: "VIDEO" and "AUDIO." The left-hand column, VIDEO, is for what will be shown; the right-hand column, AUDIO, is for what will be spoken or played such as sound effects, including music.

Generally, a script will be presented on a standard-size sheet of paper that has been divided into two columns, with the left-hand side labeled "VIDEO" and the right-hand side labeled "AUDIO." These terms, which should be at the left-hand edge of their respective columns, should be typed in capital letters. A black line may be typed beneath these terms; if so, the line should be typed all the way across the page.

Instructions explaining to the director how each scene should be shot and what should be in the scene should be typed in capital letters under "VIDEO." Abbreviations for shots may be used to conserve space.

BOX 9.1 *An Example of a Script for a Television Commercial–Nashville Zoo*

CLIENT: Nashville Zoo
JOB TITLE: 7287NZ/TV copy
DATE/VERS: March 22, 2002 / vl / abr
Nashville Zoo
:30 TV
"ELEPHANT RIDE"

VIDEO	AUDIO
OPEN ON WIDE LANDSCAPE SHOT AT ZOO.	SFX: ZOO ANIMAL SOUNDS (THROUGHOUT)
ELEPHANT SLOWLY WALKS INTO FRAME.	
ZOOM IN ON ELEPHANT, SHOWING FRONT HALF OF ELEPHANT'S BODY. A HUMAN LEG IS NOW SHOWN, REVEALING SOMEONE RIDING ON ELEPHANT.	SFX: ELEPHANT SOUND
PAN ACROSS TO REVEAL TWO CHILDREN RIDING ON ELEPHANT.	SFX: GIGGLES OF CHILDREN
RED "RECORD" SYMBOL APPEARS IN CORNER OF FRAME.	SFX: MECHANICAL CAMERA SOUND
SHOT FOLLOWS CHILD RIDING ELEPHANT. RECORD SYMBOL REMAINS.	
DISSOLVE TO WHITE WITH ZOO LOGO AND TAG. SUPER: Phone and Web address	VO: (Young girl) *The Nashville Zoo on Nolensville Road. Memories run wild.*

Courtesy of BOHAN Advertising/Marketing.

What is actually spoken should be typed in upper- and lowercase letters or "down style" under "AUDIO." Instructions for sound effects, including music, should be typed in capital letters and underlined under "AUDIO." Instructions for informing talent how to say a word or phrase should be put in parentheses and underlined. VIDEO instructions may be single-spaced, whereas AUDIO instructions and information may be double-spaced. This will make it easier for the talent to read their respective lines. Finally, shot and talent changes should be separated by at least two spaces; otherwise, the director or talent may make a mistake. The example in box 9.1, which was created by personnel at BOHAN Advertising/Marketing, Nashville, Tennessee, contains many of the suggestions mentioned above.

However, formats for scripts differ. Indeed, copywriters as well as advertising agencies follow different rules or guidelines, as the example in box 9.2—prepared by Gary Gibson (creative director), Mike Gustafson (art director), James Dalthorp (director), Mike Fisher (copywriter), and Harvey Lewis (producer) at the Richards Group, Dallas—illustrates.

THE STORYBOARD

After a copywriter writes a script for a television commercial, an artist prepares a storyboard. Each cell or frame represents each major scene in the script; the cells or frames are organized sequentially—that is, the first cell or frame depicts the action presented first in the script, the second cell or frame depicts the action presented second in the script, and so on.

Although the sizes of storyboards vary, most storyboards feature cartoon-like images in cells or frames as well as accompanying blocks of text that describe the scene and the sound. In short, storyboards usually have images of the major scenes, a description of the major scenes or what will be seen (VIDEO), and a description of what will be heard (AUDIO). Just as in scripts, VIDEO instructions, which explain how a scene moves, the desired shot, and the action, if needed, are typed in all capital letters. Only the AUDIO or what is actually heard should be typed in upper- and lowercase letters or down style.

Look at figure 9.1, which was created by personnel at O_2 ideas, Birmingham, Alabama. The instructions for the VIDEO are on the left-hand side, and the information for the AUDIO is on the right-hand

BOX 9.2 *An Example of a Script for a Television Commercial–The Home Depot*

CLIENT:	THE HOME DEPOT
JOB:	:30 TV
TITLE:	"Brownstone/L&G TV/M. Neff/Image/URL/Disclaimer :30"
JOB #:	THD-98-0708
SLATE #:	YHTO-0423
DATE:	05/05/99—As Produced

VIDEO:	Open on an older, very quaint brownstone home. A set of stairs leads up from the sidewalk where a small strip of "lawn" is next to the curb.
SFX:	(Roaring mower engine)
VIDEO:	We see a man on a Scotts riding mower.
VO:	*The 54", 25-horsepower riding mower from Scotts.*
VIDEO:	He drives straight down the steps, showing off the mower's durability.
SFX:	(Ching-ching, ching-ching)
VO:	*It's got a fully welded, steel unibody frame . . .*
SUPER:	Professional driver. Do not attempt this maneuver.
VO:	*. . . plus a solid cast iron front axle . . .*
VIDEO:	He turns and mows the strip of "lawn," then turns again.
VO:	*. . . a remarkable turning radius . . .*
VO:	*. . . and all the power you'll ever need.*
VIDEO:	He drives back up the steps.
VO:	*You'll wish you had a bigger yard.*
	Cut to art card with The Home Depot logo and full line of mowers.
VO:	*Scotts mowers. Available at The Home Depot.*
SUPER:	Internet address

The following personnel created the script for this television commercial: Gary Gibson (creative director), Mike Fisher (writer), Mike Gustafson (art director), James Dalthorp (director), and Harvey Lewis (producer).
Courtesy of The Richards Group.

side. The cells are in the center. Because the cells are in the center, the instructions for the VIDEO do not have to be typed in all capital letters. However, many advertising agencies prepare storyboards with cells that go across the page, not down. In these, instructions for the VIDEO usually are typed in all capital letters, so that they are not confused with the information for the AUDIO. Figure 9.2 contains the final version of the commercial that was prepared by personnel at O_2 ideas.

HOW TO WRITE A TELEVISION COMMERCIAL

Before a copywriter attempts to write a script for a television commercial, there are several elements that she or he must consider. First, we have the opening. How can the copywriter capture the intended consumer's attention? Capturing the intended consumer's attention is crucial. If a television commercial

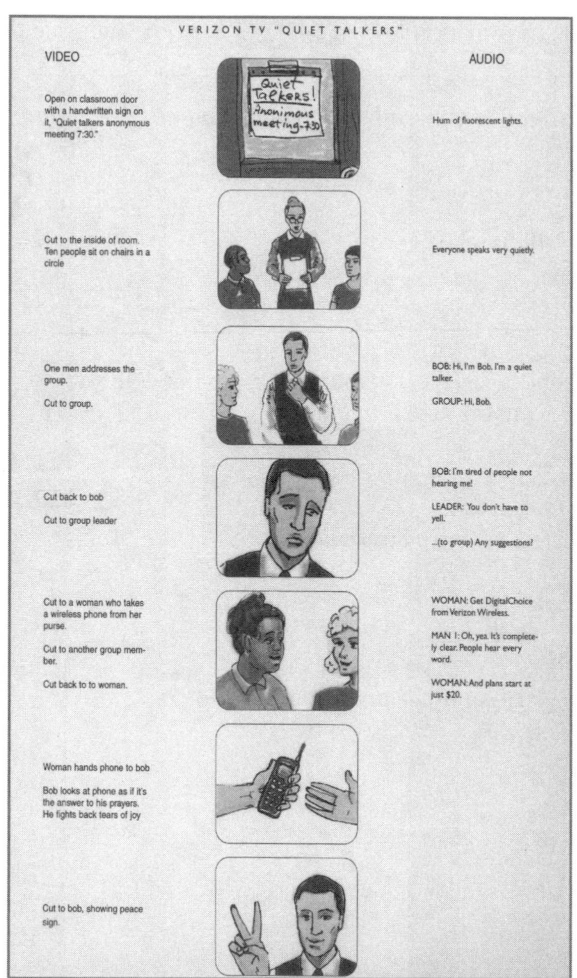

FIGURE 9.1 An example of a storyboard for a television commercial. *Courtesy of O_2 ideas.*

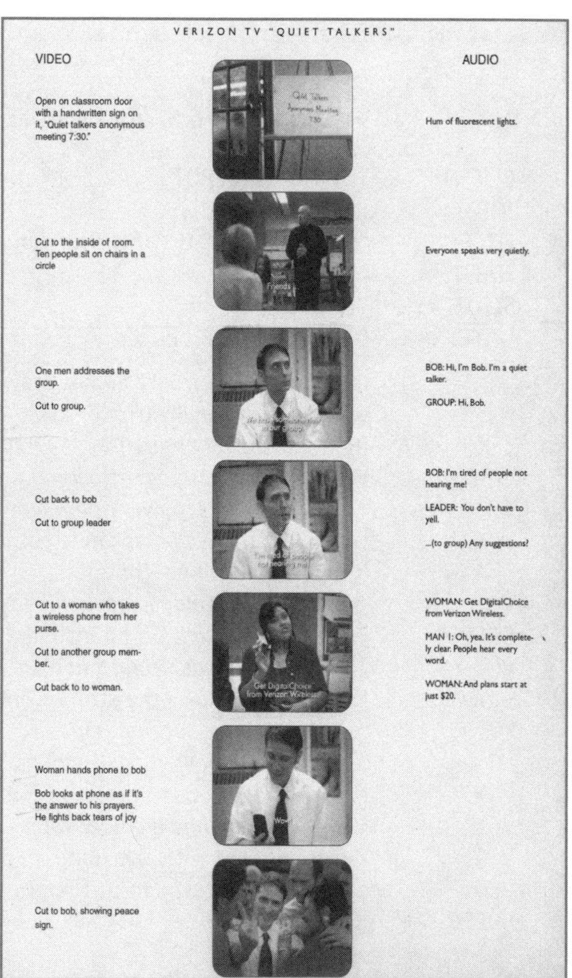

FIGURE 9.2 The photoboard based on the storyboard. (A photoboard is a series of still photographs from the commercial.) *Courtesy of O_2 ideas.*

does not capture attention within the first three to five seconds, the commercial has in all likelihood failed. One way of capturing attention is to use one of the formats previously discussed, such as the problem/solution format. If a problem is introduced that most, if not all, intended consumers have experienced, then their attention has probably been captured.

Second is the major selling point or benefit. The copywriter must make certain that the major selling point or benefit is identified and emphasized several times, not just once, in the commercial.

Third, there is the product or service. A copywriter must make certain that the product or service is integral to the commercial—that is, one of the most important elements of the commercial. Close-up shots of the product will help the intended consumer identify what is being advertised. In addition to showing the product, the talent needs to mention the product by name several times throughout the commercial. Then, whenever possible, the commercial needs to wind up on the product in the final scene or shot.

Fourth, we have the video portion of the commercial. According to the cliché, "a picture is worth a thousand words." This is true, especially of television commercials. Therefore, a copywriter should allow the video portion of a commercial to help sell the product. In other words, a copywriter should ask, "What is the best, most dramatic means of advertising the product. Showing it? Talking about it? Or both?" If the answer is "showing it," or if "showing it" carries more weight than "talking about it," then the copywriter should consider showing the product more often than having someone talking about it. Of course, the answer may depend on what the major idea or benefit is or what the copywriter believes he or she needs to emphasize. For some television commercials, the copywriter may believe that the audio portion should carry more weight than the video portion. In these cases, the audio portion should be emphasized more than the video. However, a copywriter should remember that television is a visual medium and that viewers tend to remember more of what they see than what they hear.

Television advertising is perfect for providing visuals and sounds to the intended audience, particularly sending product images to consumers at home; consequently, advertisers should think about employing it when their products can be demonstrated or shown in a positive light. The next chapter examines direct mail advertising.

EXERCISES

1. Write a 30-second television commercial that features a recording artist's greatest hits CD. You may select the recording artist. Assume that the company is packaging the product for sale exclusively through television—that is, the product will not be available in stores until after the television campaign has ended. You will need to include an 800 number, a mailing address, and of course information on how to order the product. The sales message should be strong and convincing. After you have typed your script, prepare a storyboard. A storyboard consists of sets of two frames—the top frame in each set represents a regular television screen, and the bottom frame carries a description of what the screen shows and the words that are said on camera or off by an announcer or actor(s). The number of sets of frames varies from commercial to commercial and is not necessarily dictated by the length of the commercial. Keep the following points in mind:
   a. Relate the video to the audio.
   b. Let the video carry the weight.
   c. Superimpose type, if needed, over some of the scenes.

d. Explore fully your camera possibilities.

e. Use mostly close-ups.

Remember to present representative frames on a storyboard—a picture for each scene or action and for each major change of camera position. Remember that the top frame is for the artwork. A convenient work size is 4 × 3 inches. Make sure that you keep your artwork in the safety area of each frame; do not extend the artwork to the edges of each frame. Directly under the "TV screen" frame, separated by a half-inch of space, is the description and words frame. Its size should be the same. You can create a storyboard with software, if you wish.

2. After viewing a current television commercial, write another 30-second commercial for the product or service. Your commercial should contain the theme that was present in the commercial you watched. Your commercial should expand the theme, so to speak, by presenting it differently.
3. Write a 30-second television commercial for Big Max, a quick-service restaurant that serves hamburgers, fries, various kinds of wraps, various salads, milk shakes, onion rings, and soft drinks. The purpose of the commercial is to introduce the restaurant's new menu items: submarine sandwiches and soups.
4. Write a 30-second television commercial about a natural park. You should include what the park is known for, what it offers to visitors, its hours of operation, and other information that you deem persuasive. The purpose of your commercial is to increase the number of visitors to the park and the park's lodge.
5. Write a 30-second television commercial for a retailer of your choice. The purpose of the commercial is to stimulate store traffic and consequently sales. You will need to decide on what should be advertised and how.

NOTES

1. Television Bureau of Advertising, Inc., "Television: Top Ad Medium," in *TV Basics* (New York: Television Bureau of Advertising, Inc., 2003; www.tvb.org).
2. Television Bureau of Advertising, Inc., "Station TV: Top TV Ad Component," in *TV Basics* (New York: Television Bureau of Advertising, Inc., 2003; www.tvb.org).
3. Television Bureau of Advertising, Inc., "Top 25 Spot TV Categories," in *TV Basics* (New York: Television Bureau of Advertising, Inc., 2003; www.tvb.org).
4. Television Bureau of Advertising, Inc., "Top 25 Network TV Categories," in *TV Basics* (New York: Television Bureau of Advertising, Inc., 2003; www.tvb.org).
5. Television Bureau of Advertising, Inc., "Multi-set and Color Television Households" and "Cable and VCR Households," in *TV Basics* (New York: Television Bureau of Advertising, Inc., 2003; www.tvb.org).
6. Television Bureau of Advertising, Inc., "Commercial Television Stations," in *TV Basics* (New York: Television Bureau of Advertising, Inc., 2003; www.tvb.org).
7. Television Bureau of Advertising, Inc., "Time Spent Viewing—Persons," in *TV Basics* (New York: Television Bureau of Advertising, Inc., 2003; www.tvb.org).
8. Television Bureau of Advertising, Inc., "Reach: Broadcast vs. Cable," in *TV Basics* (New York: Television Bureau of Advertising, Inc., 2003; www.tvb.org).
9. Television Bureau of Advertising, Inc., "Network TV Activity by Length of Commercial," in *TV Basics* (New York: Television Bureau of Advertising, Inc., 2003; www.tvb.org).
10. Television Bureau of Advertising, Inc., "Political Ads on Broadcast Television," in *TV Basics* (New York: Television Bureau of Advertising, Inc., 2003; www.tvb.org).
11. Jonathan Bond and Richard Kirshenbaum, *Under the Radar: Talking to Today's Cynical Consumer* (New York: John Wiley and Sons, Inc., 1998), p. 85.
12. David Ogilvy, *Ogilvy on Advertising* (New York: Vintage Books, 1985), p. 105.
13. Ogilvy, *Ogilvy on Advertising*, p. 25.

CHAPTER 10

Direct Mail Advertising

Many consumers dislike direct mail advertising, but many advertisers love it. According to the Direct Marketing Association, advertisers spent almost $50 billion in this medium in 2002, making direct mail the most preferred medium by advertisers.[1] Of course, the anthrax scare caused many advertisers to decrease their usage of direct mail for months.

There are several reasons for advertisers to be attracted to direct mail. First, the medium arrives at the consumer's residence. Indeed, direct mail allows advertisers to be more selective when it comes to identifying a target market. Of course, this is dependent on the advertiser's list of names and addresses as well as from which firm the list came. Nonetheless, advertisers can identify a prospective target market by practically any demographic or psychographic characteristic, such as age, gender, educational level or major, location, interests or hobbies, income, purchase history, credit rating, memberships, and lifestyle, among others. Second, direct mail, unlike some other media, can be easily measured based on response. Third, direct mail offers advertisers flexibility in the sense that direct mail can be presented in practically any form, including coupons and samples of the product.

As mentioned, consumers do not necessarily like direct mail. Many refer to this medium as "junk mail." Many also throw it away without opening it. And many of those who do open it do not redeem the coupons that they receive. In fact, although coupon face values have increased, coupon redemption has decreased.

Today, direct mail is divided into two categories: consumer and business to business. In 2002 advertisers spent almost $30 billion in direct mail aimed at consumers. Advertisers spent almost $20 billion in direct mail aimed at businesses.[2] According to the Direct Marketing Association, direct mail aimed at consumers will grow by almost 6 percent over the next few years, and direct mail aimed at businesses will grow by more than 7 percent.[3]

Is direct mail worth its cost to advertisers? Yes! In 2002 direct mail generated more than $636 billion in sales, making it the second most powerful medium in terms of generating sales. Only telephone marketing generated more in sales: more than $719 billion.[4]

ADVANTAGES OF DIRECT MAIL ADVERTISING

Direct mail offers advertisers several advantages. These include the following:

1. Direct mail can target prospective consumers more efficiently than other media. In fact, consumers can be targeted by any of a number of demographic and psychographic characteristics, such as age, gender, educational level or major, interests, hobbies, and lifestyle, among others.
2. Direct mail can reach every consumer by name and address the advertiser wishes in any given market.
3. Direct mail can be measured through coupon redemption or by return of cards, order forms, or telephone calls. In short, its effectiveness can be determined almost immediately.
4. Direct mail, primarily because of its flexibility, allows advertisers to use various formats, such as a letter, brochure, catalog, or card, among others, to present in-depth information about their products or services to prospective consumers.
5. Direct mail, even though it may cost more than other media based on per person reached, can be more effective, depending on the list of names and addresses used, in persuading consumers to purchase.
6. Direct mail is more personal than other media. It reaches consumers usually where they live. In addition, sales messages are more personal in the sense that individuals' names can be used in the various formats.

DISADVANTAGES OF DIRECT MAIL ADVERTISING

Direct mail has several disadvantages that advertisers need to consider. These include the following:

1. Direct mail is often thrown away without being opened.
2. Direct mail does not enjoy a high response rate.
3. Direct mail usually is more effective in reinforcing current consumers than in attracting new consumers.
4. Consumers often refer to direct mail as "junk mail," which is not a positive connotation. In short, many consumers have a low opinion of direct mail.
5. Direct mail lists may become outdated and consequently useless in a short period. Indeed, a mailing list has to be maintained in order to be effective. If it is not and an advertiser uses it, the advertiser will have wasted money on the package, its contents, and the postage.
6. Direct mail can be expensive, depending on the cost of the paper used, the production, the mailing list, and postage.
7. Direct mail campaigns that contain coupons are not as effective as they once were. Coupon redemption is decreasing, not increasing.

THE ALL-IMPORTANT MAILING LIST

Advertisers who use direct mail depend on current mailing lists in order to reach prospective consumers. Basically, the mailing list is the media plan for these advertisers. Usually, lists are compiled from various sources. An advertiser typically selects a list that will provide the greatest number of prospective consumers for the least amount of money.

Generally, there are three kinds of lists that are available to advertisers: house lists, response lists, and compiled lists. House lists are made up of an advertiser's current and past customers or past inquirers. An advertiser needs to keep accurate records of current and past customers. After all, these are the individuals or companies that have purchased something from the advertiser. Such records should provide details about these individuals or companies, such as their permanent address, the company for which they work or the type of company, their level of education, their position in the company for which they work, their current needs, their current expectations, and which direct mail campaigns caused them to respond, among other information. Of course, this information needs to be kept current. If it is not, these lists will be practically useless.

Response lists generally are made up of individuals or companies that have responded to one or more direct mail pieces produced by other advertisers. These lists can be valuable to an advertiser if the lists contain the names of individuals or companies that have purchased products or services that are similar to those of the advertiser but from the advertiser's competitors. Usually, these lists are expensive, primarily because of their quality. Generally, the information is current and accurate, and most, if not all of these lists, are restricted. For instance, in order to maintain the quality of the individuals or companies on the list, restrictions may be placed on the number of times these individuals or companies can be solicited.

Companies usually assemble compiled lists. The names of individuals or companies are gathered from published sources, such as telephone directories, yellow page listings, business transaction records, professional associations' or organizations' membership records, and real estate transaction records, among others. Then these lists are rented or sold to advertisers. Compiled lists are readily available and are relatively inexpensive in terms of cost per thousand names. However, compiled lists may not be maintained very often. Thus, the individuals or companies may not be at the addresses given. Compiled lists may suffer from duplication—that is, an individual or company may appear more than once. Finally, compiled lists are the least effective lists in generating responses. Advertisers or their advertising agencies may use the Standard Rate and Data Service volumes titled *Direct Mail List Rates and Data* to locate lists.

TESTING DIRECT MAIL

Direct mail is expensive in terms of how much it costs an advertiser to reach a potential consumer. Therefore, in order to make direct mail more cost-efficient and -effective, it should be tested. In essence, lists as well as the piece or pieces of direct mail can be tested to determine which are the most effective in generating responses.

According to Bob Stone, an advertiser should test six big areas:

1. The products or services you offer
2. The media you use
3. The propositions you make
4. The copy platform you use
5. The format you use
6. The timing you choose[5]

Regarding lists, tests can be done to determine which companies produce the best lists based on current information and response rates.

Regarding the actual piece or pieces of direct mail, tests can be done to determine the best offer: for instance, to charge a high price versus low price, to offer a free sample or not, to offer a guarantee or not, to offer two or more methods of payment versus one method of payment, to offer a send-no-money-now free trial versus a send-money-now no free trial, or to offer incentives such as discounts or gifts or not. Tests can be done to determine the format: for instance, to use a single mailing versus a series, to use a multipiece package versus a self-mailer or one piece, to use a pre- or postmailing postcard, to use a lift letter or not, to use a window envelope versus a closed envelope, to use a small envelope versus a large envelope, to use tokens versus stickers, to use a postage-paid reply card or not, to use live postage versus metered postage, to use a sales brochure or not, or to use a sales advertisement such as a folder or not.

Tests can also be done to determine what should be used in the copy: for instance, to use hard sell versus soft sell, to use a closing date or not, to use headlines or not, to personalize or not, to use a teaser on the envelope or not, to use short copy versus long copy, to use testimonials or not, or to use captions with photographs or not. Tests can be done to determine which layout or design to use: for instance, to use charts or graphs or not, to use photographs versus illustrations, to use one or two colors versus four colors, to use a small-size type versus a large-size type, to use a sans serif font versus a serif font, or to show the product alone or with models.[6] Of course, the above are some of the more common elements that are tested.

WHAT WORKS IN DIRECT MAIL ADVERTISING

Although many direct mail packages typically contain an outer envelope, a letter, a brochure, and a postage-paid reply card, there are other forms, including annual reports, booklets, broadsides, catalogs, folders, leaflets, magazines, pamphlets, and tabloids. We will focus on the most popular direct mail package.

The List

1. Select the best, most appropriate mailing list. If you do not, then you are probably trying to sell something that the prospects will not buy because they are not interested in it or they do not have a need for it.
2. Make certain that the list you have selected employs a "rifle" approach—that is, it identifies prospective consumers based on narrowly defined demographics and psychographics.
3. Make certain that the list is current. You need a list that is no more than six months old. If it is a year to two years old, some of the names and addresses in all likelihood will be incorrect.
4. Make certain that the list does not contain duplicate names and addresses. You do not want to waste postage by mailing the same package to the same person twice.
5. Make certain that you mail to a person's name, not "occupant," "resident," or some impersonal label. Otherwise, the person will know immediately that the mailing is not *that* important.

The Outer Envelope

1. Use envelopes that have quality. Inexpensive-looking envelopes tell the prospective consumer: "Don't open me, I'm cheap!"
2. Consider using a teaser or message outside the envelope. However, if a teaser is to be effective, it must be well written and appropriate to the product or service being sold. Do not include a message if it is dull or inappropriate because it may decrease response.

3. Use a standard #10 white envelope if the intended consumer is a working professional at a business or corporation. Although many companies use company stationery for their direct mail addressed to working professionals, some companies will have only their street address, city, state, and ZIP code typed in the upper left-hand corner; they do not include their company names. The primary reason for this is that the letter appear to be from an individual, perhaps someone the prospective consumer has met or knows, not a company. If you are targeting individuals at their homes, you may consider using different size and different color envelopes. However, when using different size and different color envelopes, make certain that what is inside corresponds to the size and the color. Otherwise, the mailing will not be attractive. In short, harmony will be lost.
4. Consider using textured paper stock for the envelope and its contents. Sometimes textured paper stock can help sell certain types of products, such as furniture.
5. Make certain that the postage is not indicia (postal permit number of the sender). Indicia imply third-class or bulk-rate mail. Use metering; it implies first-class mail. Or use bulk-rate stamps. Many individuals cannot discern between first-class and bulk-rate stamps.
6. Whenever first-class postage is used for direct mail, stamps should be used. In addition, have "First-Class Mail" printed on the envelopes.
7. Address labels should not be used, especially if the intended prospective consumers are working professionals at businesses or corporations. Labels indicate that others are receiving the same mailing; consequently, the addressee believes that the mailing is not important.

The Letter

1. The paper for the letter should be high quality. For instance, 20 pound should be the minimum weight used. In fact, 24 pound should be preferred because it is better. Make certain that the paper has a high rag content, such as 25 percent, especially if the paper is being used for letters that are targeting working professionals at businesses or corporations.
2. Make certain that the lead of the letter has been seriously considered. For instance, should the lead offer news, arouse curiosity, ask a question, answer a question, or present a story? Any of these may be used to begin a letter. Make certain that whichever one is used, it is relevant to what is being sold. Of course, there are other kinds of openings.
3. The message in the letter should relate well to the prospective consumer's needs. If the message is for mechanical engineers but the direct mail package is addressed to the presidents of companies, the offer that was intended for mechanical engineers will not necessarily be effective—if at all—to presidents.
4. The letter should present the major point(s) as soon as possible. Otherwise, the reader will lose interest and consequently toss the letter aside or, worse, into the trash. A good rule of thumb is to emphasize the most important point(s) in the first three to five lines of the letter. In fact, many direct mail letters emphasize the major point(s) in a headline, whether the headline stands alone or appears in a Johnson Box (a Johnson Box is a border of some kind that surrounds copy). Or if a headline does not exist, the most important point(s) should be emphasized in the first or second sentence.

5. The writing should be precise (for clarity) and concise. In short, the point(s) should be expressed in language that the prospective consumers understand. These consumers should be told specifically what is to be mailed.
6. The style of writing should be conversational, and the tone, personal. The letter should be written like any other—that is, to an individual, even if it is being mailed to thousands of prospective consumers. In short, it should be easy to read and understand.
7. Active rather than passive voice should be used. Active voice is more powerful and commanding.
8. The letter should contain short words, short and medium-length sentences, and short and medium-length paragraphs. In fact, the letter should have one or more single sentence paragraphs, depending on the length of the letter.
9. The paragraphs should be indented at least five spaces. Make certain that paragraphs are single-spaced and that two spaces separate them.
10. The letter should emphasize the benefits of the product or service. After all, benefits—not the product or service's features—are what the product or service will do for the prospective consumers. Of course, features may be included, but the letter's emphasis should be on benefits.
11. The copy in the letter should actually *sell* the product or service. In other words, the copy should cause the prospective consumer to desire the product or service enough that he or she orders the product or service, or it should at least cause the individual to respond by sending an e-mail message, sending a fax, calling a toll-free number, or returning a postage-paid reply card.
12. The letter should contain a signature of a person's name at the end. If the letter is in black ink, the signature should be in a similar color. Many companies that use direct mail have copy in a typeface that is similar to typefaces found on typewriters. Usually, these letters will have signatures that are in black or blue ink.
13. Lists using bullets or numerals should be considered for presenting features and benefits, especially if there are several mentioned.
14. The length of the letter should be seriously considered. For instance, one page with margins of white space all around is an ideal length. Sometimes letters are more than one page. Make certain that the copy has been edited as much as possible without losing anything of significance before a second or third page is used.
15. The prospective consumers should understand that whatever is being offered comes with no risk or obligation. For instance, the product or service may be tried for a certain period and then returned if the buyer is not satisfied. If the product or service has been paid for, the money will be returned. If the product or service has not been paid for, the consumer is not penalized.
16. A deadline date should be included in the letter and in any other relevant piece in the direct mail package, such as a postage-paid reply card. Deadline dates actually encourage prospective consumers to respond. They realize that they have a limited amount of time to take advantage of the offer.
17. A call to action should be included. Usually, this is put near the end of the letter. In short, do not let prospective consumers off the hook. Many direct mail marketers point out what the prospective consumers may lose if they do not act.

18. The letter should include a guarantee or warranty of some kind, if relevant. Such assures prospective consumers that the direct mail marketer is a legitimate company.
19. The letter should include one or more testimonials or endorsements, if relevant. These are usually in quotation marks and are attributed to satisfied identified customers. However, make certain that these customers have signed release or permissions forms before their comments are used.
20. The most important benefit(s) should be reiterated near the end of the letter. Such may cause the prospective consumers to desire the product or service before a call for action is presented.
21. The letter should include necessary information about the direct mail marketer, such as the firm's name and address as well as the name, title, telephone number (preferably toll free), fax number, and e-mail address of the person whose signature appears at the bottom of the letter.
22. A postscript (P.S.) should be included at the bottom of the letter, below the person's signature. The P.S. should reiterate the basic proposition in a single sentence. Sometimes it will include a second call to action.
23. Important words, phrases, and sentences should be underlined. Such attracts attention. Many direct mail marketers use letters that appear as if individuals have underlined important words, phrases, and sentences with a blue pen. Of course, individuals have not.
24. The information in the letter should be specific, not general. These specifics should be presented in some logical order. This means that the most important or strongest sales point should be presented first.
25. Whenever appropriate, phrases such as "announcing," "at last," "now," "new," "you," "free," "no obligation," "no salesperson will call," and "limited time only," among others, should be included in the letter. These words and phrases will help increase response.
26. The copy in the letter should emphasize the prospective consumers, especially what they wish to learn. In short, do not emphasize the company or the product or service as much as the consumers.
27. Make it easy for prospective consumers to respond by offering them a postage-paid reply card, order form, self-addressed postage-paid envelope, toll-free telephone number, e-mail address, or fax number.
28. If the letter contains a photograph, a cutline (caption) should appear beneath it.
29. The letter should offer something free, if possible. A gift of some kind will help increase response.
30. The letter should mention the offer, especially benefits, before the price.

The Brochure

The brochure can be one or two colors, or it can be a four-color design. It can be small or large in size. However, it should present a complete sales story—that is, if the company for which it has been designed does not have a sales staff that visits prospective consumers.

The brochure should reflect what is being offered for sale. For instance, if it offers an expensive product, the brochure should appear expensive in design. Otherwise, the brochure will "cheapen" the image of the product and consequently will not be effective. In other words, the elements, including typeface and photographs, that have been chosen for the brochure should present an image of elegance or luxury. Furthermore, these elements should be displayed in a formal manner. An easy way to achieve this is by balancing the elements on each page or panel.

If the product or service that is advertised requires excitement, the elements may border one another or even overlap. The elements will appear off balance, and as a result the brochure will be informal. Remember, a brochure's design should reflect the product or service that is advertised.

HEADLINES Headlines should focus on what is being offered and the promises that are made. If the brochure has a headline on the front cover, it may have subheads inside that correspond to blocks of copy. For instance, a headline may focus on what is being offered for sale, and several subheads may focus on several promises.

BODY COPY Body copy should be easy to read and understand. It should flow logically from one point to another throughout. If a guarantee or warranty is included, it should be displayed prominently in a box or in a tinted block. Sometimes, a guarantee or warranty is printed in italics or a different typeface from the other copy. However, no more than two different typefaces should be used in any brochure, and these should be compatible. In fact, if differences are desired, one may employ a lightface, a medium face, a boldface, an extra boldface, an italic face, an expanded face, or a condensed face of one family of type. One may use upper- and lowercase letters or all uppercase letters. In short, there are various ways in which differences can be made.

Lists of information, such as those employing bullets, may be displayed in boxes or tinted blocks. If an order form is part of the brochure, it should be placed near the bottom of the last page or panel, preferably separated by dotted lines for easy tearing or cutting. In addition, the lines for the prospective consumer's name, address, and other information that is needed by the advertiser should be wide enough so the prospective consumer can print the necessary information without any problem.

PHOTOGRAPHS Photographs that have a model demonstrating the product show the prospective consumers how the product is to be used and allow them to project themselves into the model's situation. Photographs of just the product do not have as much impact. If a photograph of a particular product feature is included, the copy should explain what the feature is and why it is important to the prospective consumers. Sometimes this explanation can be accomplished in a caption. In fact, a caption should be used whenever a photograph is used.

ILLUSTRATIONS Illustrations of a product or its features are not as powerful as photographs, especially photographs that have a model demonstrating the product. Nonetheless, an illustration may have to be used. Sometimes the reason is because a photograph does not exist or a photograph does not show what an illustration can.

FRONT COVER The front cover must be attractive. In addition to having an attractive photograph, it should have a strong selling headline that promises a benefit or reward. It should also have the company's name, and it may include the company's logo and slogan.

BACK COVER The back cover may include information about the company. Such information provides credibility and assures the prospective consumers that the company will live up to the claims and promises that have been made elsewhere in the letter and brochure. The back cover may contain an order form, as mentioned above.

THE SPECIFICS OF A BROCHURE The writing should be easy to read, yet it should contain the prospective consumers' language, just like most, if not all, other forms of advertising. The copy should include testimonials or endorsements from those who have purchased the product or service and who are completely satisfied. As mentioned, these testimonials or endorsements should be put in boxes or tinted blocks so that they are easily seen. The copy should focus on the product or service as well as the services that are provided by the company after the product or service has been purchased. Information about the product or service should emphasize benefits—that is, what the product or services does for the prospective consumers. In addition, the copy should provide details about the company offering the product or service, such as the number of years the company has been in business as well as its complete address and telephone number.

A brochure should be designed to attract attention. In essence, it should convey a sense of quality and credibility. When you are finished designing and writing the brochure, you should answer the following questions to make certain that you have not forgotten anything:

1. Is the brochure attractive?
2. Does it make a positive impression about the product or service being offered?
3. Does it make a positive impression about the company?
4. Does it feature a strong selling headline on the front cover?
5. Does it present the product or service's features and benefits in a logical manner?
6. Does it provide enough information about the product or service so that prospective consumers will not have any questions?
7. Have testimonials or endorsements about the product or service been included?
8. Have photographs, illustrations, or other graphics been used to support the sales message?
9. Is the offer reiterated at the end of the sales message?
10. Is there a call to action at the end of the sales message?
11. Is there enough information about the company so that prospective consumers will not have any questions or doubts about the company's credibility?
12. Is the brochure printed on appropriate stock paper?
13. Will the brochure fit easily in the carrier envelope?
14. Do the photographs show a model demonstrating the product?[7]

The Reply Card

The reply card or response form is important in the sense that it should present the sales message about the product or service in case the form becomes separated from the letter and brochure. It should also have information about the company, specifically its name, address, and telephone number, in case the prospective consumers wish to order the product or service by telephone. It should include lines for the prospective consumers to print their names, addresses, and other information that the company needs to insure that the product or service gets to them in a short period.

The response form should be identified with a label, such as "Risk-Free Trial Card," "Savings Certificate," "Urgent Reply Form," "Claim Ticket," "Free Trial Acceptance Form," or "Information Request Card." The label should reflect the sales message, however, not mislead the prospective consumers into thinking that they will receive something other than what is offered. If a guarantee or warranty has been discussed in the letter or brochure, it should be emphasized on the response form. Sometimes a guarantee will cause a response.

In order for the above information to appear on a response form, it is necessary to make certain that the copy contains simple words, short sentences, and brief paragraphs; otherwise, the response form may be as long as the letter and brochure. Once the response form has been roughly designed and written, answer the following questions so that nothing has been overlooked:

1. Does the response form have a label so that prospective consumers will know what it is?
2. Does the response form appear attractive?
3. Does it contain a sales message about the product or service?
4. Does it explain the guarantee or warranty?
5. Is the offer clear?
6. Does the response form have the company's name, address, and telephone number?
7. Does it have wide lines for the prospective consumers to print their names, addresses, and other information the company needs to fill the order or respond to questions?
8. Does it explain the company's policies about returns or claims?
9. Does it have a code printed on it for testing or statistical purposes?
10. Does it have an involvement technique, such as a token or sticker, for the prospective consumers?

EXAMINING DIRECT MAIL

One firm that has been successful in creating direct mail is Alan Rosenspan & Associates. For instance, for American Express CreditAware, the firm created two direct mail packages that were tested against each other. Both were designed to generate orders for a credit-monitoring service. The outside of one window envelope contained the following:

Who's looking over your credit report?

The outside of the second window envelope contained the following copy:

How would you know if someone is using your name to open accounts?

The second envelope and its copy generated more responses than the first. This envelope contained a letter with a tear-off CreditAware Membership Activation form, a multipanel folder, a small sheet announcing a free gift, and a postage-paid self-addressed reply envelope.

The letter contained the following headline:

They say they're
John Doe.

They're using your name
to open credit accounts,
take out bank loans,
and commit fraud.

How would you know?

The body of the letter contained information about identity theft and how one could protect oneself against it. The letter contained information that was presented in italics as well as boldface type. In addition, some of the copy was presented in a list, and some of it was centered, with plenty of white space above and below it. White space was also used to separate paragraphs, which were brief. The letter contained a postscript, too, that summarized the important part of the letter and included a call to action statement.

The tear-off form contained information about the CreditAware program and provided plenty of space for the person to print his or her social security number, home telephone number, signature, and date. The person's address had been printed on the form. At least two call to action statements appeared on the form, as well as the company's name, address, and toll-free telephone number.

The multipanel folder's first panel contained the following headline:

Preserve your
good name
with CreditAware from
American Express.

On the inside, the following headline crossed three panels:

CreditAware from American Express
lets you identify potential identity theft
and other inaccuracies on your credit file
before they take their toll.

Small blue subheads introduced blocks of body copy, which explained the program. On the third panel a call to action statement closed the body copy. A toll-free telephone number as well as information about the "free 30-day trial" followed. The back of the fourth panel contained information about identity theft and how the program could help. The back of the third panel contained questions and answers, a call to action statement, and information about American Express.

The sheet announcing the free gift contained the following headline on one side:

Only you can make sure
your credit history is accurate and up-to-date.

This side contained information about enrolling in the program. The other side of the sheet contained the following headline:

You'll also
receive a free gift

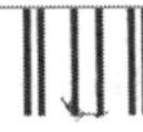

NO POSTAGE NECESSARY IF MAILED IN THE UNITED STATES

BUSINESS REPLY MAIL

FIRST-CLASS MAIL PERMIT NO. 9576 CHANTILLY VA 20153

POSTAGE WILL BE PAID BY ADDRESSEE

They say they're
Pat Sample.

They're using your name
to open credit accounts,
take out bank loans,
and commit fraud.

How would you know?

Identity Theft
Cell Code 288
January 2000 Direct Mail

Dear Pat Sample:

It can happen to *anyone* — over 300,000* identity theft inquiries are made in America every year, and that number is growing.

Someone you don't know could be using your name right now to obtain bank loans, get credit cards, and even apply for jobs.

And most people never even find out about it, *until the harm has been done.*

That's why you should keep an eye on your credit history with **CreditAware® from American Express.**

And you are invited to take advantage of our **free 30-day trial.**

It's the fast, easy way to help keep an eye on your credit history now and in the future. And, as a Platinum Card® member, you are cordially invited to accept our free 30-day trial.

CreditAware Provides You With Three Levels of Service

1. **Your personal credit profile.** The first thing you'll get when you join is your **comprehensive 3-Bureau Credit Profile** that lets you know your credit history with all three major credit bureaus.

   We make it easy for you to compare what each bureau has to say — because they don't always get information from the same sources or at the same time. And as a CreditAware member you will receive a new comprehensive profile every year.

2. **Notification if there are any changes.** We will monitor your files at all 3 bureaus on an ongoing basis, and send you a **Notification Report** if there are any significant changes. You will know if any new accounts have been opened in your name, if changes occurred in your account status, or if any negative information has been added. We'll also notify you with a list of those who have inquired about your credit, as often as once a month.

3. **Fast, professional assistance.** If you do find an inaccuracy on your report, you need to

*U.S., Congress, House, Committee on Commerce, Financial Identity Theft, 106th Con., 1st sess., 1999

(Continued on back)

ILLPL100

FIGURE 10.1 The successful direct mail advertisement for CreditAware from American Express.
Courtesy of Alan Rosenspan & Associates.

FIGURE 10.1 (continued)

The body copy described the free gift and contained a call to action statement. See figure 10.1.

Perhaps the best-known marketer that uses direct mail is the Reader's Digest Association. The Reader's Digest Association publishes *Reader's Digest* and numerous handsome books that concern specific topics. One way the Reader's Digest Association attracts attention to its magazine and books, among other items, is to announce a sweepstakes. For instance, look at figure 10.2, an example of letters that were enclosed in a business-size window envelope that was glued to a much larger manila envelope.

The letter reads:

> Dear Mrs. Doe:
>
> *The Letters of Instruction in the attached brown envelope need your immediate approval.*
>
> Each letter contains important details about prize payments and notification that our bank and two internal departments would follow if you are selected the winner, Mrs. Doe.
>
> These steps were taken for individuals like you, Mrs. Doe, who now have secured a chance to win up to $2,770,000.00. So please review your Letters of Instruction very carefully. Then initial each one in the red-stamped area on the bottom of the page. All three Letters must be returned along with your Certified Cash Dispatch by July 25th to be considered valid for entry.
>
> The initialed Letters of Instruction would confirm your acceptance of full eligibility to win a prize—and should our Prize Judge select your Certified Cash Dispatch as the winning entry, within 30 days of the drawing, you'd be collecting your share of $2,770,000.00, Mrs. Doe.
>
> I urge you to use the YES reply envelope to return all your documents. By doing so, you'll secure your chance to win up to $2,770,000.00 in Sweepstakes prizes and guarantee priority processing of your copy of THE AMERICAN PRESIDENT and a special companion book GEORGE W. BUSH, A HEROIC FIRST YEAR. (See the full-color brochure enclosed with your Letters of Instruction.) If you use the NO reply envelope, I will just enter your chance to win up to $2,770,000.00 in Sweepstakes prizes. I won't be able to authorize priority processing of these memorable books.
>
> Kindly initial all three Letters of Instruction to indicate your acceptance of full eligibility to win up to $2,770,000.00 and return them with your validated Certified Cash Dispatch Entry. Arrangements would be made to send you your prize winnings as outlined in the Letters should you be selected the winner. Your entry must be postmarked by midnight, July 25th to be accepted.
>
> Yours sincerely,
>
> Ronald J Leslie
>
> Ronald J. Leslie
> Sweepstakes Director

In addition to having the company's logo and address at the top, the letter contains a blocked area for the person's name and address. An "ATTENTION" box also appears directly across from the person's name and address. This box, which is actually a label, should be affixed to the back of the Certified Cash Dispatch Entry form, which was enclosed with the letter above. The bottom of the letter contains two postscripts. The first instructs the person to attach the "ATTENTION" label to the back of the entry form. The second informs the person about earning a free gift, possibly more, by saying "YES" to the book.

OS0349/PA

FINAL

RONALD J. LESLIE • SWEEPSTAKES DIRECTOR • READER'S DIGEST • PLEASANTVILLE, NY

**********AUTO** 5-DIGIT 89117
OS0349-P*0112667*P11-T00-B29
MRS

ATTENTION

IF SELECTED WINNING ENTRY, PROCESS ACCORDING TO LETTERS OF INSTRUCTION

AFFIX THIS LABEL TO THE BACK OF YOUR CERTIFIED CASH DISPATCH ENTRY

Dear Mrs :

The Letters of Instruction in the attached brown envelope need your immediate approval.

Each Letter contains important details about prize payments and notification that our bank and two internal departments would follow if you are selected the winner, Mrs .

These steps were taken for individuals like you, Mrs , who now have secured a chance to win up to $2,770,000.00. So please review your Letters of Instruction very carefully. Then initial each one in the red-stamped area on the bottom of the page. All three Letters must be returned along with your Certified Cash Dispatch by July 25th to be considered valid for entry.

The initialed Letters of Instruction would confirm your acceptance of full eligibility to win a prize -- and should our Prize Judge select your Certified Cash Dispatch as the winning entry, within 30 days of the drawing, you'd be collecting your share of $2,770,000.00, Mrs .

I urge you to use the YES reply envelope to return all your documents. By doing so, you'll secure your chance to win up to $2,770,000.00 in Sweepstakes prizes and guarantee priority processing of your copy of THE AMERICAN PRESIDENT and a special companion book GEORGE W. BUSH, A HEROIC FIRST YEAR. (See the full-color brochure enclosed with your Letters of Instruction.) If you use the NO reply envelope, I will just enter your chance to win up to $2,770,000.00 in Sweepstakes prizes. I won't be able to authorize priority processing of these memorable books.

Kindly initial all three Letters of Instruction to indicate your acceptance of full eligibility to win up to $2,770,000.00 and return them with your validated Certified Cash Dispatch Entry. Arrangements would be made to send you your prize winnings as outlined in the Letters should you be selected the winner. Your entry must be postmarked by midnight, July 25th to be accepted.

Yours sincerely,

Ronald J. Leslie

Ronald J. Leslie
Sweepstakes Director

P.S. Remove the "ATTENTION" label from this letter and affix it to the back of your Certified Cash Dispatch Entry. If your entry document is selected the winner, the Prize Judge will know that Letters of Instruction are enclosed upon seeing this label.

P.P.S. See the Free Gift "Credit Card" in the attached envelope to discover how many Free Gifts you can claim when you say "YES" to THE AMERICAN PRESIDENT.

FIGURE 10.2 The primary letter to "Jane Doe" from the Reader's Digest Association. *Courtesy of the Reader's Digest Association.*

The large manila envelope contains a four-page folded letter, a large four-color folder containing information about the book, a "Draft" letter concerning funds for the grand prize, a second "Draft" letter concerning funds to cover the federal taxes on the first $1 million of the grand prize, a third "Draft" letter concerning a "Quick Cash Prize" of $20,000, a free gift "credit card," a fact sheet about the sweepstakes, a "Yes" envelope, and a "No" envelope for the person's perusal. The "No" envelope contains a printed insert reminding the person to reconsider the offer. See figures 10.3–10.10.

CD-OS0349-P

IMPORTANT: The enclosed Letters of Instruction clearly show our intent to award $2,770,000.00 in prizes in our Sweepstakes. Return your Certified Cash Dispatch Entry by July 25th along with your three Letters. If you are selected the winner, arrangements would be made to send you your prize winnings. Make sure you initial each Letter where indicated for eligibility to win in the Sweepstakes.

Plus, see the enclosed Free Gift "Credit Card" to discover how many Free Gifts you can claim when you say "YES" to...

THE AMERICAN PRESIDENT

An Intimate Look At The Lives Of The Leaders Who Brought Our Nation To Glory

Dear Reader,

Inspiring tales of bravery!

Dazzling stories of romance!

Moving accounts of personal tragedy and triumph!

This might not be exactly what you'd expect from a book about America's highest-ranking elected official.

But THE AMERICAN PRESIDENT takes you beyond the press conferences and interviews, the campaign promises and handshakes. And it introduces you to 42 men with lives as full of hopes, dreams and passions as our own. Fascinating, surprising men like...

Harry Truman who worked on his family farm until he was 30 years old and never took to the work. "Corn-shucking," he said, was "a job invented by Satan."

(over, please)

Lyndon Johnson who, during a meeting, might suddenly stalk to the White House pool, strip off his clothes, dive in naked, and badger his associates until they followed!

George Bush who, despite the protests of his father, enlisted in the Navy becoming the youngest pilot then serving in the armed forces. On one mission, Bush parachuted from his burning plane and floated for hours in the ocean avoiding enemy fire.

THE AMERICAN PRESIDENT will take you deeper into the lives, minds and hearts of our presidents than any book ever has!

Before he held the highest office in the land, each American president led a life that would determine how he would guide his country. Our leaders were little boys, big dreamers, and passionate thinkers long before they became "Mr. President."

And when they did take office, they embarked upon the most poignant and life-altering journey one can take. THE AMERICAN PRESIDENT invites you to share that journey...

Stand alongside **Franklin Pierce** as he struggles to get through his inauguration just two months after the death of his only son.

Find out what led **Abraham Lincoln** to declare: "I claim not to have controlled events, but confess plainly that events have controlled me."

Spend two terms with **Ronald Reagan** as he restores American pride and confidence even as he fights against the private anguish of declining health.

In this one-of-a-kind book, you'll read fascinating accounts of extraordinary lives. You'll find rare eye-opening photos and illustrations -- many of which have never been seen before. And you'll get to know each President as more than just a name in the history books or a familiar face on TV.

FIGURE 10.3 The four-page letter about the book, *The American President*. *Courtesy of the Reader's Digest Association.*

As you examine the letter and other forms, see if the copywriter used any of the suggestions mentioned earlier. In addition, try to identify the words and phrases that encourage a person to read further and even respond to the offer.

SUMMARY OF WHAT MAKES DIRECT MAIL EFFECTIVE

When writing direct mail, remember to begin by offering a benefit in the headline or at least the first paragraph. Then emphasize this benefit in the following paragraph. This benefit should be the most important benefit that the product or service offers the consumer.

In the body copy, mention the product or service's features and then explain in depth these features' benefits. Try to make the product or service distinct—that is, different or unique from its competitors. Provide documented evidence (performance tests, endorsements, scientific studies, reports, etc.) that supports your claim. Try to build integrity and reliability for the advertiser. End by repeating the major benefit that the product or service offers the consumer and urge action, such as buying the product or service.

You'll meet...

A lonely child... Picked on as a little boy, **Richard Nixon** wasn't comfortable around anyone outside his family. He said he didn't like riding the school bus "because the other children didn't smell good."

A doting husband... "After much pleading my own sweet, pretty darling consented to be my wife," **Teddy Roosevelt** wrote of his first wife Alice who died at the age of 22. "The aim of my whole life will be to make her happy."

A devoted fisherman... Fly fishing was **Herbert Hoover's** favorite pastime and metaphor for democracy. He once said: "All men are equal before fishes."

Public men. Private people. From Washington's humility to Lincoln's vanity, Jackson's ferociousness to Buchanan's timidity, Madison's caution to Johnson's ambition, you'll discover the diverse temperaments that have gone hand in hand with the presidency.

And, because THE AMERICAN PRESIDENT groups our leaders according to their personalities and leadership styles, you'll find striking similarities even between presidents separated by centuries!

In their own words... Find out what made our presidents tick as you read their own words on a multitude of topics...

> **On Trouble:** "If you see ten troubles coming down the road, you can be sure that nine will run into the ditch before they reach you and you have to battle with only one..."
> *Calvin Coolidge*
>
> **On American business:** "The only trouble with capitalism is capitalists. They're too damned greedy." *Herbert Hoover*
>
> **On life:** "Everything goes wrong with a man until he gets on the right road."
> *Woodrow Wilson*

EXTRA BOOK – GEORGE W. BUSH, A HEROIC FIRST YEAR

Along with THE AMERICAN PRESIDENT you'll receive a special companion book that gives you an inside look at our 43rd President's historic first year in office, from the controversial election to the tragic events of September 11, 2001 and the war on terrorism.

"I do solemnly swear that I will faithfully execute the office of the President of the United States, and will, to the best of my ability preserve, protect and defend the Constitution of the United States."

Only 43 men have placed their hand upon the Bible, spoken these words, and changed their lives -- and America's destiny -- forever. Come, enjoy their intriguing, enlightening stories...

Send for THE AMERICAN PRESIDENT and GEORGE W. BUSH, A HEROIC FIRST YEAR today. And enter the Sweepstakes too!

Send no money now. Just return your validated Certified Cash Dispatch Entry and signed Letters of Instruction in the enclosed "YES" reply envelope. We'll enter you in the Sweepstakes with a chance to win up to $2,770,000.00 in prizes and we'll send you THE AMERICAN PRESIDENT right away. You can also claim your free gifts with the enclosed Free Gift "Credit Card."

You can keep this insightful, picture-packed book and the special companion book for just $34.96 payable in 4 monthly installments of only $8.74 each. No interest, no charge for credit. And you have the Reader's Digest Complete Money-Back Guarantee of Satisfaction.

You can enter the Sweepstakes without sending for THE AMERICAN PRESIDENT and the special companion book. Just return your validated Certified Cash Dispatch Entry and signed Letters of Instruction in the enclosed NO reply envelope instead. We'll enter you in the Sweepstakes with a chance to win up to $2,770,000.00 in prizes, but you'll miss out on this one-of-a-kind chance to go behind the scenes and meet the men who have held the most powerful political office in the world.

Whatever you decide, reply by July 25 to ensure your chance to win. All prizes are guaranteed to be given away!

Sincerely,

Carolyn Davis

Carolyn Davis

FIGURE 10.3 (continued)

Letters

Begin a letter with a brief paragraph. In fact, it may be one sentence. Make sure that no paragraph is very long. However, the paragraphs should vary in length. In addition, think about creating a list for some of the information. Make sure that white space is used to separate paragraphs. Finally, close with a brief paragraph that prompts action.

Brochures and Folders

Begin a brochure or folder with a strong headline and an appealing illustration or photograph. A brief block of copy may also appear on the first page or panel. The next two pages or panels should be treated as one page or panel by having a strong headline spreading across them. In addition, have a large dominant illustration or photograph with a cutline or caption occupying part of each page or panel. Use subheads that sell to break up blocks of body copy. These subheads should summarize or emphasize the most important point of a block or blocks of copy. Smaller illustrations or photographs may be used on these pages or panels. If so, use a cutline with each. The last page or panel should be as interesting as the first, primarily because it may be examined before the inside pages or panels. The last page or panel may contain a list of important points, a guarantee or warranty, or a special offer. In addition, it may contain an urge to action as well as information about the company, such as the company's logo, address, telephone number, and website.

Directing potential buyers to visit the World Wide Web can be essential. I will discuss Internet advertising in the next chapter.

FIGURE 10.4 (FRONT) The large four-color folder about the book, *The American President*. *Courtesy of the Reader's Digest Association.*

A Fresh View Of The Presidents And The Presidency Itself!

By grouping our presidents according to their personalities, leadership styles, and the conditions that brought them to office, **THE AMERICAN PRESIDENT** will let you gain new insight into one of the oldest offices in the land!

Here's how the book is organized ...

CHAPTER ONE:
THE HEROIC POSTURE
National heroes before they were candidates...
George Washington America's First Hero
Ulysses S. Grant In Over His Head
Dwight D. Eisenhower The Heroic Image
William Henry Harrison A Manufactured Hero

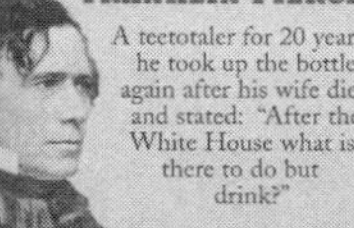

FRANKLIN PIERCE
A teetotaler for 20 years, he took up the bottle again after his wife died and stated: "After the White House what is there to do but drink?"

CHAPTER TWO:
COMPROMISE CHOICES
Elected for who they weren't, rather than for who they were ...
Franklin Pierce The Dark Horse President
James A. Garfield Awaiting Destiny
Gerald Ford Healing the Nation
Warren G. Harding "I Should Never Have Been Here"

CHAPTER THREE:
THE PROFESSIONAL POLITICIAN
Lives spent in training for the Presidency ...
Martin Van Buren The Little Magician
James Buchanan Avoiding Conflict
Abraham Lincoln Politics with a Purpose
Lyndon B. Johnson The Art of Political Bluster

CHAPTER FOUR:
AN INDEPENDENT CAST OF MIND
Political loners with strong political vision ...
John Adams Going It Alone
Zachary Taylor Old Rough and Ready
Jimmy Carter The Outsider
Rutherford B. Hayes The President Without a Nickname

CHAPTER FIVE:
FAMILY TIES
Born to hold the high office ...
John Quincy Adams His Father's Son
Benjamin Harrison Nobody's Grandson
Franklin D. Roosevelt Possession by Right
John F. Kennedy Vindicating the Irish

CHAPTER SIX:
HAPPENSTANCE
Presidents through accident or national tragedy...
John Tyler Establishing the Precedent
Millard Fillmore "Called by a Bereavement"
Andrew Johnson "Elect of an Assassin"
Chester A. Arthur Gentleman Boss
Harry S. Truman American Optimist

CHAPTER SEVEN:
THE AMERICAN WAY
Men suspicious of Big Government ...
Thomas Jefferson His "Empire of Liberty"
Calvin Coolidge Preacher of Prosperity
Herbert C. Hoover American Individualist
Ronald Reagan An American Dreamer

CHAPTER EIGHT:
THE WORLD STAGE
Leaders who helped bring America into the international arena ...
James Monroe A Vision for the Hemisphere
William McKinley Reluctant Apostle
Woodrow Wilson American Idealism
George Bush Personal Contact

CHAPTER NINE:
EXPANDING POWER
Men who deliberately stretched the power of their office...
Andrew Jackson The Power of the People
Grover Cleveland Ugly Honest
Theodore Roosevelt Rough Rider
Richard M. Nixon Abuse of Power

WILLIAM J. CLINTON
"My mother taught me three things: never give up; never forget where you came from; and never lose your compassion for people who are less fortunate than you are."

CHAPTER TEN:
THE BALANCE OF POWER
Presidents immersed in the checks and balances of our government ...
James Madison Creating the Balance
James K. Polk Young Hickory
William Jefferson Clinton Second Chances
William Howard Taft Preserving the Balance

SEND NO MONEY NOW!

Simply return your YES reply. We'll send you the THE AMERICAN PRESIDENT and GEORGE W. BUSH, A HEROIC FIRST YEAR for the low price of just $34.96 payable in 4 easy monthly installments of just $8.74 each, plus delivery. No interest, no charge for credit. And you are 100% protected by...

THE READER'S DIGEST COMPLETE MONEY-BACK GUARANTEE OF SATISFACTION

You always come first, and your satisfaction is fully guaranteed. This means that if you are not completely satisfied with THE AMERICAN PRESIDENT, you may return it and your money will be promptly refunded. For more than 80 years, Reader's Digest has practiced this policy, and we will continue to serve you as friends with this one aim in mind: You must be entirely satisfied.

Reader's Digest. EDITORS' CHOICE

B-OS0349-P

Reader's Digest Presents
A Book 210 Years In The Making

Your invitation to take a private look at the men who've held the most public office in the land

GEORGE BUSH
Bush campaigns his way in 1992. "I resisted people trying to make me something I wasn't," he said. "Wear this! Do your hair with a bouffant do! There's too much of that."

JOHN F. KENNEDY
Always happiest at sea, Jack once said: "It is an interesting biological fact that all of us have in our veins the exact same percentage of salt ... that exists in the ocean. We are tied to the sea."

FASCINATING BIOGRAPHIES OF ALL 42 PRESIDENTS!

FRANKLIN D. ROOSEVELT
Even though he was confined to a wheelchair by polio for all four of his terms in office, nothing could defeat FDR. Here he is seen reviewing the troops in Sicily in 1943.

GEORGE WASHINGTON
Our first president not only loved music but also valued courtesy and thoughtfulness. By age 16 he had copied 110 etiquette rules into his school notebook.

BOLD MEN. SHY MEN. PASSIONATE MEN. THE MEN WHO BUILT AMERICA. THEIR STORIES BROUGHT TO YOU IN VIVID DETAIL IN THE AMERICAN PRESIDENT. SEE INSIDE ...

FIGURE 10.4 (BACK)

FIGURE 10.4 (INSIDE SPREAD)

FIGURE 10.4 (INSIDE SPREAD)

OS0349/P

W.H. Magill
Vice President and Treasurer

Pleasantville, NY
Office 3C-1

To: John T. Forstrom, Citizens State Bank
Fr: W.H. Magill
RE: TRANSFER OF PRIZE FUNDS TO WINNER(S)

Mr. Forstrom:

Pursuant to the agreement between Reader's Digest and Citizens State Bank, please confirm arrangements to transfer prize funds to winner when selected within 30 days thereof.

At the time this draft was written, funds held on deposit at Citizens State Bank cover both first installment and lump-sum payments offered in our Sweepstakes for prizes totalling $2,020,000.00.

When the Prize Judge selects the winning entry document, I will let you know to expedite prize payment.

Kind regards,

W.H. Magill

W.H. Magill

Copy to all qualified entrants, including: Mrs [redacted]

001832679086

0112667

JS

INITIAL HERE & RETURN

By initialing this box, entrant accepts full eligibility to win up to $2,770,000.00 in prizes.

0170583

THE READER'S DIGEST ASSOCIATION, INC.

FIGURE 10.5 The "Draft" letter about the grand prize. *Courtesy of the Reader's Digest Association.*

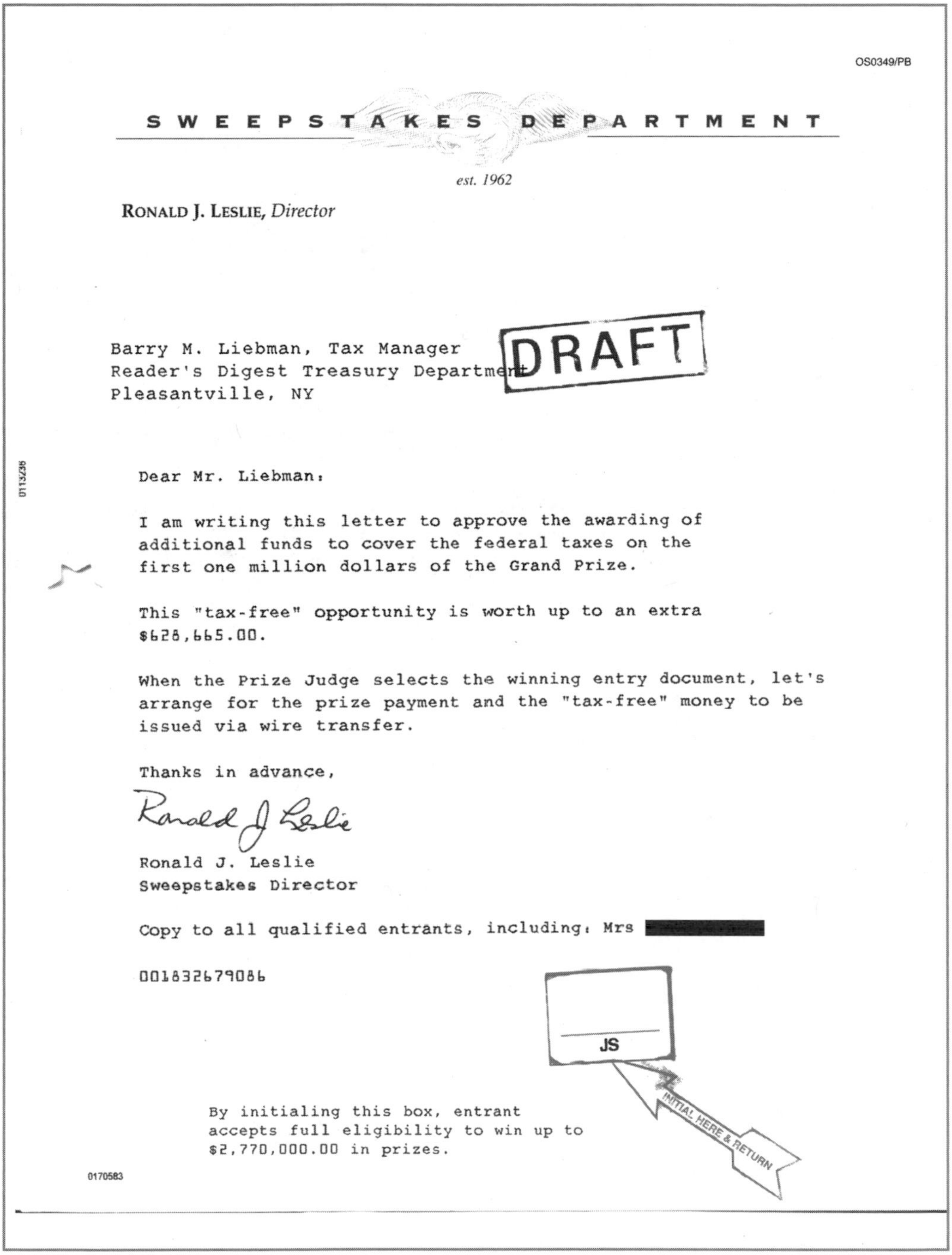

OS0349/PB

SWEEPSTAKES DEPARTMENT

est. 1962

RONALD J. LESLIE, *Director*

Barry M. Liebman, Tax Manager
Reader's Digest Treasury Department
Pleasantville, NY

0113238

Dear Mr. Liebman:

I am writing this letter to approve the awarding of additional funds to cover the federal taxes on the first one million dollars of the Grand Prize.

This "tax-free" opportunity is worth up to an extra $628,665.00.

When the Prize Judge selects the winning entry document, let's arrange for the prize payment and the "tax-free" money to be issued via wire transfer.

Thanks in advance,

Ronald J. Leslie

Ronald J. Leslie
Sweepstakes Director

Copy to all qualified entrants, including: Mrs

001832679086

JS

INITIAL HERE & RETURN

By initialing this box, entrant accepts full eligibility to win up to $2,770,000.00 in prizes.

0170583

FIGURE 10.6 The "Draft" letter about the funds for federal taxes. *Courtesy of the Reader's Digest Association.*

OS0349/PB

Reader's Digest®

U.S. Marketing — Books and Home Entertainment Home Division

DRAFT

Attention: Public Relations Department

I have approved the funding of a new $20,000.00 Quick Cash Prize that those individuals receiving our exclusive book offer for THE AMERICAN PRESIDENT and a special companion book GEORGE W. BUSH, A HEROIC FIRST YEAR will be given a chance to win.

The winning entry document will be selected by the Prize Judge on August 14. If the selected winner approves, please issue a press release to their local newspaper regarding this special $20,000.00 prize award.

Please contact me directly should you have any questions.

Sincerely,

D.C. Nelson

D.C. Nelson
Associate Director
Home Division

Copy to all qualified entrants, including: [redacted]

001832679086

JS

INITIAL HERE & RETURN

By initialing this box, entrant accepts full eligibility to win up to $2,770,000.00 in prizes.

OS0349-P

0170583 The Reader's Digest Association, Inc. • Reader's Digest Road • Pleasantville, NY 10570

FIGURE 10.7 The "Draft" letter about the Quick Cash Prize. *Courtesy of the Reader's Digest Association.*

FIGURE 10.8 The Free Gift "Credit Card." *Courtesy of the Reader's Digest Association.*

Sweepstakes Facts

Prize	Retail Value	Number of Prizes	Odds	Final Closing Date
Grand Prize #902	$2,000,000.00	1	1 in 105,000,000	8/09/02
Cash On Demand Prize #982	$125,000.00	1	1 in 120,000,000	8/09/02
$250,000.00 Cash Sweepstakes #131	$250,000.00	1	1 in 75,000,000	3/07/03
$100,000.00 Cash Sweepstakes #132	$100,000.00	1	1 in 75,000,000	3/07/03
$50,000.00 Cash Sweepstakes #133	$50,000.00	1	1 in 75,000,000	3/07/03
$25,000.00 Cash Sweepstakes #134	$25,000.00	1	1 in 75,000,000	3/07/03
$10,000.00 Cash Sweepstakes #135	$10,000.00	1	1 in 75,000,000	3/07/03
$5,000.00 Cash Sweepstakes #136	$5,000.00	1	1 in 75,000,000	3/07/03
The 50 Winners Jackpot #137	$1,000.00	50	1 in 1,500,000	3/07/03
Fast Cash Sweepstakes #138	$100.00	100	1 in 750,000	3/07/03
The $20,000.00 Quick Cash Prize #885	$20,000.00	1	1 in 552,000	8/01/02

You Have Not Yet Won.
All Entries Have The Same Chance Of Winning.

No one will know who the winner is until after the sweepstakes ends. Final Closing Date is the last date entries are accepted. Your entry deadline may vary, see enclosed entry materials.

Entry Is Free.

You don't have to buy anything to enter. Just mail the enclosed Entry as directed. You will be entered for each prize offered in this mailing.

Buying Won't Help You Win.

Your chances of winning without a purchase are just as good as the chances of someone who buys something.

FIGURE 10.9 The Fact Sheet about the Sweepstakes. *Courtesy of the Reader's Digest Association.*

FIGURE 10.10 The "Yes" and "No" Envelopes. *Courtesy of the Reader's Digest Association.*

EXERCISES

1. Create a direct mail piece such as a letter, card, flyer, or brochure that promotes a book that can be ordered by mail. Read the following descriptive information about the book's contents:
   - The book explains how people can achieve whatever goals they set for themselves in a competitive society. Each chapter—there are 13—describes in depth one of 13 rules that, if followed, not only will make a positive impression on superiors but also will help the people who live by the rules succeed. The author, Thomas Fielding, has come upon these rules the hard way, by trial and error. The book costs $19.95. A charge of $4.95 is added for postage and handling.
   - You will need to come up with the title for the book, write the copy, and then present it in the format you think is best. Remember, this is direct mail. You must attract your prospective consumer immediately.
2. From a local resort, secure information on services available and other information and then prepare copy for a four-color envelope enclosure that might also be distributed in gasoline stations, chamber of commerce offices, and the like. The size of the mailing piece is to be such that it will fit a business-size envelope. The purpose of the mailer is to secure inquiries and reservations for the resort.
3. Think about your favorite restaurant's specialty. Is it burgers, chicken, fish, pizza, or what? Identify it and then write copy that offers the restaurant's specialty at a reduced price for a limited period of time, for a two-color self-mailing card. Although one side of the card should contain the copy about the specialty, as well as offering it at a reduced price for a limited period of time, the other side should have space for the restaurant's logo, address, telephone number, and hours of operation as well as space for the addressee's name and address.

NOTES

1. Direct Marketing Association, "Economic Impact: U.S. Direct and Interactive Marketing Today Executive Summary—2002: DM Advertising Expenditures by Medium and Market" (New York: Direct Marketing Association, 2002; www.the-dma.org).
2. Direct Marketing Association, "Economic Impact."
3. Direct Marketing Association, "Economic Impact."
4. Direct Marketing Association, "Economic Impact."
5. Bob Stone, *Successful Direct Marketing Methods*, 4th ed. (Lincolnwood, IL: NTC Business Books, 1988), p. 478.
6. See Pat Friesen, "Direct Response Creative: What to Test First," *Target Marketing*, Vol. 22, No. 5 (May 1999): p. 50; Alicia Orr, "The Mechanics of a Direct Mail Test," *Target Marketing*, Vol. 17, No. 5 (May 1994): p. 10-11; John Fraser-Robinson, *The Secrets of Effective Direct Mail* (London: McGraw-Hill Book Co., 1989), pp. 163–166.
7. See David Wilkinson, "The Brochure," *Direct Marketing*, Vol. 50, No. 1 (May 1987): pp. 62–63, 123; Ellen Looyen, "The Art of Brochures," *Guerrilla Tactics* (www.gmarketing.com/tactics/weekly_85.html); Kirwood Inc., "Corporate Brochures: Are Yours Helping or Hurting Your Company?" (www.kirwood.com/brochwpd.htm); Stone, *Successful Direct Marketing Methods*, pp. 329–330; Donna Baier Stein and Floyd Kemske, *Write on Target: The Direct Marketer's Copywriting Handbook* (Lincolnwood, IL: NTC Business Books, 1997), pp. 137–151.

CHAPTER 11

Internet Advertising

The Internet is growing as an advertising medium. In 2000, advertisers spent $4.85 billion on Internet advertising.[1] A year later, advertisers spent $5.8 billion.[2] However, numerous companies that advertised on the Internet also existed by the Internet, and these companies have gone out of business. As a result, advertising on the Internet has slowed somewhat. If advertising on the Internet is to pick up, advertisers must be willing to cut their advertising expenditures in other media or enlarge their advertising budgets.

According to a report that was published in 2002, Internet advertising was expected to grow from almost 3 percent of total media spending in 2001 to almost 4 percent of total media spending in three years, thus indicating that advertisers are willing to move funds from one medium to another or enlarge their advertising budgets.[3] There are several reasons for prognosticators to believe that Internet advertising will increase. One is that more people will use the Internet. Consequently, advertisers will attempt to reach these individuals with advertisements. A second reason is that the number of households having access to broadband will increase, and broadband allows users to download pages faster. Third, more people are making more purchases on the Internet, which is attractive to advertisers. A fourth reason is that finally the Interactive Advertising Bureau, in agreement with several companies and organizations, has introduced guidelines that make advertising on the Internet easier to purchase.[4]

WHO USES THE INTERNET?

There are more than 150 million users of the Internet in the United States. Many of these users are affluent and spend a lot of time in front of computers. Many have actually purchased products or services through the Internet. In addition, most executives in corporations spend some time on the Internet as part of their jobs. In fact, some executives spend more hours on the Internet than they do with any other medium, and they actually prefer to learn about products through this medium. They also tend to look at the advertisements.[5]

ADVANTAGES OF THE INTERNET

1. The Internet has an extremely large audience. The Internet is global, reaching more than half a billion people worldwide. In fact, more than 75 million people get online every year. Of course, as more people who are economically able to get online do so, the number of new users will not be as great.
2. The Internet is an interactive medium. It allows users to actually interact with advertisers. Other media do not.
3. The Internet allows for an immediate response. The Internet allows advertisers to reach educated affluent users who can immediately order the merchandise that is advertised.
4. The Internet is an exciting medium. People all over the world are experiencing the Internet for the first time. Therefore, it is an exciting medium in the sense that it allows users the opportunity to explore websites and learn about new products and services.
5. The Internet is a flexible medium. It allows advertisers the opportunity to change their advertising messages often.
6. The Internet can be used to target specific users. It allows advertisers to target specific users by placing advertisements on certain websites that appeal to these users.
7. The Internet may be a cost-effective medium, depending on how many intended users actually see and respond to an advertiser's advertisement.
8. The Internet reaches the affluent. It is used by the affluent; consequently, advertisers interested in reaching these individuals should consider using the Internet.
9. The Internet reaches executives. It allows advertisers to reach those who work for corporations, primarily because these individuals tend to use the Internet as part of their jobs.
10. The Internet can present the whole story. It allows advertisers the opportunity to design websites that present in-depth information about themselves and their products or services. In fact, many companies actually present their entire catalogs on the Internet so that users can shop online.

DISADVANTAGES OF THE INTERNET

1. The Internet is an untested medium. As an advertising medium it has not been shown to be effective. In fact, there are too many questions that have not been answered regarding the Internet's impact on consumers.
2. The Internet may be perceived in a negative light. Many users of the Internet do not enjoy being bombarded with advertisements, especially when they are paying to get online. In addition, many users may block countless advertisements with software or close/delete those advertisements that happen to appear on their screens.
3. The Internet may cause concern when it comes to shopping. Many users of the Internet are skeptical about ordering products or services online. In fact, many do not wish to provide their credit card numbers or other personal information because they are afraid that such information may be stolen or sold. In short, they question the security of the Internet or the website.
4. The Internet may take too much time. Most users of the Internet use modems that are connected to telephone lines. These modems are slow. If an advertiser's website has sounds and

graphics, many users will go back to the previous page before the advertiser's page downloads. The reason is that it takes too long for such pages to download, unless the advertiser has employed a company that used the latest technology to create the website or the user has access to broadband.

Of course, there may be other disadvantages, but these are the most common.

WHAT IS WRONG WITH THE INTERNET

The Internet presents problems for users. According to Creative Good, "The Web is an intimidating, foreign environment to many customers. Pages are a jungle of links, buttons, forms, blinking graphics, and baffling jargon. Accusatory error messages leap out at any time."[6] Indeed, according to Zona Research, "62 percent of online shoppers had given up at least once while looking for products, and 42 percent had turned to traditional channels to make their purchase."[7] Although corporations are spending money to entice users to their websites, some users find these websites too difficult to use or too slow to download; consequently, they go to another website. As a result, corporations are losing potential customers.

According to Creative Good, "Customers want simplicity, but the Web offers complexity. Customers want service, but the Web offers technology. Customers want to accomplish their goal, but the Web offers 'compelling features.'"[8] In essence, the consumer's Internet experience is not necessarily to his or her liking. This is particularly true of Internet advertising, which is more of a bother than a help, and users are less inclined to click on an advertisement today primarily because of a previous bad experience. According to Forrester Research, if customers have a bad experience on a website, they express their displeasure to about 10 people.[9] Of course, this action can soon destroy a business that sells most, if not all, of its goods or services online. Therefore, it is imperative that an e-business provide prospective customers with a very positive experience.

How can an e-business make certain that it offers a positive experience to prospective consumers? First, an e-business must assure the prospects that its website is easy to use and fast. Prospects are interested in learning whether an e-business has the product they desire, and they do not wish to waste time trying to find it. Therefore, the navigation system must be easy to operate. Second, an e-business must assure prospects that its website is secure. In short, an e-business should inform users about its security system and guarantees.[10] Third, an e-business must assure prospects that the products or services it carries are at least equal in quality to what is carried by other businesses. Fourth, an e-business must assure consumers that its products or services are competitively priced; otherwise, there is no reason for a prospect to shop online, except that it may be more convenient than driving to a store. Actually, an e-business should strive to price its goods or services lower than the competition because prospects usually have to pay for shipping.

INTERNET ADVERTISEMENTS

There are several kinds of advertisements that appear on the Internet. These include banners, buttons, interstitials, keywords, pop-ups, rectangles, skyscrapers, and "webmercials." Banner advertisements are similar to miniature outdoor advertisements, in that they spread across or down the screen usually at the top, bottom, or side of the website. Banner advertisements vary in size:

- Full Banner (468 × 60 pixels—about 4½" wide × ½" high)
- Half Banner (234 × 60 pixels)
- Vertical Banner (120 × 240 pixels)
- Micro Bar (88 × 31 pixels)[11]

In addition, a banner may expand to as large as 468 × 240 pixels when it is clicked. It may play audio or video content when it is clicked.

Button advertisements are small or scaled-down versions of banner advertisements. Usually, when these are clicked they move the user to the advertisers' websites. Button advertisements vary in size as well:

- Button 1 (120 × 90 pixels)
- Button 2 (120 × 60 pixels)
- Square Button (125 × 125 pixels)[12]

Interstitial advertisements or transitional advertisements appear on the screen as website downloads. Usually, these advertisements are 336 × 280 pixels in size and may have audio or video content.

Keyword advertisements or meta-advertisements appear on the screen when a user has typed a term to be searched. For instance, if a user desires to learn about jackets, an advertiser who sells jackets may have a keyword advertisement linked to the term. In other words, advertisers link keyword advertisements to related terms that may be typed by users who are interested in learning about a specific item or topic.

Pop-up advertisements are similar to interstitial advertisements, in that they pop up on the screen when a website downloads. Pop-up advertisements vary in size:

- Pop-up 1 (Square Pop-up 250 × 250 pixels)
- Pop-up 2 (Square Pop-up 550 × 550 pixels)[13]

Rectangle advertisements are similar to banner advertisements and may play audio or video content when they are clicked. Rectangle ads vary in size:

- Large Rectangle (336 × 280 pixels)
- Medium Rectangle (300 × 250 pixels)
- Vertical Rectangle (240 × 400 pixels)
- Rectangle (180 × 150 pixels)

Finally, skyscraper advertisements are vertical advertisements that may play audio or video content when they are clicked. These advertisements vary in size too:

- Wide Skyscraper (160 × 600 pixels)
- Skyscraper (120 × 600 pixels)[14]

Many advertisers use their websites as advertisements. Some advertisers sponsor pages of other websites or entire websites for a certain period. Many use e-mail advertisements to reach potential customers. In fact, this form of Internet advertising is growing faster than perhaps any other form. E-mail advertisements are similar to direct mail advertisements in that they reach prospects at home or at work. E-mail advertisements are fast and are usually responded to within two days, according to Jupiter Research as well as Digital Impact.[15] Also, e-mail advertisements can enhance brand equity when they are delivered to subscribers' inboxes on a regular basis.[16] In the early 2000s, advertisers were spending more than $2 billion on e-mail advertisements.[17] According to eMarketer, "E-mail can be highly personalized to individual customers' needs. Messages sent on behalf of companies from messaging solution providers can be targeted and customized using sophisticated database-marketing techniques. The technology can capture and track individual responses throughout the campaign, 'learn' more about customers from response and purchase behavior, and refine customer profiles for future communications."[18]

E-mail advertisements, if they are not solicited or sent to subscribers, are considered *spam*. Spam is nothing more than "junk e-mail," and many users have grown frustrated as a result of receiving numerous advertisements that they did not request. In fact, many users whose inboxes are filled with spam refuse to purchase any of the products or services advertised, primarily because these advertisements were sent without permission. In order for e-mail advertisements to be effective, they should be requested by the user or at least sent to a user who has shown interest in the product.

Webmercials are similar to television commercials in that they occupy the full screen and contain audio and video content. Studios such as KMGI in New York are revolutionizing Internet advertising. These firms specialize in creating rich media flash banners, skyscrapers, and webmercials, among other forms. These advertisements contain audio and video content similar to television commercials. In fact, webmercials last from 10 to 45 seconds. KMGI Studios can produce webmercials that occupy the entire screen with audio and video content in such a way that these advertisements can be accessed with no download time, no matter which modem is used. Figure 11.1 is a print from one frame of a webmerical for Coca-Cola that KMGI created. Of course, the webmercial is in color, not black and white.

FIGURE 11.1 One frame of a "webmercial" created by KMGI. *Courtesy of KMGI.*

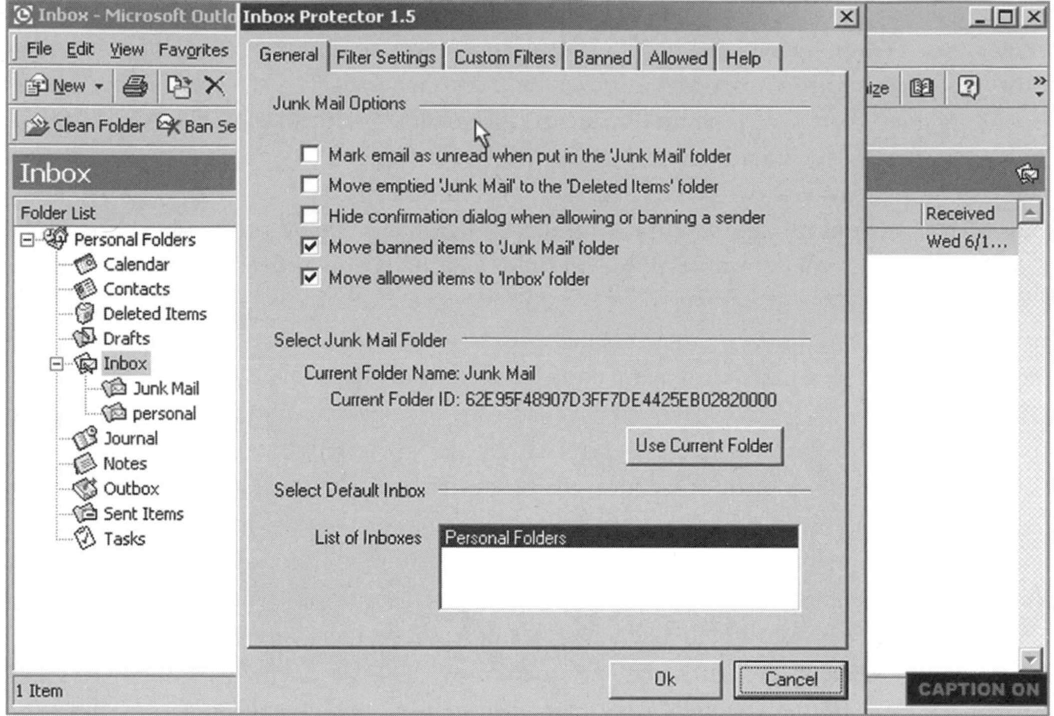

FIGURE 11.2 The last frame from a "WebPresentation" created by KMGI. *Courtesy of KMGI.*

KMGI also develops "WebPresentations" for clients so that they can demonstrate a product or provide a manual for a product online to a prospective buyer or current customer. WebPresentations employ audio and video content. Figure 11.2 is a print of the last frame from a WebPresentation for Inbox Protector, a software program. The WebPresentation is in color, not black and white.

CREATING EFFECTIVE INTERNET ADVERTISING

Before I discuss how to create effective advertisements for the Internet, I must reiterate that the Internet contains websites that contain pages. Users get to pages by links or connections. For instance, if a user goes to a bookseller's website, he or she will in all likelihood find several headings on the website's home page. These headings may include "Home," "Books," "Audio Books," and "Software," which allow the user to choose according to the product category he or she is interested in browsing. Smaller headings may include "Shopping Cart," "Order History," "User Profile," "Help," "About Us," "Browse Subjects," and "Affiliate's Network," which allow the user to learn the answer to practically any question or concern he or she may have about the company, its products, its services, and the consumer's ordering history. Each of these headings will bring the user to a different page. However, each page is designed similarly to another. For instance, the company's logo appears in the same typeface, type size, color, and position on every page. The navigation bar contains the same headings in the same typeface and type size. The basic page design is consistent from one page to another. The reason for the consistency is simple: the firm desires a website that is user friendly and, concurrently, builds brand equity. In short, the user can access any page without any trouble, and the pages are easy to understand.

Building an effective website may not be easy. However, it may be easier if the following points are kept in mind:

1. Identify the users or prospects the company wishes to reach. Try to learn as much as you possibly can about them.
2. Identify the website's purpose. Make sure that the purpose is based on a sound business or marketing plan. In short, the website should focus on a specific objective.
3. Make certain that the website's purpose relates well to the intended prospects' needs or desires.
4. The website should have few links or connections that take users to other pages. You do not wish to possibly lose prospects.
5. The website should contain pages that are consistent in design, much like a newspaper's pages or a magazine's pages.
6. The website should contain enough headings for pages so as to answer any question or concern the user may have, such as an explanation of a guarantee, shipping costs, return policies, refund policies, security, and ordering.

In addition to these points, the following should be kept in mind about the website's content:

1. The website should be easy to navigate. In fact, the website's structure should be based on what the prospects wish or desire, not on the company's needs.
2. The website's pages should be simple in design and should be easy to use. Prospects are interested in achieving a particular objective, not learning that a company's website has features and links or connections that are not relevant to them.
3. The website's pages should download quickly. If it takes longer than three to five seconds for a page to download, some prospects will leave.
4. The website should have an appropriate width so that its contents fit most screens.
5. The website's language should be precise, easy to understand, and concise. It should not have more than one or two brief paragraphs of copy because prospective consumers may not wish to read lots of copy. Such activity takes time, and prospects' time is valuable.[19]

Creating advertisements for the Internet should be based on objectives. Basically, the purpose of the advertisement must be identified before the advertisement is created. Remember, less than 1 percent of all Internet advertisements are clicked, according to eMarketer.[20] If you wish to have your advertisement seen, you must make sure that it is based on a sound objective and that it is directed to a specific target market. Furthermore, the kind of advertisement must be determined before the advertisement is created. If these have not been determined, then the advertisement will in all likelihood fail.

The size of the advertisement must be considered as well. The bigger the advertisement is, the greater the potential brand awareness. The use of audio and video content in such forms as webmercials or WebPresentations increases potential brand awareness even more. Frequency or how often an advertisement appears before a user or prospect effects potential brand awareness too and may actually encourage brand favorability and purchase of the product or service.

In addition to what has been mentioned, it is important to remember the following when creating advertisements for the Internet:

1. Gain the user's attention immediately. Try using one or two words for the headline and an arresting visual element to accomplish this, especially if the user needs to click on the advertisement to learn more. If a user needs to click, make sure that you use the words "Click here" on the advertisement.
2. Change the offer as often as possible. Users of the Internet expect change. Try not to disappoint them.
3. If a user has to go to a second page to learn more about the offer, keep the copy brief and the audio and video contents at a minimum, unless a studio such as KMGI has been hired to help produce the advertisement.
4. Emphasize a unique selling proposition in the copy.
5. Emphasize benefits, not features, in the copy.
6. Use abundant amounts of white space between blocks of copy.
7. Have no more than four or five lines of copy for any paragraph. In fact, try using one or two sentences as paragraphs.
8. Try to present some or all of the information in the copy in a bullet-type list.
9. Use testimonials or endorsements, if relevant, as part of the copy.
10. Include a "call to action" statement in the copy, if relevant.
11. Explain how the offer can be ordered.
12. Show how the offer can be ordered.
13. Offer a bonus to a user who has responded as intended.
14. Explain policies such as guarantees, warranties, returns, refunds, and shipping costs.
15. Explain the policy concerning security. Users need to be informed that their personal information is safe.
16. Try to choose colors for the advertisement that will complement the colors of the website, no matter which website the advertisement will be placed on.

And when creating e-mail advertisements, it is important to remember the following points:

1. Identify the sender of the e-mail advertisement.
2. Identify the receiver of the e-mail advertisement.
3. The e-mail advertisement should have a brief headline.
4. The e-mail advertisement should be personal. After all, a person has asked for it; it should be written to one person.
5. The language should be conversational and informal, unless the e-mail advertisement is for a company or its products or services and is being sent to an executive at another company.
6. The e-mail advertisement should be brief and to the point. Try not to have more than 250 words of copy.
7. Paragraphs should be brief—that is, each should not have more than four or five lines of copy.
8. Paragraphs should be separated by at least one line of white space.

9. Include copy that persuades, even if the e-mail advertisement is not about a product or service. An e-mail advertisement may attempt to persuade a person to go to a company's website, for instance.
10. The e-mail advertisement should concern one product, service, or subject, not several.
11. Include a "call to action" statement, even if the purpose of the e-mail advertisement is to direct the person to a company's website.

TERMS THAT MAY BE IMPORTANT

In order to create advertisements for the Internet, you may need to know some of the following:

broadband transmission—a single medium that can carry several signals at once, such as cable or DSL

click through—the process of a user clicking on an Internet advertisement, which brings the user to the advertiser's website

Flash—vector-graphic technology that is used for interactive animations

HTML (hypertext markup language)—a language that is used for formatting purposes. Browsers can easily translate this language.

hyperlink—a piece of text or a visual element on a website that when clicked takes a user to a new website or page

interstitial—an advertisement that appears while a user waits for a website or page to load

Java—advanced programming language for use with the World Wide Web. Java is more flexible and functional than HTML.

JavaScript—a scripting language that is actually a scaled-down version of Java. JavaScript can go into an HTML document and be interpreted by a browser.

pixel (picture element)—a single point in a graphic image. Pixels are arranged in rows and columns. VGA systems display 300,000 pixels. SVGA systems display 480,000 pixels.

RealAudio—used for streaming audio data over the World Wide Web

RealVideo—used for streaming video data over the Internet

server (hosting company)—provides space on its server (computer) to websites in exchange for a fee

Shockwave—technology that allows websites or pages to include multimedia, such as animation, audio, and video content

site map—a hierarchical visual display of a website's pages. A site map helps users navigate through a website by showing the user a diagram of the website's contents.

splash page—the page of a website that a user sees first. A splash page usually advertises a company or its products or services and usually consists of audio and video content.

streaming—transferring data continuously so that it can be processed as it is received

superstitial—an interactive advertisement that can be of any size on the screen. Usually, it features animation, audio, and video content.

URL (universal or uniform resource locator)—website address or domain name. This is created by registering the domain name through one of the numerous domain name registration sites.

The next chapter focuses on advertising in other media.

EXERCISES

1. Examine several pop-up ads for a particular advertiser and then create a Pop-up 1 that continues the idea for the advertiser.
2. Write and develop a Full Banner advertisement for a particular advertiser of your choice. Make sure that you think about the intended target market before you develop the ad.

NOTES

1. Radio Advertising Bureau, *Media Facts* (Irving, TX: Radio Advertising Bureau, 2002), p. 14.
2. AdAge.com, *Fact Pack: A Handy Guide to the Advertising Business: 2002 Edition*, *Advertising Age* (New York: AdAge.com, September 9, 2002; www.AdAge.com), p. 17.
3. eMarketer, *Online Advertising Update: A Review of Research Data Measuring the Growth and Effectiveness of Online Advertising in the U.S.* (New York: eMarketer, March 2002; www.emarketer.com), p. 9.
4. eMarketer, *Online Advertising Update*, pp. 13–18.
5. eMarketer, *Online Advertising Update*, pp. 21–29.
6. Creative Good, *White Paper One: Building a Great Customer Experience to Develop Brand, Increase Loyalty and Grow Revenue* (New York: Creative Good; www.creativegood.com), p. 2.
7. Creative Good, *White Paper One*, p. 3.
8. Creative Good, *White Paper One*, p. 4.
9. Creative Good, *White Paper One*, p. 5.
10. Creative Good, *White Paper One*, pp. 7–8.
11. Interactive Advertising Bureau, "Ad Unit Guidelines—Interactive Marketing Units" (New York: Interactive Advertising Bureau, 2002; www.iab.net).
12. Interactive Advertising Bureau.
13. Interactive Advertising Bureau.
14. Interactive Advertising Bureau.
15. eMarketer, *The E-mail Marketing Report: Executive Summary* (New York: eMarketer, 2001; www.emarketer.com), p. 6.
16. eMarketer, *The E-mail Marketing Report*, p. 7.
17. eMarketer, *The E-mail Marketing Report*, p. 9.
18. eMarketer, *The E-mail Marketing Report*, p. 9.
19. See Creative Good, *White Paper One*, p. 14.
20. eMarketer, *Online Advertising Update*, p. 33.

CHAPTER 12

Other Media Advertising

This chapter focuses on additional media in which advertisers try to reach intended target markets. The first medium we will examine is outdoor or transit advertising.

OUTDOOR OR TRANSIT ADVERTISING

In the United States, outdoor advertising started in the early 1800s. In the early 2000s, advertisers spent more than $5 billion in this medium.[1] Of this amount, outdoor displays or posters accounted for about 60 percent, transit accounted for about 17 percent, street furniture accounted for about 17 percent, and alternative outdoor formats accounted for about 6 percent.[2]

Outdoor Bulletins and Poster Panels

Bulletins usually are printed by computer and are located in high traffic areas. These are purchased for a specific period, normally for several months or longer. Most bulletins are 48 feet wide × 14 feet high or 36 feet wide × 10.6 feet high. These bulletins may have extensions, if needed.

Electronic spectacular displays usually are 60 feet wide × 20 feet high. These displays, which are generally in the heart of major cities, feature arresting messages that can be seen day or night.

Wall murals, which are generally in downtown business areas, are painted on sides of buildings and vary in size.

Posters, which are printed in sheets, may actually be identified by the number of sheets, such as *30-sheet posters*, which typically are found by primary and secondary highways or roads and are 25 feet wide × 12 feet high; *8-sheet posters*, which are 12 feet wide × 6 feet high; *wrapped posters*, which are 25 feet wide × 12 feet high; and *square-wrapped posters*, which are 25 feet wide × 24 feet high.[3]

Street Furniture

Advertising displays that can be found on the street are called *street furniture*. Such displays are positioned so that potential shoppers, whether walking, driving, or riding in some form of transit, can see the message. Street furniture includes bus bench panels, bus shelter panels, convenience store advertising, information kiosk panels, in-store advertising, newsstand or news-rack panels, one-sheet posters, pedestrian panels, public telephone panels, shopping mall advertising measures, and urban panels.[4]

Transit Displays

Transit displays actually are found on the outside of taxis, trailers, and trucks or positioned at transit stations or terminals and airports. Transit displays may appear on the inside and outside of buses. They include airport panels; rail panels; subway panels; taxi tops; truck-side advertising; vinyl-wrapped bus advertising; king panels, which are 144 inches wide × 30 inches high; super king panels, which are 240 inches wide × 30 inches high; and queen panels, which are 88 inches wide × 30 inches high.[5]

Alternative Outdoor Formats

Alternative outdoor formats vary in size and execution, depending on the advertiser's objective and message. Alternative outdoor formats include arena or stadium advertising, airborne advertising, marine advertising, beach advertising, golf course advertising, ski resort advertising, rest area advertising, gas pump advertising, and parking meter advertising, among other formats.[6]

Advertisers That Use Outdoor or Transit Advertising

Various advertisers use the outdoors as part of their advertising media. However, some of the advertisers that use this medium the most include retailers, hotel and motel chains, resorts, restaurants, automotive dealerships, insurance agents, and real estate agents, among others.

Advantages of Outdoor or Transit Advertising

There are several advantages of outdoor or transit advertising. These include the following:

1. Outdoor or transit advertising is precise, concise, and consequently effective.
2. Outdoor or transit advertising is generally lower in cost than any other advertising medium.
3. Outdoor or transit advertising captures attention primarily because of its size, color, and position.
4. Outdoor or transit advertising can appear for a brief or long period of time in strategic locations.
5. Exposure to outdoor or transit advertising may be frequent, depending on the viewer's method of transportation.
6. Outdoor or transit advertising may be seen by large and diverse groups of individuals.
7. Outdoor or transit advertising may be timely, depending on the viewer's location in proximity to the advertiser.
8. Outdoor or transit advertising generally reaches its intended target market.
9. Outdoor or transit advertising works well with other media.

Disadvantages of Outdoor or Transit Advertising

There are several disadvantages of outdoor or transit advertising. These include the following:

1. Outdoor or transit advertising does not allow the advertiser to communicate product features and benefits or the product's advantages over its competition.

2. Outdoor or transit locations or positions may be limited or not available when advertisers desire them.
3. Outdoor or transit advertising may not be seen as a result of inclement weather or other conditions.
4. Outdoor or transit advertising is not necessarily flexible, in that the message must be brief and the advertising must stay in place for a specified period of time.
5. Outdoor or transit advertising may reach people who are not necessarily interested in what is advertised.
6. Outdoor or transit formats may not exist in some markets. Not every city has mass transit, for instance.
7. Outdoor or transit advertising's effectiveness is difficult to measure.
8. Outdoor or transit advertising may be destroyed by inclement weather.

How to Write Outdoor or Transit Advertising

Outdoor or transit advertising can be creative. For instance, it can be humorous or intriguing, surprising or aesthetically pleasing, depending on the advertiser's objective or purpose and the target market. However, outdoor or transit advertising, primarily because its intended audience is mobile, must focus on one idea. The copy should concern the most important benefit. After all, this is the major reason for prospective consumers to be interested in the product or service. The design elements or graphics should be simple and relate well to the copy. You should not include too many design elements or graphics because these may cause the intended target market to work too hard in order to understand the message. Also, it may cause them to take their eyes off of what they are doing, which, if they happen to be driving, could cause an accident.

Outdoor or transit advertising can be filled with brilliant color. However, you should choose colors that contrast in both hue and value. Hue is the color's identity, such as red or blue. Value is the measure of lightness (tint) or darkness (shade). Colors that should be considered include blue and yellow, black and any color of light value, and white and any color of dark value. You should not use pastels.

What about typefaces or fonts? Typefaces or fonts should be easy to read from different distances. If the copy has few words, such as three or four, you may use all capital letters. If the copy has several words—more than four—you should use upper- and lowercase letters. In fact, upper- and lowercase letters are easier to read. Also, serif typefaces or fonts are easier to read than sans serif. Of course, you should not use compressed type; rather, you should leave space in between letters.[7] Refer to the following points whenever you have to create outdoor or transit advertising:

1. Use little copy—no more than seven words, if possible.
2. Use simple words. Simple words are easy to understand.
3. Use typefaces or fonts that are legible. Remember to leave space in between letters.
4. Use large illustrations or photographs or graphics. Outdoor or transit advertising usually has plenty of space for visual elements.
5. Use bold, contrasting colors, not pastels.
6. Identify the product by showing it, not just mentioning it by name.

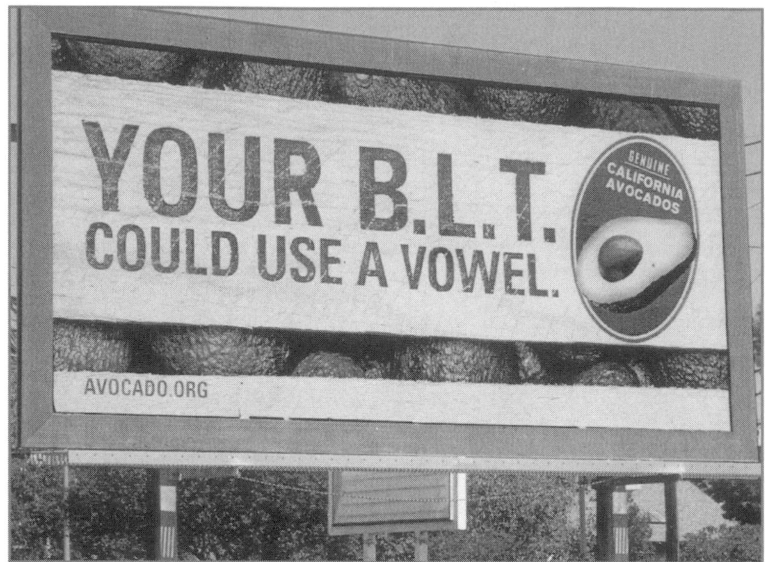

FIGURE 12.1 An outdoor display for California avocados. *Courtesy of Colby & Partners.*

FIGURE 12.2 A transit panel for California avocados. *Courtesy of Colby & Partners.*

FIGURE 12.3 A truck-side panel for California avocados. *Courtesy of Colby & Partners.*

Examples of Outdoor or Transit Advertising

Examine figures 12.1–12.3, which include an outdoor display, a transit panel, and a truck-side panel for California avocados. This outdoor or transit advertising campaign was created for the California Avocado Commission by Colby & Partners. The agency used radio and outdoor formats. Outdoor displays located close to supermarkets were used primarily to remind consumers that they love avocados. Box 12.1 is the agency's case study.

BOX 12.1 ***California Avocado Commission Case Study***

PROBLEM: Strong household penetration in core markets, but these consumers were largely composed of light and moderate users who were restricting consumption due to calorie and cost concerns.

CREATIVE STRATEGY: To remind consumers that California Avocados are a delicious, healthy indulgence you can't get enough of and assure them it's okay to treat themselves.

EXECUTIONAL ELEMENTS: The campaign reminds consumers of how irresistible California Avocados are. Outdoor prominently displays the avocado—a rich communication device and a reminder of taste. Radio utilizes popular cooking show formats to offer various usage suggestions to make listeners hungry and stimulate purchases.

MARKET RESULT: Light and moderate users have transitioned into heavy purchases. Crop value has steadily increased over time.

KEY INSIGHT: Although shoppers were only light to moderate users, they were very much in love with California Avocados. They restricted usage on a rational level, rather than giving in on an emotional one. All we had to do was remind them of their love and make them hungry to overcome their barriers.

Courtesy of Colby & Partners and the California Avocado Commission.

Examine figure 12.4 (next page), which is an outdoor display for Chick-fil-A created by Doug Rucker (creative director), David Ring (art director), and Gail Barlow (writer) of the Richards Group, Dallas. Box 12.2 is the agency's creative brief.

POINT-OF-PURCHASE ADVERTISING

The second medium we will examine is point-of-purchase (P-O-P) advertising. P-O-P started in the 1800s and has grown into a major medium. Advertisers invested $15.5 billion in this medium in 2001, when spending on advertising dropped as a result of the terrorist attacks on September 11. This amount accounted for 6.6 percent of the total dollars spent on advertising for the year. It is estimated that advertisers will spend almost $17 billion on P-O-P by 2004.[8]

The Point-of-Purchase Advertising Institute (POPAI), an organization that represents the P-O-P advertising industry, has studied the impact of this medium and has learned that in-store advertising captures a consumer's attention in convenience stores. In fact, based on interviews, 40 percent of the respondents recalled in-store advertising, especially when the advertisements were in the main shopping aisles.[9]

P-O-P advertising is used primarily because it benefits manufacturers or advertisers. For instance, P-O-P advertising not only keeps the advertiser's name in front of consumers, it advertises the product or brand usually within arm's reach and at eye level. It is also very good for promoting a sale or a sweepstakes.

P-O-P advertising benefits retailers, too. For instance, it increases consumers' interest in shopping, which, of course, increases retailers' revenues and profits. It may help retailers to utilize floor and shelf space more efficiently.

FIGURE 12.4 An outdoor display for Chick-fil-A. *Courtesy of The Richards Group.*

P-O-P advertising benefits consumers by providing helpful information about a company and its products. When it is used in conjunction with advertising appearing in or on other media, it reinforces the advertiser's message and may increase sales.

According to POPAI, P-O-P signs and displays have four functions: informing, reminding, persuading, and merchandising. Signs and displays inform consumers that a specific brand or a category of goods is available or on sale. P-O-P signs and displays can remind consumers of advertising that they have seen or heard in other media by reiterating a phrase from that advertising. Thus, P-O-P advertising reinforces the message and increases consumers' awareness. P-O-P signs and displays can persuade consumers to purchase a product by presenting its features and benefits, the reasons for buying it, and other information. P-O-P displays perform the last function by attracting consumers' attention to a particular product. They achieve this by isolating a great quantity of a product. In short, because the product is not necessarily on a store's shelves, other products do not surround it.[10]

Advantages of P-O-P Advertising

P-O-P advertising enjoys several advantages. These include the following:

1. P-O-P advertising helps retailers to inform consumers about products' availability and features.
2. P-O-P advertising is flexible, in that it uses different forms and these forms can be placed almost anywhere in stores.
3. P-O-P advertising can persuade members of a specific target market when they are ready to purchase.
4. P-O-P advertising has progressed technologically speaking, offering advertisers a variety of innovative forms to present a commercial message.
5. P-O-P advertising can be used to change or improve a store's image or direct store traffic.[11]

Disadvantages of P-O-P Advertising

P-O-P advertising has at least two disadvantages:

1. P-O-P advertising only reaches those consumers who are in proximity to it when they are shopping. It does not necessarily reach a large group of potential consumers.

2. P-O-P advertising does not influence consumers to patronize certain businesses; it only influences consumers to buy certain products or brands.

P-O-P advertising also suffers when retailers do not use it, and not every retailer that receives it from advertisers will use it. This is so for a variety of reasons, some of which include the fact that it may be too large or bulky for the store's aisles, it may use colors that do not complement the colors of the store, it may not be strong enough to display the product, or it may not generate enough income for the time and space it requires.

P-O-P Displays

Basically, P-O-P displays may be categorized as short-term promotional displays or permanent long-term displays. The former is for up to six months; the latter is for more than six months.[12] P-O-P displays include the following: cart advertising, which are signs that fit on shopping carts; dump bins, which are bins that usually contain graphics as well as hold the samples of the product; end-of-aisle displays;

BOX 12.2 ***The Richards Group Creative Brief–Chick-fil-A***

Warning: People don't like ads. People don't trust ads. People don't remember ads. How do we make sure this one will be different?

WHY ARE WE ADVERTISING?

To position the Chick-fil-A chicken sandwich as the best alternative to other fast food sandwiches and remind people how much they like them.

WHOM ARE WE TALKING TO?

Adults, 18–49, who are infrequent or nonusers of Chick-fil-A. They are primarily women, college graduates, in white-collar jobs. They associate chicken with a healthy lifestyle and believe that quality food is better for you and worth the money.

WHAT DO THEY CURRENTLY THINK?

"Unless I'm in the mall, I just don't think of Chick-fil-A. I guess they're pretty good, but I haven't been there in a long time."

WHAT WOULD WE LIKE THEM TO THINK?

"I'd rather have a chicken sandwich than a hamburger. And Chick-fil-A makes the best one."

WHAT IS THE SINGLE MOST PERSUASIVE IDEA WE CAN CONVEY?

Every other sandwich is second-rate.

WHY SHOULD THEY BELIEVE IT?

Chick-fil-A is simple, wholesome and doesn't take itself too seriously.

ARE THERE ANY CREATIVE GUIDELINES?

14 × 48 outdoor.

Courtesy of The Richards Group.

floor stands, which are displays that stand upright; mobiles or banners, which are signs that hang from ceilings; door or window signs, which identify or advertise businesses or brands; small displays that will fit on cash registers, counters, and shelves; signs that are illuminated; displays that move; kiosks that dispense coupons or information; and signs that attach to shelves, among others.[13]

How to Write P-O-P Advertising

Use the following points whenever you have to write advertising for a point-of-purchase sign or display:

1. The sign or display should capture consumers' attention. For instance, graphics and colors that are used in the advertiser's other advertising, especially print, should be considered in order to trigger or remind consumers of something they saw or heard in a previous advertisement or commercial.
2. Focus on one objective. Some signs and displays attempt to do too much. Identify the major objective or purpose of the sign or display and then create the appropriate message. In many instances, you need only a brief headline or a brief headline and subhead. If the sign or display concerns a sweepstakes, address the sweepstakes but let a tear-off explain the details and rules.
3. The client's name or brand should be clear. In fact, try not to allow the consumer to forget the name or brand by making it the heart of the message.
4. Present the major feature or benefit in a brief easy-to-understand sentence. In short, you do not wish for consumers to have to read the offer twice in order to understand it; they will not bother.
5. If relevant, make certain that an area exists in the sign or display for the price to be included by the retailer.[14]

FIGURE 12.5 A point-of-purchase display for Classico. *Courtesy of Interesting Displays & Ideas.*

If possible, make certain that the sign or display is designed so that it is the appropriate size and type, it complements the store's decor, it can be assembled or used easily and quickly by the retailer, it is delivered when needed, it is tied to a current advertising campaign, and it is appealing and informative.[15] Examine figure 12.5, which is a photograph of a nice and simple display for Classico.

YELLOW PAGES ADVERTISING

The third medium we will examine is *Yellow Pages* advertising. The first *Yellow Pages* directory was published in the late 1800s. For years, until AT&T was divested in 1984, the telephone company published the major *Yellow Pages* directories. However, more than 200 companies publish more than 6,000 different *Yellow Pages* directories today. In the early 2000s, advertisers spent more than $13 billion in this medium.[16] Local advertisers spent more than $11 billion, and regional and national advertisers spent more than $2 billion.[17] The reason advertisers are interested in the *Yellow Pages* is because 76 percent of the adults in the United States use the medium at least once a month and 56 percent use it at least once a week.[18]

Types of Yellow Pages *Directories*

Publishers that are not associated with telephone companies publish directories that are aimed at specific targets. These include area-wide or overlap directories, suburban or neighborhood directories, special interest or niche directories, business-to-business directories, and the electronic *Yellow Pages*, which are online versions of the printed directories.[19]

Directories typically provide the names, addresses, and telephone numbers of businesses that have telephone numbers and are located in the geographic areas covered by the directories. Headings or groupings are arranged alphabetically. There are more than 4,000 headings or groupings under which businesses may choose to be listed. Generally, headings pertain to professions, such as attorneys or podiatrists; products, such as books or paint; services, such as automobile repair and service or kitchen remodeling; or types of businesses, such as motels or restaurants. Directories usually have in-column advertisements in which businesses may have messages under their listings. They also have display advertisements, which are similar to other print advertisements in that they may contain headlines, body copy, and illustrations.[20]

Advantages of the Yellow Pages

The *Yellow Pages* has several advantages. These include the following:

1. Practically every home and every business has at least one *Yellow Pages*.
2. Almost every adult living in the United States uses the *Yellow Pages* at least once a month.
3. The *Yellow Pages* generally is used when individuals intend to spend money.
4. Advertisements in the *Yellow Pages* appeal to individuals who have particular needs to fill.
5. An advertisement in the *Yellow Pages* exists for the entire year; thus, potentially many may see it.
6. An advertisement in the *Yellow Pages* may create a positive image of the business in a consumer's mind even if she or he has never heard of the business.
7. An advertisement in the *Yellow Pages* is paid for each month, not all at one time.

Disadvantages of the Yellow Pages

The *Yellow Pages* has several disadvantages. These include the following:

1. The advertiser must advertise using the same message for an entire year.
2. The advertiser's advertisement is positioned with other advertisements for the same profession, product, service, or type of business. Thus, potential consumers will be exposed to the advertiser's competitors' advertisements.
3. The advertiser's ad may be hidden by larger advertisements, depending on the advertisement's size.
4. Slightly more than 50 percent of the adults in the United States refer to the *Yellow Pages* in a typical week. Many of these adults will not be searching for an advertiser's advertisement.

Thus, the *Yellow Pages* may not reach the intended target market and consequently may not be the right medium for an advertiser.
5. Advertisements in the *Yellow Pages* do not necessarily create awareness. Other advertisements in other media must be used to create awareness of a business or product in a consumer's mind.
6. The *Yellow Pages* may not be readily available outside the home. Thus, consumers may not refer to it when they are outside the home and ready to buy.
7. Advertisements for the *Yellow Pages* must be purchased and created in advance of the publication date, which is once a year. Timely changes in advertisements as a result of trends in markets are impossible to implement once the date nears or passes.
8. The *Yellow Pages* has competition. Publishers not affiliated with telephone companies are printing *Yellow Pages*–type directories. Other companies are offering similar information on the Web.

How to Write Advertisements for the Yellow Pages

Creating advertisements for the *Yellow Pages* is similar to creating advertisements for other print media. In essence, the advertiser must decide on the objective or purpose of the advertising; the target market—specifically, what it desires or needs; and the advertising message. Of course, the advertiser must consider the tone and the approach of the advertising message as well as the size. Generally, the latter is based on the advertiser's competition and their advertisements in the *Yellow Pages*, as well as the advertiser's advertising budget. After these issues are considered, the advertiser must create the advertisement.

SIZE OF THE ADVERTISEMENT There is a direct relationship between the size of the advertisement and selectivity. In short, the larger the advertisement, the more effective it is. Indeed, consumers respond more often to large advertisements in the *Yellow Pages*. According to the Advertising Research Corporation, the advertisement's placement under a heading can affect its selection as well. For instance, large advertisements placed near the heading will usually enjoy more selections than large advertisements that are placed away from the heading.[21]

HEADLINES Headlines used in advertisements that appear in the *Yellow Pages* should perform the following:

1. Capture the reader's attention. Using a bold statement or asking a question can accomplish this.
2. Employ a unique selling proposition, if possible, about the advertiser's business. A unique selling proposition will separate the advertiser from the competition, which is important.

Many advertisers that place display advertisements in the *Yellow Pages* merely use the names of their businesses for their headlines. This practice is usually a mistake unless the advertisers are well established and well known. A headline should attract attention and actually encourage consumers to read more about the business. For instance, a headline may provide a reason that the business is of interest to the consumer, or it may address the consumer's needs by mentioning what the business does.

When writing a headline for an advertisement that will appear in the *Yellow Pages*, make certain that it relates to the target market's needs or expectations. Such will inform consumers that the advertiser understands them and what they are interested in or need. As a result, a bridge will link the advertiser to the target market.

BODY COPY Body copy should provide the consumer with information, including features and benefits, about the profession, product, service, or business. If you adhere to the following guidelines, your body copy should succeed:

1. Limit the amount of words in your body copy. In addition to being clear and easy to understand, body copy should be brief.
2. Focus on the benefits that the profession, product, service, or business offers the consumer. Benefits work, even in the *Yellow Pages*.
3. If appropriate, emphasize areas of expertise or specific brand names in the body copy. For instance, if the advertiser repairs cars, inform consumers about the types of repairs performed as well as the models of cars serviced.
4. Emphasize information that the advertiser's competitors have overlooked. This information will help the advertiser appear different or unique from the competition.
5. Include essential information, such as the address or location of the business, hours of operation, days open, credit cards accepted, parking spaces or lots available, and website, among other information.
6. Emphasize the telephone number; try putting a small rectangular box around it or printing it in large, bold numerals. Some advertisers will print it in a different color, whereas other advertisers will put some graphics or artwork around it.
7. The advertiser may wish to emphasize the location of the business by including a small box with two lines that intersect. These lines represent streets and are identified as such. A small square representing the business would appear near one of the lines. This small box informs consumers where the business is located, and it is usually better than just a street address and name.

GRAPHICS AND LOGOS Graphics, such as borders and illustrations, and logos provide important information and concurrently attract a consumer's attention. In particular, borders can help establish a mood for the advertisement and the advertiser. If borders are bold, the advertisement appears separated from other advertisements on the page, which may be desired by the advertiser. However, borders should not be so bold that they overwhelm the other elements within the advertisement. If borders are broken by some graphics element, such as an illustration, the advertisement will attract attention. Before a decision about breaking a border is reached, it should be based on the fact that the graphics element is relevant to the advertising message and is appropriate for the advertisement and the image the advertiser wishes for consumers to have. Otherwise, the graphics element may appear out of place and even cause consumers to look at other advertisements on the page. In short, graphics elements, such as illustrations, should cause the consumer's eyes to look at the advertiser's message, not a competitor's advertisement.

Graphics elements, including illustrations, should be unique or different from those used by the advertiser's competitors. These elements should be large and appealing and should represent the products or brands that are mentioned. In fact, if an illustration representing a product is done well, it may eliminate the need for mentioning the product by name in the copy. Finally, the logo, which is the name of

BOX 12.3 ***An Advertisement for the* Yellow Pages**

TWO-HOUR

TV Repair Co.

- **All Makes and Models**
- **Trained Professionals**
- **Warranty on Service**

345 ROOSEVELT ST.
(One block from the city sq.)
351-4545

the advertiser's business, should be distinctive in design and positioned in the advertisement so that it is easy to read.

DESIGN An advertisement for the *Yellow Pages* should be designed so that the elements are positioned in such a manner that the consumer's eyes move easily from one component to another without the consumer losing concentration. Basically, when designing such an advertisement, it is important to remember that the elements should be positioned so that the consumer's eyes move toward the advertiser's telephone number. In order to achieve this logical flow, refer to the following:

1. The size of the type may be varied. That is, it may be bold, medium, and light. It may be large and small. Such will maintain the consumer's interest.
2. Do not use typefaces or fonts that are ornate or difficult to read, especially for the body copy.
3. If appropriate, use reverse type for the advertiser's name and telephone number to make either or both stand out.
4. Make sure that the advertisement is uncluttered. Space between elements within the advertisement lends emphasis to the elements and the advertisement overall. Space also provides a "clean" appearance, which should be desired.
5. One additional color can increase an advertisement's visibility. Try using color to attract the consumer's attention and stimulate interest. Color can enhance the image that the consumer has of the advertiser, especially if the advertisement is the only one on the page that has color.[22]

Examine box 12.3. This advertisement is representative of those that appear in the *Yellow Pages*. Notice the brief copy as well as the abundant space between the elements within the advertisement.

The *Yellow Pages* offers advertisers the opportunity to advertise for a long time in a widely used medium; however, their ads must be created well in order to be effective. We look at public relations and corporate advertising in the next chapter.

EXERCISES

1. Write the copy for an outdoor poster that promotes Burger King. Emphasize the name more than the restaurant's menu items. You will need to write a brief headline and subhead. The subhead may act as the copy because few words should appear on an outdoor poster. You may wish to identify what will be in your illustration—that is, if you have an illustration.
2. Develop a point-of-purchase display that will be used in grocery stores to remind consumers to buy Quaker Oats cereal. You will need to develop the theme, write the copy, and create the artwork. Remember that a P-O-P display must contain a complete sales message, not just offer the product.
3. Create a small-space *Yellow Pages* ad for L-L-Laundry. The ad should include an illustration, a small map that shows where the business is located, and copy. The business is located on the corners of Thompson Road and 15th Street. The laundry is unique because it can have clothes clean in 15 minutes. The store's hours are 6 A.M. to 11 P.M., Monday–Saturday. It is closed on Sundays. The store's telephone number is 456-1000.
4. Create a display ad for the *Yellow Pages* of your local telephone directory. Write the copy on a copy sheet. Create a layout that includes at least one piece of art. You may use lines to indicate lines of type for your copy, or you may type the copy on the layout. The size of your ad should be 4 × 5 inches. The company is the following:
   - A-One Car Service offers complete service on all foreign and domestic cars. This includes service on the engine, wheel alignment, brakes, tires, automatic transmission, air conditioning, electrical system, and exhaust system. It also provides complete lubrication, complete tune-up, safety check, and computer balancing. The telephone number is 456-2000; the address is 4100 North Broadway. The owner is "Doc" Wheeler.

NOTES

1. AdAge.com, *Fact Pack: A Handy Guide to the Advertising Business: 2002 Edition*, *Advertising Age* (New York: AdAge.com, September 9, 2002; www.AdAge.com), p. 17.
2. Outdoor Advertising Association of America, Inc., *Basic Facts about the Outdoor Advertising Industry* (Washington, DC: Outdoor Advertising Association of America, Inc., n.d.), p. 5.
3. Outdoor Advertising Association of America, *Basic Facts about the Outdoor Advertising Industry*, pp. 5–6.
4. Outdoor Advertising Association of America, *Basic Facts about the Outdoor Advertising Industry*, p. 7.
5. Outdoor Advertising Association of America, *Basic Facts about the Outdoor Advertising Industry*, p. 8.
6. Outdoor Advertising Association of America, *Basic Facts about the Outdoor Advertising Industry*, p. 9.
7. See Outdoor Advertising Association of America, *Creating Award Winning Outdoor: A Guide for Designing Effective Advertising* (Washington, DC: Outdoor Advertising Association of America, 2000).
8. Laurie Najjar and Lyndsey Erwin, "The Fourth Annual Top POP Buyers Report," *Point of Purchase*, August 2002: pp. 16–20.
9. Dick Blatt, "In-Store Ads Compel Attention: Study Shows That In-Store Ads Disseminate Key Message in Convenience Stores," *Snack Food and Wholesale Bakery*, Vol. 91, No. 8 (August 2002): p. 40.

10. Point-of-Purchase Advertising Institute, *P/O/P: The Last Word in Advertising* (Washington, DC: Point-of-Purchase Advertising Institute, n.d.), pp. 4–5.
11. See Point-of-Purchase Advertising Institute, "The Point-of-Purchase Advertising Industry" (Washington, DC: Point-of-Purchase Advertising Institute, n.d.; www.popai.com).
12. Point-of-Purchase Advertising Institute, *The Point-of-Purchase Advertising Institute's Retailer Guide to Maximizing In-Store Advertising Effectiveness* (Washington, DC: Point-of-Purchase Advertising Institute, 1999), p. 4.
13. Point-of-Purchase Advertising Institute, *The Point-of-Purchase Advertising Institute's Retailer Guide to Maximizing In-Store Advertising Effectiveness*, pp. 5–7.
14. See Don E. Schultz, *Essentials of Advertising Strategy* (Chicago: Crain Books, 1981), p. 113.
15. See Terence A. Shimp, *Advertising and Promotion: Supplemental Aspects of Integrated Marketing Communications* (Orlando, FL: Harcourt, Inc., 2000), pp. 249–250.
16. Yellow Pages Publishers Association, *Yellow Pages Facts and Media Guide: 2001* (Troy, MI: Yellow Pages Publishers Association, 2001; www.yppa.com), pp. 4–6.
17. Yellow Pages Publishers Association, *Yellow Pages Facts and Media Guide*, p. 5.
18. Yellow Pages Publishers Association, *Yellow Pages Facts and Media Guide*, p. 8.
19. Yellow Pages Publishers Association, *Yellow Pages Facts and Media Guide*, p. 6.
20. Joel J. Davis, *Understanding Yellow Pages* (Troy, MI: Yellow Pages Publishers Association, 1998), p. 5.
21. Davis, *Understanding Yellow Pages*, p. 22.
22. See Davis, *Understanding Yellow Pages*, pp. 22–24; Yellow Pages Publishers Association, *Yellow Pages Facts and Media Guide*, pp. 19–20; Yellow Pages Publishers Association, "Section IV: Creating Yellow Pages Advertising" (Troy, MI: Yellow Pages Publishers Association, n.d.; www.yppa-currentadissues.org), pp. 1–4.

CHAPTER 13

Public Relations and Corporate Advertising

Public relations is not normally performed by advertising agencies or advertising personnel; however, advertising personnel are asked from time to time to perform some types of public relations on behalf of a client. Therefore, I will discuss some of the public relations tools that an advertising copywriter may be asked to wield on occasion.

Public relations practitioners attempt to create goodwill between a client and the public. According to the Public Relations Society of America, "Public relations helps an organization and its publics adapt mutually to each other."[1] Public relations began in the early 1900s, when people like Ivy Lee and Edward Bernays wrote publicity for clients primarily for the purpose of shaping public opinion. Today, more than 125,000 people work in public relations. In 2001, public relations firms in the United States earned almost $4 billion.[2]

Public relations practitioners work for various entities, including associations, businesses, colleges, foundations, government agencies, hospitals, religious institutions, schools, unions, and universities. These practitioners help these entities achieve their goals by communicating to different audiences, such as customers, employees, members of the federal government, members of local and state governments, and other entities. In order to be successful, practitioners must understand their client's various audiences and be able to communicate information for their client. Such information may be a news release about an improved or new product, information regarding a new plant, or an advertorial about the client's position toward an issue.

According to the Public Relations Society of America, public relations encompasses the following:

- Anticipating, analyzing, and interpreting public opinion, attitudes, and issues that might impact, for good or ill, the operations and plans of the organization.
- Counseling management at all levels in the organization with regard to policy decisions, courses of action, and communications, taking into account their public ramifications and the organization's social or citizenship responsibilities.

- Researching, conducting, and evaluating, on a continuing basis, programs of action and communication to achieve the informed public understanding necessary to the success of an organization's aims. These may include marketing; finances; fund-raising; employee, community, or government relations; and other programs.
- Planning and implementing the organization's efforts to influence or change public policy. This may involve setting objectives, planning, budgeting, recruiting and training staff, developing facilities—in short, managing the resources needed to perform all of the above.[3]

Public relations practitioners realize that audiences or publics change. Consequently, public relations practitioners must understand what caused this change and address it properly and effectively, especially if the client caused the change.

HOW PUBLIC RELATIONS DIFFERS FROM ADVERTISING

Public relations firms use various public relations communications tools to present information about their clients. These communications tools are sent to editors and other employees of the media in hopes that they will use the information. Only a few public relations communications tools are charged fees by the media. In contrast, advertising agencies, on behalf of their clients, purchase space and airtime in media for the advertisements and commercials they have produced. The advertisements and commercials appear as they were created, with no changes whatsoever. This is not necessarily true of public relations communications tools. For instance, a medium's employee may edit a news release or some other public relations communications tool—that is, if the employee accepts it at all—before it appears in the medium.

Even though the news release or some other public relations communications tool may be edited, if it is published or used, it will tend to be more credible, primarily because it appears as a story written by a journalist or presented by a commentator, not as an advertisement or commercial. However, advertisers have more control over the advertisements or commercials that are produced for them by their advertising agencies. The messages will not be changed or edited by media personnel. Of course, the advertisers are paying for the space or airtime, which may not be the case for a public relations communications tool.

ADVANTAGES OF PUBLIC RELATIONS

Public relations enjoys several advantages. These include the following:

1. Public relations enjoys credibility. This was mentioned earlier. Basically, public relations communications tools tend to be believed primarily because these tools do not necessarily appear as advertisements, especially the tools that appear as stories or articles in the media. In short, readers, listeners, and viewers assume that the media's journalists have gathered the information and written the stories or articles, not a public relations practitioner.
2. Public relations communications tools typically enjoy low cost. These tools do not cost as much as advertisements or commercials to produce. Nor do these tools cost a lot when they appear in the media, especially the tools that are sent to media personnel for consideration. In fact, only a few forms of public relations tools appear in media as a result of the client paying a fee.
3. Public relations tools do not necessarily compete with other public relations tools, primarily

because these communications usually appear as stories or articles. Unfortunately, advertisements and commercials have to compete with other advertisements and commercials in the media.

4. Public relations communications tools can be effective in developing a positive image in the minds of various publics for a product, service, or whatever else a client wishes to address.

DISADVANTAGES OF PUBLIC RELATIONS

Public relations has a few disadvantages, too. These include the following:

1. Public relations communications tools may not appear in media, especially the tools that are merely sent to media personnel for consideration.
2. Public relations communications tools may be read, seen, or heard, but members of the intended public may not link the messages to the client.
3. Public relations communications tools may fail to achieve the objective for which they were created. If this is the case, the client may never know it, primarily because the effectiveness of public relations is difficult to measure.
4. Public relations communications tools usually have a brief life. In fact, in order for a public relations tool to have any impact, it must be changed frequently with new information.
5. Public relations may have difficulty changing an intended public's perception of a product, service, or whatever else a client addresses. Generally, changing someone's perception of something takes a multitude of communications tools over a long period. Public relations communications tools may not be able to achieve this.

TOOLS OF PUBLIC RELATIONS

Public relations practitioners use various kinds of communications tools to present information to various publics. Some of the more popular include annual reports, audiovisual materials, brochures, corporate or institutional advertisements, exhibits, feature articles, house advertisements, letters, media or press kits, news or press releases, newsletters, photographs, and video news releases, among others. Let us examine some of these in depth:

Annual reports are about companies and are directed to stockholders, prospective stockholders, and other audiences. An annual report provides information about a company, such as its key personnel, its history, its activities, and its financial situation. The annual report may be a company's most important form of communication. Consequently, a company may spend a considerable amount of money on the content and appearance of this document.

Audiovisual materials may be used to present information about companies. Usually, these are very well produced, primarily to enhance the image that various publics have of the companies.

Brochures are typically about companies or their products or services and are directed to specific external publics, such as customers, dealers, and suppliers. Brochures, unlike newsletters, are not published periodically. Usually, a brochure is published for a specific purpose, such as to introduce a new company, association, or organization. Therefore, a brochure must be well designed in order to attract attention and well written so that a reader easily understands the message.

Corporate or institutional advertisements are used when companies wish to present public relations messages without the interference of media employees. These advertisements are nonproduct advertisements and generally serve to increase awareness of companies and enhance companies' images.

Exhibits may be used to present the history of the company or discuss a new product. They may even explain how a company's product is manufactured. Exhibits may be for fairs or trade shows. Some are designed exclusively for elementary schools, high schools, community colleges, and universities.

Feature articles are used to discuss the history of a product or a company or to present information as to how a product should be used or how a product or company has changed as a result of technological innovations. Of course, feature articles can concern other topics.

House advertisements typically are displayed in a company's media and concern something that the company deems important.

Letters generally concern a company and its policies, a company's position toward an issue, or a company's response to a question or concern. Of course, other topics may be discussed. Letters can be very effective, especially if they are well written. Indeed, the message in a letter can be tailored to the individual to whom it is being sent. Although a letter can be personal, it should not be too personal. Letters usually represent someone at a company, not a personal acquaintance; consequently, they should appear professional.

Media or press kits are created for special events, such as press conferences. Usually, media or press kits include a fact sheet about the event, a list of participants and their biographies, a schedule of the event's activities, a news story or article about the event, a photograph of the event or the participants, and other information.

News or press releases are popular. In fact, the news or press release is the most popular public relations communications tool. Generally, news or press releases are written in the form of news stories and typically concern a new product, a new service, a newly promoted employee, the opening of a new plant, the closing of an old plant, or some other timely topic. I will discuss this tool in depth later in the chapter.

Newsletters may be for internal publics, such as workers, or for external publics, such as customers. Newsletters are publications that contain articles about the company, employees, policies, products, and services, among other information. A newsletter may be a single sheet or a multipage, full-color publication, depending on its purpose, its audience, and the amount of money its sponsor has allocated for its production. Many newsletters are directed at internal audiences, such as employees. Writers must understand who these audiences are and consequently write with them in mind.

Photographs may be used with a news or press release, feature article, or some other public relations communications tool, or they may be sent with captions that identify what or who is shown. Sometimes media personnel request photographs, especially when they are writing stories about companies, products, services, or personnel.

Video news releases may be used because the messages are seen as well as heard. A video news release can be a brief news story produced on videotape and then distributed locally, or it can be a lengthy feature produced on film and then distributed nationally. If a broadcast station uses a video news release, it is generally used during a news broadcast. In short, it has excellent credibility because the viewer assumes that the broadcast journalists produced it. However, video news releases may be expensive to produce, especially those produced on film and distributed nationally. And, like news or press releases, video news releases may not be used whatsoever by media personnel. To offset some of the expense of producing a broadcast commercial, a company will allow part of its video news release, if relevant, to be incorporated, thus decreasing the amount of footage needed for producing its broadcast commercial.

Writing the News or Press Release

As mentioned, the news or press release is one of the most popular communications tools used by public relations practitioners. Whenever an advertising copywriter is given the task of writing one of these for a client, the copywriter must remember that a release should be written in the form of a news story. That is, it should follow a particular journalistic style and emphasize something that an editor will find newsworthy. This "something" will have to contain one or more news values, such as conflict, impact, prominence, proximity, timeliness, and unusualness.

Let us examine each of these. *Conflict* or a clash between individuals, businesses, or groups of individuals generally is newsworthy, especially if the individuals, businesses, or groups of individuals are well known. *Impact* applies to any event that affects individuals' lives, even if the event involves only a few individuals. *Prominence* refers to how well known or revered a person is, whether the person happens to be a business executive, a celebrity, or a politician. *Proximity* refers to where an event occurs. If the event is not close to an editor's medium's market, the editor will not necessarily consider the event newsworthy to the medium's readers, listeners, or viewers. *Timeliness* refers to when the event occurred. If an event occurred last month, for instance, it will not necessarily be considered newsworthy. The *unusual*, whether it is an unusual event or an individual doing something out of the ordinary, generally is newsworthy.

In addition, a news or press release should identify who, what, when, where, why, and how, if relevant. *Who* is the person or persons related to the story. *What* is the major event of the story. *When* is the time and date the event will occur or occurred. *Where* is the place or location of the event. *Why* is the reason or explanation for the event's occurrence. *How* is the explanation of the planning and staging of the event.

Even though an advertising copywriter may be aware of news values and incorporate one or more in a news or press release, there is no assurance that an editor will use it. In fact, editors do not use many, if not most, of the releases they receive. One reason is that they receive too many to use. There is only so much space or airtime; it is impossible for editors to use every release they receive. Another reason is that not every release is newsworthy to the editor's medium's market. Still another reason is that editors may have a bias against using releases; after all, many releases may not be anything other than advertisements for products or companies, and editors are not interested in providing free space or airtime to advertisers. Consequently, every editor who receives a copy of an advertising copywriter's news or press release may not use it. However, if the advertising copywriter writes the release in the inverted pyramid style, the release stands a better chance of at least being considered.

The inverted pyramid style, which journalists use, means that the most important information is presented first. The editor should be able to identify the major points of the release by reading the lead or first sentence. In fact, this first sentence may be the first paragraph. The remaining information should be presented in descending order of importance. This means that the next most important piece of information is presented in the next sentence or next paragraph. The least important information is presented last. The reason the inverted pyramid style is used is because a story may have to be cut to fit the space that has been allotted for it. If the story is cut from the bottom up, the least important information is deleted. The most important information is saved. Another reason the inverted pyramid style is used is because it allows readers to grasp the major points of the story without having to read every paragraph, especially those toward the end of the story.

Generally, news or press releases should be typed or printed on the company's stationery or letterhead or with a heading that includes the company's name, address, telephone number, fax number, and website information. At the top of the first page, "NEWS RELEASE" should be typed in uppercase letters. This lets an editor know immediately what the information is. In addition, a name and telephone number of a person who can be contacted should be typed. The person should be available to answer any questions or provide additional information. The release should specify whether it is immediate, such as "FOR IMMEDIATE RELEASE," or for a later date, such as "FOR RELEASE ON NOVEMBER 15, 20—." Sometimes it may be necessary to put "FOR RELEASE AFTER NOVEMBER 15, 20—." A headline or slug line should also be typed at the top of the first page. The headline or slug line should identify what the news or press release concerns. In many instances, headlines will include the name of the company—that is, if it is relevant.

At the beginning of the lead or first paragraph, a "dateline" that includes the city from which the information originated and the date should be typed. The name of the city is typed in uppercase letters, followed by the state usually in uppercase letters. The date follows and is put in parentheses. The date should be the date the release arrives at the media, not necessarily the date the release was actually typed. For example, "NEW YORK, NY (December 1, 20—)—Henderson Communications President William Hart." As mentioned, the information in the body of the news or press release should be presented in order of importance, with the most important information at the beginning, then the next most important information, and then the next, until the least important information is near the end.

Examine box 13.1, which concerns Wendy's Southwest Chicken Caesar entrée salad. This press release begins with the name, telephone number, and e-mail address of the person to contact if additional information is desired, and then it presents a relevant headline and subhead that an editor may use. The first and second paragraphs present the most important information, basically announcing the "new Southwest Chicken Caesar entrée" that is available at Wendy's. Additional information about the salad is presented in descending order of importance in the paragraphs that follow. The last paragraph concerns the company.

This press release was available at the company's website. Unfortunately, a sans serif typeface was used. The typeface should have been a serif, such as Times New Roman, because of the length. Furthermore, if you desire to have editors use your press releases, you need to use a typeface that they are familiar with or use.

Look at box 13.2, which concerns Frito-Lay. If this press release had been sent to media personnel, the writer would have included a contact name and an address and telephone number, not just the company's name and the words "Press Release." However, this press release was for the company's website. Consequently, readers had to be at the company's website in order to read it; there was no need for a contact name, address, or telephone number because the readers could contact the company through the website's "Contact" icon.

On the other hand, if it had been sent to media personnel, the copywriters probably would have begun the press release differently. For instance, to editors the company's name is not necessarily as important as the main subject, the "line of snacks." Thus, the main subject and the company's name likely would have been transposed. Some writers would have started the story with information about the tests that were done in four key markets. After all, this is the reason for the company launching the "line of snacks."

BOX 13.1 ***Press Release–Wendy's***

Contact: Bob Bertini
Wendy's International, Inc.
614/764-3327
Bob_Bertini@wendys.com

FRESH AND SPICY FLAVORS SERVED UP WITH INTRODUCTION OF WENDY'S NEW SOUTHWEST CHICKEN CAESAR SALAD

Wendy's Offering Three Lighter Dressing Alternatives

DUBLIN, Ohio, June 2, 2003—Call it "Caesar with a kick."

A new Southwest Chicken Caesar entrée salad is now available at Wendy's Restaurants in the U.S. and Canada.

The Company rolled out the latest addition to the successful Garden Sensations™ salad line in May, and now has achieved full distribution.

The launch is being supported with extensive broadcast, print and in-store advertising. National television advertising efforts began May 26 in Canada and June 1 in the U.S.

Accompanying the launch will be placement early this month of a new lighted menuboard sign in all Wendy's restaurants, highlighting the availability of three lighter salad dressings options: fat-free French, low-fat honey mustard and reduced-fat creamy ranch.

Available for a limited time, the Southwest Chicken Caesar Salad will be featured through August.

Made with fresh romaine lettuce, spicy pieces of all-white chicken breast fillet, a blend of roasted corn and seasoned black beans, grape tomatoes and shredded Parmesan cheese, and served with home-style garlic croutons and a special Southwest Caesar dressing, this salad is designed to meet consumers' demands for quality, freshness and variety. The suggested price for the Southwest Chicken Caesar Salad is $3.99 (U.S.) and $5.99 (Canada). As with the other salads in the Garden Sensations line, select toppings for the Southwest Chicken Caesar are customizable and served on the side.

"We know that today, more than ever, our customers are looking for variety and taste excitement. They want high-quality salads that offer different flavors, colors and textures at an exceptional value," said Lori Estrada, Wendy's vice president of new product development. "We believe our new salad offering has a terrific flavor combination that our customers will truly enjoy."

Wendy's has a legacy of innovations in the Quick Service Restaurant (QSR) category. In 1979, the chain introduced the salad bar nationwide and, in 1992, it created "Fresh Salads To-Go" in response to changing consumer lifestyles.

Considered one of the most successful introductions in the history of the QSR industry, Garden Sensations launched in February 2002. The line-up includes Mandarin Chicken, Chicken BLT, Taco Supremo and Spring Mix.

Wendy's International, Inc., is one of the world's largest restaurant operating and franchising companies with more than $9.4 billion in systemwide sales, and three brands: Wendy's Old Fashioned Hamburgers, Tim Hortons and Baja Fresh Mexican Grill. Wendy's Old Fashioned Hamburgers was founded in 1969 by Dave Thomas and is the third-largest quick-service hamburger chain in the world with more than 6,250 restaurants in North America and international markets.

# # #

BOX 13.2 *Press Release–Frito-Lay*

FRITO-LAY LAUNCHES LINE OF SNACKS FOR HISPANICS IN KEY URBAN MARKETS ACROSS THE COUNTRY

PLANO, TX (May 22, 2002)–Frito-Lay, Inc., the world's favorite convenience fun foods company, announced today the launch of a line of snacks targeted specifically at Hispanics, the fastest growing ethnic group in the United States.

The snacks include:

- Sabritas Adobadas tomato and chile potato chips
- Sabritones puffed wheat snacks with chile and lime seasonings
- Churrumais fried corn strips with chile and lime seasonings
- Crujitos queso and chile flavor puffed corn twists
- Doritos Ranchero tortilla chips
- Lay's Limon potato chips
- Fritos Sabrositas lime and chile corn chips
- Doritos Salsa Verde tortilla chips
- Cheetos Flamin' Hot cheese-flavored snacks
- El Isleno Plantains

"This product lineup offers great tasting snacks with unique flavors and textures that are both appealing and familiar to Hispanic consumers," said Rebeca Johnson, Frito-Lay's Vice President, Marketing.

Frito-Lay conducted extensive consumer testing in four key markets (Miami, New York, Los Angeles, Houston) to determine the snack flavors and textures with the strongest appeal among Hispanics. The research showed that Hispanics had the greatest interest in snacks flavored with chile, citrus and cheese seasonings.

Next, Frito-Lay teamed up with its Mexico-based sister company Sabritas to select top selling brands that are familiar to Mexican-American and Latino consumers, including Sabritas Adobadas, Sabritones Churrumais and Crujitos among others. Then, Frito-Lay added to the line its own Doritos and Lay's varieties as well as Cheetos Flamin' Hot, which has emerged as the country's number one selling single serve salty snack.

Beginning now, the complete line of products will be distributed in key urban markets including several Southwest cities. The markets include Los Angeles, CA, San Francisco, CA, San Jose, CA, San Diego, CA, Phoenix, AZ, Tucson, AZ, Austin, TX, Laredo, TX, Houston, TX, Dallas/Ft. Worth, TX, Rio Grande Valley, TX, San Antonio, TX, Albuquerque, NM, Chicago, IL, Detroit, MI, Miami, FL and New York City.

Frito-Lay North America is the convenience fun foods division of PepsiCo, Inc., which is headquartered in Purchase, NY. Frito-Lay makes and sells some of America's favorite snack brands including Lay's potato chips, Ruffles potato chips, Doritos tortilla chips, Tostitos tortilla chips and Cheetos cheese-flavored snacks. The company also makes and sells Quaker Chewy granola bars, Fruit and Oatmeal bars, Gatorade energy bars and Quaker rice snacks.

# # #

Courtesy of Frito-Lay.

BOX 13.3 ***Press Release–United Methodist Communications***

FOR IMMEDIATE RELEASE

Contact: Jeffrey Buntin
The Buntin Group
615-244-5720

UNITED METHODISTS NAME THE BUNTIN GROUP TO CREATE NATIONAL CAMPAIGN

Nashville, Tenn. (Nov. 27, 2000)–United Methodist Communications (UMCom), the communications agency of The United Methodist Church, has chosen The Buntin Group, Nashville, as agency of record.

Buntin is developing creative and placing media for "Igniting Ministry," a $20 million national television campaign, supplemented by multimedia regional and local efforts. Launching in Fall 2001, the campaign will increase awareness of The United Methodist Church and its ministries and encourage attendance across the 36,000 United Methodist congregations in the United States. The campaign is already underway, with creative strategy approval and initial media planning having occurred this month.

"From the first of the screening process, Buntin demonstrated great insight into our target audience and what motivators would appeal to them," says Rev. Steve Horswill-Johnston, Associate General Secretary and Executive Director, Igniting Ministry media campaign. "In their strategies, they proposed a combination of conventional and unconventional methods that we found unique and have helped us completely understand the complexities of our target."

"This campaign serves a higher purpose," says Jeffrey Buntin. "The United Methodist Church is reaching out to those who are seeking answers in their lives. Offering deeper meaning in life and spiritual well being, we are extending an invitation for them to join a welcoming community. Our consumer-fluent approach will help ensure that the invitation is delivered in the appropriate way."

United Methodist Communications selected Buntin to create and place their 2001–2004 campaign utilizing in-church, outdoor, Internet, TV, radio and print media. The only Tennessee agency considered during UMCom's agency review, Buntin won the account over several agencies including Doe-Anderson, Louisville and BBDO, Chicago.

The Buntin Group is the largest marketing communications agency in Tennessee. Founded in 1972, the agency offers integrated marketing services and is renowned for its results-oriented creative work.

# # #

Courtesy of The Buntin Group.

This press release was also originally in a sans serif typeface, which may be used for some copy on websites. However, if it had been sent to media personnel, it should have been typed in a serif typeface because of its length. Serif typefaces are easier to read, especially when there is a lot of copy. In addition, it would have been typed double-spaced. If major newspapers had published information from the release, many editors at these newspapers would have edited the information for regular columns that concern businesses. This was the case in several, including the *New York Times*.

Advertising agencies, like other firms, write news releases about new business. For instance, personnel at the Buntin Group, an advertising agency in Nashville, Tennessee, wrote the press release in box 13.3. The news release begins with contact information, which is important if editors have questions about the information. The writer also provides a headline that features the most important point—that United Methodists has hired the Buntin Group to do a national advertising campaign. The first paragraph reiterates the information in the headline. The second paragraph identifies the specific advertising campaign, including its allocation, when it will begin, and what it hopes to achieve. The third and fourth paragraphs contain quotations from a representative of United Methodists and Mr. Jeffrey Buntin of the Buntin Group, respectively. The fifth paragraph claims that the Buntin Group was the only advertising agency in Tennessee to be considered by United Methodists. The last paragraph provides additional information about the Buntin Group.

Box 13.4 contains a second news release about the Buntin Group. The press release begins with contact information and a headline that may be used by an editor. The first paragraph elaborates on the information in the headline. The second paragraph provides the reason for the contract between the Tennessee Valley Authority and the Buntin Group: "Projects will be geared toward programs designed to help residential consumers in the Tennessee Valley use electricity wisely and protect the environment." The third paragraph contains a quotation from Jeffrey Buntin, the president of the Buntin Group. The fifth paragraph provides information about the Tennessee Valley Authority, the client, and the last paragraph provides information about the Buntin Group, the advertising agency.

BOX 13.4 *Press Release–TVA and The Buntin Group*

FOR IMMEDIATE RELEASE
Contact: Jeffrey Buntin
The Buntin Group
615-244-5720

BUNTIN ANNOUNCES CONTRACT WITH TVA FOR MARKETING SERVICES

NASHVILLE, Tenn. (November 16, 2001)–The Buntin Group announced that it has entered into a contract to provide creative material, marketing planing and media for the marketing division of Tennessee Valley Authority (TVA).

Buntin was selected from among a number of agencies operating withint the TVA footprint that submitted proposals. Projects will be geared toward programs designed to help residential consumers in the Tennessee Valley use electricity wisely and protect the environment.

"We consider TVA a vital part of the success of our region," said Jeffrey Buntin, President of The Buntin Group. "It is with great pleasure that we enter into this relationship. We are very excited."

The account adds a new category to The Buntin Group's list of category and market leading clients.

Founded in 1937, TVA is the nation's largest public power producer, providing power to large industries and 158 power distributors that serve 8.3 million customers in seven southeastern states. TVA serves the people of the Tennessee Valley by supporting sustainable economic development, supplying affordable, reliable power, developing new energy sources, protecting the environment and managing a thriving river system.

The Buntin Group is the largest marketing communications firm in Tennessee. Founded in 1972, the agency offers integrated marketing services and is known for its results-oriented creative work.

# # #

Courtesy of The Buntin Group.

BOX 13.5 ***Press Release—U.S. Census Bureau***

UNITED STATES DEPARTMENT OF COMMERCE NEWS
WASHINGTON, DC 20230
EMBARGOED UNTIL: 12:01 A.M. EDT, JULY 18, 2002 (THURSDAY)

Mike Bergman CB02-95
Public Information Office
(301) 763-3030/457-3670 (fax)
(301) 457-1037 (TDD)
e-mail: pio@census.gov

Quotes & radio sound bites

CENSUS BUREAU REPORT SHOWS "BIG PAYOFF" FROM EDUCATIONAL DEGREES

Over an adult's working life, high school graduates can expect, on average, to earn $1.2 million; those with a bachelor's degree, $2.1 million; and people with a master's degree, $2.5 million, according to a report released today by the Commerce Department's Census Bureau.

People with doctoral ($3.4 million) and professional degrees ($4.4 million) do even better.

"At most ages, more education equates with higher earnings, and the payoff is most notable at the highest educational level," said Jennifer Cheeseman Day, co-author of *The Big Payoff: Educational Attainment and Synthetic Estimates of Work-Life Earnings* [PDF].

The estimates of work-life earnings are based on 1999 earnings projected over a typical work life, defined as the period from ages 25 through 64.

In 2000, 84 percent of American adults age 25 and over had at least completed high school and 26 percent had a bachelor's degree or higher, both all-time highs.

Some additional highlights:

- In 1999, average annual earnings ranged from $18,900 for high school dropouts to $25,900 for high school graduates, $45,400 for college graduates and $99,300 for the holders of professional degrees (medical doctors, dentists, veterinarians and lawyers).
- Over a work life, earnings for a worker with a bachelor's degree compared with one who had just a high school diploma increase by about $1 million for non-Hispanic Whites and about $700,000 for African Americans; Asians and Pacific Islanders; and Hispanics.
- Men with professional degrees may expect to cumulatively earn almost $2 million more than their female counterparts over their work lives.
- More American women than men have received bachelor's degrees every year since 1982.
- Currently, almost 9-in-10 young adults graduate from high school and about 6-in-10 high school seniors go on to college the following year.

A separate report released last year (*What's It Worth? Field of Training and Economic Status: 1996*) said among people with bachelor's degrees, those working full time in engineering earned the highest average monthly pay ($4,680), while those with education degrees earned the lowest ($2,802) in 1996.

The work-life earnings data were collected in the March supplement to the Current Population Survey for 1998–2000. The data regarding earnings by specific degree fields were collected as part of the 1996 panel of the Survey of Income and Program Participation. Statistics from all surveys are subject to sampling and nonsampling error.

Source: U.S. Census Bureau
Public Information Office
(301) 763-3030
Last Revised: July 18, 2002 at 08:46:21 AM

Look at box 13.5 (page 207), which is a press release for the U.S. Department of Commerce, specifically the U.S. Census Bureau. This press release identifies whom to contact and other information if an editor or anyone has questions about its content. Also, note the phrase beginning with the words "Embargoed until." These words inform the editor that the information should not be used until a certain time and date.

Guidelines for Writing News or Press Releases

1. Double-space all body text so it can be easily read.
2. Indent all paragraphs.
3. Have at least a 1-inch margin on the left- and right-hand sides of the paper so that the release can be easily read and, if necessary, easily edited by the editor.
4. Type on only one side of an 8½ × 11-inch piece of paper.
5. Use factual information as well as strong verbs. Do not use adjectives that exaggerate.
6. Explain how the information will benefit the reader, listener, or viewer.
7. Check the spellings of names of individuals, products, and companies.
8. If initials or acronyms are used, make sure that the words for which these initials or acronyms stand have been spelled out once.
9. Use the active, not the passive, voice.
10. Use a quotation or quotations from the company's president or some other official or expert that relate to the subject discussed, especially if the quotations are opinionated or offer interpretation. A quotation adds color or flavor to a release.
11. Explain to the reader, listener, or viewer how they can obtain additional information.
12. Do not use jargon or terms that may not be understood.
13. As mentioned, use short sentences and short paragraphs.
14. Use words that are easily understood.
15. Edit the release. Try to replace a phrase, for instance, with a word.
16. If possible, try to get all of the information on one side of one page.
17. If the release continues to a second page, make sure that the first page ends with a completed paragraph or sentence. Sometimes, editors use scissors to cut releases into paragraphs so that they can arrange the information. Make it easy for them to do so.
18. If the release continues to a second page, type "More" in the center at the bottom of the first page. This informs the editor that there is more information on the next page.
19. If the release continues to a second page, type a brief heading either flush left or flush right that identifies the company, the date, the page number, and what the release concerns at the top of the second page. Sometimes, pages can become separated on editors' desks.
20. In a two-page news or press release, use at least one subhead, if relevant, to break up the copy.
21. At the end of the release, type "30," "# # #," or "End" in the center. This informs the editor that there is no additional information.
22. If needed, a fact sheet or illustration or photograph may be included with the release. If an illustration or photograph is included, make sure that a cutline or caption explaining the artwork is included as well.

23. Study the medium or media to which the news or press release is being sent. For instance, if the medium is a newspaper, learn if the publication publishes stories that are similar. If so, find out in which sections such stories appear. Then learn who is responsible for this section or these sections. This may be the editor or editors you need to contact.

CORPORATE ADVERTISING

Corporate advertising is designed to enhance the image that one or more target markets have of a company. Numerous service and product advertisers, including manufacturers of automobiles and computers as well as oil companies, use corporate advertising. And these companies use various media, including magazines, newspapers, and television, for their corporate print advertisements and broadcast commercials. In fact, magazines and newspapers are used primarily because they allow advertisers to employ whatever space is necessary to deliver their messages. Magazines are also used because they reach specific target markets or readers. Advertisers use television because it can deliver messages that appeal to viewers' emotions.

Basically, corporate advertising includes advocacy advertising, image or institutional advertising, and recruitment advertising. Let us examine these in depth.

Advocacy advertising, which often appears as so-called advertorials, actually attempts to influence readers, listeners, and viewers about important environmental, political, or social issues by presenting the company's perspectives toward these issues. Advocacy advertising is not easy to write. In fact, oftentimes these advertisements are merely headlines and body copy, not illustrations or photographs. Consequently, it is up to a copywriter to do all of the persuading. In order to write an advocacy advertisement, a copywriter must understand upper management, specifically its position toward the issue that needs to be addressed. Then the copywriter should present this position slowly—that is, using factual information that supports or reinforces the position. This information should be incorporated into the body copy—one fact on top of another—until the reader is convinced that the advertiser's position is the "right" position.

Image or institutional advertising is very popular among companies. It attempts to enhance the image of a company in people's minds. These people may include customers or prospective customers as well as employees. However, changing the image someone has of a company is not easy to do; nor is it immediate. Indeed, it may take months or years of running image or institutional advertisements and commercials before peoples' perception of a company is changed. Even then not all members of the intended target market will be persuaded. For those who have become persuaded, the company may have an easier time convincing these people that they should purchase the company's products. Of course, this is not necessarily the purpose of image or institutional advertising, but it cannot keep from having some impact on sales.

Companies use recruitment advertising primarily to interest prospective employees. These copy and display advertisements typically appear in the help wanted sections of major daily newspapers and some weekly and monthly magazines, especially magazines that are directed toward professional audiences. Usually, these advertisements originate in a company's human resources department, not in its advertising, marketing, or public relations department. Nonetheless, an advertising copywriter may be asked to write one of these advertisements from time to time.

A recruitment advertisement may be nothing more than one to three lines of copy announcing a position; it may be a typical classified advertisement that has the copy inside borders or a "box"; or it may be a larger display advertisement that contains an illustration or photograph as well as copy. No matter which of these has been assigned, it is important for the copywriter to remember that the advertisement should mention the position by title and include a description of the responsibilities. The advertisement should also provide information about the attributes, education, experience, and skills required, if relevant, of an applicant. Of course, the contact person's name and the company's name, address, and telephone number may be included. The first two kinds of advertisements may include only a telephone number, not a contact person's name or the company's name or address.

In the next chapter, we will examine advertising copy research.

EXERCISE

1. You work for an advertising agency that creates all kinds of ads for large firms. The agency has created corporate or institutional ads for such firms as East Tennessee Electric and Power, Inc. (ETE&P). Recently, as a result of a reporter investigating a story, it was discovered that ETE&P was breaking laws established by the federal government. In short, the company was not cooling the water it was using to make power to the Environmental Protection Agency's prescribed temperature before releasing it into the Cumberland River. Consequently, aquatic life died. The reporter's scoop was published in several newspapers in Tennessee, picked up by the wire services, published in larger newspapers that enjoy a national audience, picked up by several television stations, and mentioned by several news anchors at the major networks. The company was embarrassed. Not only that, the company may have to pay fines for breaking environmental statutes.

   Your job is to (1) write a press release that plays down the event—in other words, make it appear as though the company was not at fault or that its employees were unaware of any problem; and (2) write a reading notice (an ad that appears as editorial copy but includes the word *advertisement* in either 4 or 6 point type, usually placed at the top or bottom of the column—several oil companies, for instance, have used this format). The reading notice is important. Remember, it is an ad in the form of an article. It will have, in most instances, a headline similar to those found in newspaper or magazine articles, and it will contain copy that is very positive. Basically, it attempts to create a positive image of the advertiser. It does not sell products or services; it sells images.

   The purpose of the press release is to inform the public about the incident—but from the company's perspective. It will be distributed to various media, including newspapers, television stations, and the major networks. The reading notice (ad) will appear in newspapers and magazines.

NOTES

1. Public Relations Society of America, "About Public Relations" (New York: Public Relations Society of America, 2002; www.prsa.org), p. 1.
2. Council of Public Relations Firms, "2001 Public Relations Industry Revenue Documentation and Rankings: FACT SHEET" (New York: Council of Public Relations Firms, 2002; www.prfirms.org), p. 2.
3. Public Relations Society of America, "About Public Relations," p. 3.

CHAPTER 14

Advertising Copy Research

We examined several methods of research in chapter 2 that could be employed to help create an advertising campaign or integrated marketing communications campaign. Now we need to examine methods of research that can help determine (1) whether the message in the advertisements is understood correctly by representatives of the intended target market(s) before the advertisements are placed in media and (2) whether the message in the advertisements is understood correctly by members of the intended target market(s)—and, more important, with what effect—after the advertisements are placed in media.

When advertisers or their advertising agencies test advertising messages, they generally hire outside specialty firms that perform tests before advertisements are placed in media. These tests are called pretests. Then outside specialty firms may be hired to perform tests after advertisements are placed in media. These tests are called posttests. There are various pretests and posttests available, but none is completely accurate. Before a pretest or posttest is selected, it is important that the advertiser or its advertising agency have identified the question or questions that need an answer or answers; otherwise, they may order a pretest or posttest that is not appropriate. For instance, advertisers may like to know how the advertisement compares with similar previous advertisements. The advertising agency may like to know if the advertisement is doing what it is supposed to do.

On the other hand, creative personnel may not care for these tests. They realize that tests are not accurate and do not necessarily prove anything. Of course, creative personnel are biased; they assume that their work is good or great. They fear that the results of a test may be used against what they have created and they will be forced to change the advertisement. Contrary to the opinions of creative personnel, some testing may prove beneficial. Remember, placing advertisements in the media is expensive. Wouldn't it be better to place an advertisement that has been tested instead of one that has not?

GUIDELINES FOR TESTING

The Association of National Advertisers (ANA) published *Choosing the Best Advertising Alternative: A Management Guide to Identifying the Most Effective Copy Testing Technique* in 1971. The book was printed again in 1986. The ANA recommended four steps in testing advertising messages:

1. *Select a single criterion measure.* (It is difficult for a test to measure several criteria.)
2. *Design the test so that, when the respondents are interviewed, they do not know that they are being interviewed about their exposure to an advertisement or commercial. They should perceive the interview as merely being an attitude survey.*
3. *Expose the individuals to the commercial or print advertisement in their homes, so that they have no idea that their viewing is part of a test.*
4. *Set up multiple exposure situations.*[1] (This ensures a more realistic assessment of the effects of the advertisement.)

Responding to advertisers and their advertising agencies' concerns about copy testing, research directors at 21 major advertising agencies developed nine principles on which a sound copy test should be based. These principles, which were presented in Positioning Advertising Copy Testing (PACT), which was distributed to every member of the American Association of Advertising Agencies, included the following:

1. *A good copy-testing system provides measurements that are relevant to the objectives of the advertising.* (Basically, a copy test should be designed to assess the advertisement's potential for achieving its stated objectives.)
2. *A good copy-testing system is one that requires agreement about how the results will be used in advance of each specific test.* (Specifying how the results will be used before the results are in insures that there is mutual understanding on the goals of the test.)
3. *A good copy-testing system provides multiple measurements—because single measurements are generally inadequate to assess the performance of an advertisement.* (Multiple measurements may differ in weight in evaluating the advertising.)
4. *A good copy-testing system is based on a model of human response to communication—the reception of a stimulus, the comprehension of the stimulus, and the response to the stimulus.* (Advertising performs on several levels; consequently, an advertisement must have an effect:
   - on the "eye," on the "ear" [it must be received—reception]
   - on the "mind" [it must be understood—comprehension]
   - on the "heart" [it must make an impression—response])
5. *A good copy-testing system allows for consideration of whether the advertising stimulus should be exposed more than once.* (Situations exist in which a single exposure is sufficient, but other situations exist in which multiple exposures are needed.)
6. *A good copy-testing system recognizes that the more finished a piece of copy is, the more soundly it can be evaluated, and requires, as a minimum, that alternative executions be tested in the same degree of finish.* (If alternative executions are tested in different stages of completion within the same test, the results may be biased because of the varying degrees of finish.)
7. *A good copy-testing system provides controls to avoid the biasing effects of the exposure context.* (Recall of the same commercial can vary depending on a number of conditions, such as whether exposure to the commercial is off air versus on air, a clutter reel of commercials versus a program context, or one specific program context versus another specific program context.)
8. *A good copy-testing system is one that takes into account basic considerations of sample definition.*

(The test should be conducted among a sizable sample of the intended target market so that the data help with decision making.)

9. *A good copy-testing system is one that can demonstrate reliability and validity*. (The copy-testing system should yield the same results each time the advertising is tested, and it should provide results that are relevant to marketplace performance.)[2]

WHAT SHOULD BE EVALUATED

Determining what should be evaluated may not be easy. However, usually advertisers or their advertising agencies wish to know one or more of the following:

- Does the advertisement attract attention?
- Is the advertisement communicating what is desired?
- Does the advertisement cause people to buy the product?
- What attitudes do people have toward the advertisement?
- What attitudes do people have toward the brand?
- Does the advertisement have credibility?

Of course, there are other questions that could be asked and answered. As mentioned, an advertiser or advertising agency must have something in mind before a firm is hired to conduct a test.

PRETESTS

To determine whether an advertising message is doing what it is supposed to do before the advertisements are placed, there are several pretests that can be performed. The most common pretests include the following:

- Focus Group Sessions
- One-to-One Interviews
- Telephone Interviews
- Observation
- Projective Techniques
- Mechanical or Physiological Tests
- Large Group or Theater Tests

Focus Groups

As mentioned in chapter 2, members of a focus group are invited to participate in a focus group session by employees of an advertising agency or outside specialty firm for the purpose of discussing a specific subject. Generally, a skilled moderator will have certain topics that he or she wishes for the 8 to 12 members of the group to examine.

When asking members about advertisements, specifically headlines, subheads, body copy, slogans, logos, layout or design, and so on, it is important to ensure that they represent the intended target market(s) and either subscribe to or read, listen to, or watch the media vehicles that will be selected for the placement of the advertisements. In short, you do not want members who are not representative of the intended target market(s). In addition, you want to make sure that these individuals buy or will buy the product or service being advertised or at least will purchase a similar product or service from one of the advertiser's competitors. These individuals must have a desire or need for the product or service being advertised. You do not want to include individuals who have not bought or will not buy the product or service being advertised.

In most instances, focus group sessions are recorded as well as observed through a one-way mirror by one or more individuals who work for the advertiser or the advertiser's advertising agency. Focus group sessions can provide a great deal of information, even if each session lasts only an hour. For instance, these individuals may express how they feel toward an advertisement. They may point out that they do not like the headline because of a particular word or phrase. Or they may mention that the first line of body copy does not relate to the headline and consequently causes confusion. They may not like the design of the advertisement because of the artwork. They may not care for the artwork's colors or the typefaces or fonts that have been used. Or they may not like the slogan. Focus group sessions can provide information for questions for formal surveys, too. In fact, focus group sessions are often conducted when at least one formal survey has been planned.

Members of focus groups may be asked to rank in order of merit two or more advertisements for the same product or service. This is usually referred to as an Order-of-Merit Ranking Test. Members of focus groups may be asked to compare various pairs of advertisements. Generally, these advertisements are alike except for one element, such as the headline, or subhead, or body copy, or slogan, or artwork and so forth. Members are asked to rate each pair of advertisements based on their preferences. This is usually referred to as a Paired-Comparison Test.

Focus groups usually are preferred over depth interviews or in-depth interviews primarily because group sessions generate more information in less time. Depth interviews or in-depth interviews are one to one and are more time-consuming and consequently more expensive.

One-to-One Interviews

The one-to-one interview is an alternative to the focus group session. Generally, a person will offer more information when she or he is the only one being asked questions about an advertisement; whereas, in a focus group session, individuals may not respond as often or as in depth when they notice others looking at them.

Advertisers and their advertising agencies usually hire specialty firms to conduct one-to-one interviews. Often these firms are located in or near shopping malls, where prospects are easy to find. The MSW Group, formerly McCollum Spielman Worldwide, uses the AD*VANTAGE/ACT copy test, which was developed in 1968 primarily to measure respondents' reactions to television commercials. The test measures *Liking/Disliking* as well as *Effectiveness* and uses AD*MAP to define the commercial's level of effectiveness. To put it simply, the two evaluative scores (Liking/Disliking and Effectiveness) are positioned on a graph that contains four quadrants. Where the scores intersect on the graph reveals the level of effectiveness.[3]

The BUY©Test, which is conducted by Taylor Nelson Sofres, uses an emotional response scale to measure the creativity in advertisements. This test identifies the communication elements of an advertisement that should be emphasized. The BUY©Scale is based on a series of questions that measure the involvement and persuasion of respondents. As a result, respondents are classified as Persuaded, Involved, or Recall Only. In addition to being administered in interviews, the test is administered online.[4]

Telephone Interviews

Advertisers and their advertising agencies usually hire specialty firms to conduct interviews over the telephone. Generally, the firm hired will recruit prospects to read a magazine or view a specific program on television. A day later a representative of the firm telephones these prospects to learn what they remember about a print advertisement or a broadcast commercial.

Ipsos-ASI: The Advertising Research Company offers clients its Next brand of pretests for print advertisements and television commercials. The Next*Print test arrives at a recruited respondent's home in a magazine and actually parallels the firm's Next*TV test in design and scope. The test measures recall of the advertisement and its relationship with the brand as well as its persuasiveness. The Next*TV test is conducted in a recruited respondent's home as well, where the individual views a program with commercials. The following day a representative of the firm calls the respondent and asks questions about what the individual watched, especially the commercials. The respondent's answers are recorded and later analyzed.[5]

Gallup & Robinson offers clients its InTeleTest, which arrives at a recruited respondent's home so that the respondent may view a television program with commercials. The respondent is instructed to fill out a questionnaire before watching the program as well as another questionnaire after watching the program. A representative of the firm calls the respondent the following day and asks questions about the commercials.[6]

Observation

Advertisers and their advertising agencies may hire specialty firms that conduct observational or ethnographic research. Basically, an observation researcher will observe consumers where they live or work. Sometimes they will observe consumers when they are engaged in athletic activities. In short, the researcher records consumers while active in their natural environments. Usually, the researcher will use a camera to videotape subjects. Although observation has the advantage of showing what consumers actually do, it does not provide an explanation as to why they do what they do. Generally, advertisers and their advertising agencies hire specialty firms to conduct other tests in addition to observational research.

Projective Techniques or Approaches

These approaches or techniques developed out of motivational research, which is typically done by psychologists and sociologists. In essence, motivational research examines the basis (motivations) for thinking, learning, and actions.

Advertisers or their agencies hire specialty firms that perform tests, such as *depth* or *in-depth interviews*, *free associations*, *sentence completions*, *picture completions*, *dialogue balloons* or *bubbles*, and *story constructions*. Of course, depth or in-depth interviews are one-to-one interviews and typically last from one to two hours. The purpose of these interviews is to record responses to direct and indirect questions and to learn the respondents' motivations.

Free association tests are open-ended and allow respondents to express their thoughts or feelings after a product, brand name, or some other element has been mentioned or some element has been shown to them. In sentence and picture completion techniques, an incomplete sentence or picture is shown to a respondent who is asked to fill in the blank(s). The purpose of this approach is to obtain an immediate and (hopefully) honest thought or feeling (response).

Dialogue balloons or bubbles allow respondents to provide the dialogue for a cartoon-like character and his or her relationship with a product. Basically, the purpose is to learn what the respondent thinks the cartoon character's attitude is toward the product. Story constructions allow respondents to interpret a picture or illustration or to tell a story based on what is in the picture or illustration. Respondents may be asked to provide a story about the characters in the picture or illustration or asked to describe the characters' personalities.

Mechanical or Physiological Tests

Mechanical or physiological tests include *pupil dilation*, *eye movement* or *tracking*, *galvanic skin response*, the *tachistoscope*, and the *electroencephalograph*. These techniques attempt to measure individuals' physical reactions to advertisements before the advertisements are placed in media.

Advertisers or their agencies have used the pupillometer to measure the dilation and constriction of the pupils of the eyes when the eyes are exposed to advertisements. Generally, the pupils increase in size when a participant is interested in an advertisement. An electronic camera is used to track eye movement. Basically, the camera follows the individual's eyes, usually one, as he or she examines an advertisement. This technique allows advertisers and their agencies to determine which elements are noticed first, second, third, and so on as well as which elements are not.

Perception Research Services (PRS), which was founded in 1972, has conducted thousands of studies for hundreds of clients. These studies have been conducted nationally through focus group facilities and research centers in malls. One of the most popular PRS tests is PRS Eye-Tracking, which measures the effectiveness of print and out-of-home advertising, such as outdoor ad formats. PRS Eye-Tracking measures print advertisements' ability to capture and hold readers' attention. It also determines which elements are looked at first, second, third, and so on.[7]

A psychogalvanometer measures galvanic skin response. This instrument measures electrodermal response, or perspiration, when the individual is exposed to an advertisement. If the individual finds the advertisement interesting, perspiration increases. Advertisers or their agencies do not use this test very often, primarily because it does not measure whether the person's interest to the advertisement is positive or negative. The tachistoscope allows an individual to view different parts of an advertisement for a certain period. In short, the entire advertisement is not revealed all at once. The purpose is to determine how long it takes the individual to understand the parts that are revealed.

The electroencephalograph measures brain waves and can actually inform researchers whether an individual is paying attention to an advertisement. However, most advertisers or their agencies have not used this instrument for advertising purposes. Although advertisers or their agencies have used the devices mentioned above for copy-testing purposes, it is still unknown what most of these devices actually measure.

Large Group or Theater Tests

Large group or theater tests involve several hundred participants who have been recruited by telephone or at malls. Sometimes tickets are mailed to individuals inviting them to view a new program for television. Broadcast commercials are shown as well, and then the participants are asked to fill out an evaluation form. Occasionally, participants are provided with an electronic device that contains buttons. Participants are encouraged to record their reactions to what is being shown. This device allows respondents to react to segments of a broadcast commercial, not just to the entire commercial.

Today, some specialty firms send videotaped programs with broadcast commercials interspersed to individuals so that they may view the programs and commercials in the luxury of their homes or offices. Other specialty firms have their own viewing rooms or rent hotel conference rooms. In other words, tests very similar to theater tests are performed but on a smaller scale.

The ARS Group, which was founded in 1974 and is also known as RSC, the Quality Measurement Company, offers clients its ARS Persuasion measure, among other tests. The ARS Persuasion measure is conducted on a group of individuals who represent the intended target market. They are informed that there will be a drawing for a prize and are asked to select products they would like to receive, and then they are asked to view pilot programs for television that contain commercials. After viewing, a representative of the firm asks the individuals about the programs and, of course, the commercials. Then they are asked to select products again. If more people select one of the advertised products after the commercials have been shown than before the commercials were shown, the commercials are considered persuasive.[8]

POSTTESTS

Specialty firms conduct posttests after the advertisements have been placed in the media. Advertisers and their agencies are interested in learning how advertisements or advertising campaigns are perceived by sizable representative samples of the intended target market. Basically, they are interested in learning if the advertisements have reached members of the intended target market and if the advertisements have done what they were supposed to do—that is, achieve the creative objectives. Posttests include the following:

- Readership Study Tests (Memory)
- Attitude or Persuasion Tests
- Inquiry Tests
- Sales or In-Market Tests

Readership Study or Memory Tests

Specialty firms perform these tests primarily for the purpose of learning what consumers remember about advertisements. These tests are classified as recognition tests and recall tests.

RECOGNITION TESTS Specialty firms use recognition tests to determine if readers of newspapers and magazines as well as viewers of television remember having seen specific advertisements or commercials and, if so, if they can identify the advertisers. One of the most prominent firms that use recognition tests is Roper ASW, which conducts the "Starch Ad Readership" for various clients. Starch measures more than 25,000 advertisements in more than 400 magazine issues. It conducts one-to-one interviews with at least 100 to 200 individuals (readers) and provides the following data:

Noted—The percentage of readers who remember having seen part of the advertisement.
Associated—The percentage of readers who remember having seen the advertiser's name or logo.
Read Some—The percentage of readers who read part of the advertisement's copy.
Read Most—The percentage of readers who read more than 50 percent of the advertisement's copy.

In addition to the above, Starch ranks the advertisements against other advertisements in the magazine as well as against other advertisements in the advertisement's product category over the past two years.[9]

Another firm that uses recognition tests is Readex, which conducts "Branded Ad Readership Studies" that measure advertisements' effectiveness. These studies are conducted by mail or e-mail, and each is based on at least 100 responses. Readex offers four different Ad Readership Studies to clients: "Ad Perception Studies," "Red Sticker Studies," "Message Impact Studies," and "On Target Studies." The first two measure similar variables, and the last two measure similar variables.[10]

The Bruzzone Research Company (BRC) is another firm that offers clients several different tests. These tests measure advertising's effectiveness, particularly *likability*, after the advertising has appeared in the media. Basically, BRC uses diagnostic measures to determine if advertisements have affected those who have been exposed to them.[11]

Another firm that uses recognition tests is Communicus, which offers clients its Advertising Campaign Evaluation test. This test is conducted after a client's advertising has appeared in the media and measures the campaign's overall impact, including advertising awareness and strength as well as media selected, among other elements.[12]

RECALL TESTS Although recognition tests refer to advertisements that are shown, *recall tests* do not necessarily emphasize advertisements. Indeed, recall tests attempt to measure what people remember about advertisements after they have appeared in the media.

Recall tests may be classified as *aided recall* or *unaided recall*. In the former, researchers ask questions that attempt to learn if an individual remembers seeing an advertisement for a particular brand or product. In the latter, researchers ask questions that attempt to learn if an individual remembers seeing an advertisement for a particular product category, not a specific brand or product. In both, researchers ask additional questions based on the individuals' responses.

Gallup & Robinson, Inc., which offers clients the Magazine Impact Research Service (MIRS), among other services, was founded in 1948 by Dr. George Gallup and Dr. Claude Robinson for the purpose of measuring advertising effectiveness. MIRS invites more than 100 respondents to read a major magazine in the luxury of their homes. Representatives of the firm interview the respondents the following day to determine which advertisements are remembered. For the advertisements that are recalled, the representatives learn about the respondents' overall impressions of the advertisements as well as the advertisements' sales points. Gallup & Robinson also measures recall of television commercials with its In-View service.[13]

Mapes and Ross, Inc., uses its Natural Exposure tests to measure television commercials, radio commercials, magazine advertisements, and newspaper advertisements. Each test conducted is similar in design and scope. Based on "real-world" exposure of the client's commercials or advertisements, respondents see the commercials or advertisements as they watch television, listen to the radio, read a magazine, or read a newspaper in their own homes. Recruited by telephone, respondents are asked to watch, listen, or read a regularly scheduled program or magazine.

When participants are recruited, their pre-exposure levels of brand preference in the advertiser's product category are recorded, along with five other categories. Questions, however, do not concern advertising; even brand names are not mentioned. The next day, after the respondents have viewed or listened to the program or read the publication, the same questions are asked to determine postexposure levels of brand preference in the advertiser's product category. In addition, questions pertaining to the client's advertisements are asked. If respondents have seen or heard the client's advertisements, additional questions are asked to determine the level of recall. The comparison of pre-exposure responses to postexposure responses provides the level of persuasion.[14]

Attitude or Persuasion Tests

These tests are closely related to recall tests primarily because they are usually conducted after advertisements have appeared in the media. However, attitude tests or persuasion tests attempt to determine respondents' changes in attitude toward advertisers and their products or brands. These changes are learned as a result of asking questions before the respondents view or listen to a program or read a magazine or newspaper. Then the responses are compared with the responses to the same questions asked after the respondents have viewed or listened to a program or have read a magazine or newspaper.

More in-depth tests that are conducted over a longer period after broadcast commercials and print advertisements have appeared in the media also measure changes in attitudes. These are typically called *tracking studies*. Basically, tracking studies include periodic sampling of the target market to determine the effectiveness of an advertising campaign. Generally, advertisers are interested in learning whether members of the target market are aware of their advertising and brands, which elements of the advertisements are remembered, the beliefs or attitudes that these members have toward the advertisers and brands as a result of having seen their advertising, and which products or brands that these members prefer, among other measures. In short, advertisers are interested in learning whether their advertising campaigns have had impacts on their target markets over time. Are these target markets aware of the advertisers' brands? If so, what are their attitudes toward the brands? Tracking studies are conducted primarily through mail surveys, telephone surveys, and personal interviews and usually include from 200 to 500 representative members of the target markets each time they are conducted, which may be once every three months or twice a year. Tracking studies, primarily because they are conducted several times over a long period, are expensive.

Inquiry Tests

These tests are conducted to determine advertising's effectiveness and are based on the number of inquiries generated by advertisements appearing in the media, especially print. Inquiries may be in the form of coupons placed by advertisers or their agencies in print media, direct inquiries through reader cards that typically appear in the backs of magazines, telephone calls generated by toll-free numbers included in advertisements, or responses made online as a result of advertisers' websites included in advertisements.

Another version of an inquiry test is the *split-run test*, which refers to placing two or more variations of an advertisement in different copies of the same issue of a magazine or newspaper. Today, split-run tests can be conducted on cable television. Cable stations can broadcast different commercials concurrently to different subscribers. Based on the number of responses, advertisers can determine which advertisement was the most effective. Although split-run tests can be performed after advertisements have appeared in the media, generally these tests are conducted before advertisements are placed in the media to determine which ads are the most effective.

Inquiry tests are not as expensive as other posttests. However, these tests do not provide a lot of information about respondents or the specific elements within the advertisements that prompted them to respond.

Sales or In-Market Tests

Most, if not all, advertisers track sales, and with scanners in most retail stores, advertisers can learn how well their products are selling in different countries, regions, or states within a relatively short period of time as a result of orders. In fact, sales may be used to evaluate the effectiveness of an advertising campaign by some advertisers, even though various factors other than advertising affect sales. Still, advertisers may base their advertising budgets on previous sales. Unfortunately, sales are not a very good means of measuring the effectiveness of an advertisement. By the time advertisers have sales figures for a certain period, a new advertisement may have appeared in the media or a new advertising campaign may be under way. Consequently, advertisers should not necessarily measure the effectiveness of their advertising by sales figures.

Although advertisers will continue to hire firms to conduct pretests and posttests, they must realize that these tests are not accurate 100 percent of the time. I discuss finding a job in advertising and preparing a cover letter and résumé in the next chapter.

NOTES

1. Joel N. Axelrod, *Choosing the Best Advertising Alternative: A Management Guide to Identifying the Most Effective Copy Testing Technique* (New York: Association of National Advertisers, Inc., 1971), p. 26.
2. "21 Ad Agencies Endorse Copy Testing Principles," *Marketing News*, Vol. 15, No. 17 (February 19, 1982): pp. 1, 9; "Positioning Advertising Copy Testing," *Journal of Advertising*, Vol. 11, No. 4 (1982): pp. 3–29.
3. MSW Research, "Brand and Advertising Research: AD*VANTAGE/ACT®" (Lake Success, NY: MSW Research, 2002; www.mswresearch.com).
4. Taylor Nelson Sofres, "Maximize Your Advertising Effectiveness" (London: Taylor Nelson Sofres, 2002; www.tnsofres.com).
5. Ipsos, "Advertising Research" (New York: Ipsos, 2002; www.ipsospa.com).
6. Gallup & Robinson, "Gallup & Robinson: Services" (Pennington, NJ: Gallup & Robinson, 2002; www.gallup-robinson.com).
7. Perception Research Services, "*PRS Eye-Tracking* Sample Data" (Fort Lee, NJ: Perception Research Services, 2002; www.prsresearch.com).
8. The ARS Group, "Advertising Measurement" (Evansville, IN: The ARS Group, 2002; www.ars-group.com).
9. Roper ASW, "Products and Services" (New York: Roper ASW, 2002; www.roperasw.com).
10. Readex, "Readex" (Stillwater, MN: Readex, 2002; www.readexresearch.com).
11. Bruzzone Research Co., "Bruzzone Research Company" (Alameda, CA: Bruzzone Research Co., 2002; www.bruzzone-research.com).
12. Communicus, "Communicus" (Santa Monica, CA: Communicus, 2002; www.communicus.com).
13. Gallup & Robinson, "Gallup & Robinson."
14. Mapes and Ross, Inc., "Communication Research: Services Offered" (Princeton, NJ: Mapes and Ross, Inc., 2002; www.mapesandross.com).

CHAPTER 15

Advice on How to Get a Job in Advertising

Getting a job in advertising is not easy. However, if you follow the advice in this chapter, you should have an advantage over some who apply for the same or a similar position.

In the United States, there are more than 10,000 advertising agencies. This figure does not include specialty firms, such as those that focus on creativity, interactive, media-buying, public relations, or some other area of marketing communications. According to the federal government and other entities, the outlook for careers in this industry is positive. In short, jobs should be available. In the near future, many employees will be retiring or pursuing other careers; consequently, additional jobs should become available. Before you begin your search for a job, however, there are several things that you should do.

WHAT DO YOU WANT TO DO?

You need to ask yourself, "What do I want to do?" Do you want to get a job or go on to graduate school? If you want to get a job, you need to decide on what kind of job. For instance, do you want to work in an advertising agency? If so, do you want to work for a full-service advertising agency? Or do you want to work for a medium-size or small-size advertising agency? Do you want to work for a company's advertising department or in-house advertising agency? Do you want to work at a specialty firm, such as a specialty firm that focuses on creative? Or media? Or research? Do you want to work for one of the media, such as a radio station? Television station? Magazine? Newspaper? Or a firm that specializes in outdoor formats? Or the yellow pages? Or the Internet? In other words, you should decide on what kind of company you want to work for before you think about your next step.

WHAT ABOUT GRADUATE SCHOOL?

If you have decided to go on to graduate school, you will need to take a graduate examination, such as the Graduate Record Examination or the Graduate Management Admissions Test, before you are formally admitted to a quality program. There are graduate programs in mass communications that allow students to emphasize advertising as well as graduate programs in advertising. (See "Appendix: Graduate Programs.") There are programs in business administration and marketing, too. Some graduate programs that offer the master's in business administration actually allow students to emphasize marketing. These programs as well as those that offer the master's of science in marketing should be considered. After all, advertising is merely an aspect of marketing. In fact, many professionals who aspire to move up in companies and businesses often have a graduate degree in some area of business.

However, if you have no professional experience, you should try to find a job before you go on to graduate school. In fact, if you have no professional experience but you have a graduate degree, you may not find a job because a prospective employer may not wish to pay you what he or she thinks you would expect, especially if the position is entry level. Of course, there are exceptions. For instance, in a major city that has numerous advertising agencies, such as New York or Chicago, a prospective employee with a master's degree may have an advantage over a prospective employee who has only a bachelor's.

WHAT ARE YOUR SELLING POINTS?

Specifically, what are your selling points? Think about what you majored in. What are your majors? Minors? What other courses did you enroll in? For instance, did you enroll in courses in art? Can you draw or paint? Did you enroll in courses in graphics? If so, what did you learn? Do you know how to use specific software programs? If so, which ones? Did you enroll in courses in English, especially the courses that focus on certain types or forms of writing, such as technical writing or professional writing? If so, what did you learn? Did you enroll in courses in sociology? If so, what did you learn? Did you enroll in courses in psychology? If so, which courses? Did you enroll in other liberal arts courses? If so, what were these courses? Did you do an internship? If so, what did you do and for what company or business? The answers to these questions and others may help you to identify your strengths or selling points, some of which should be emphasized in your cover letter and at least mentioned in your résumé.

HOW DOES YOUR WORK COMPARE WITH THAT OF OTHERS, ESPECIALLY PROFESSIONALS?

If you have creative work, how does it compare with professional quality work? In order to answer this question, examine similar creative work in publications or other media. How does your work compare? Is it as good? Or does it lack something? Try to get a feel for what is being done by personnel at companies where you would like to work. Remember, your work should be close in quality to what you see being produced by those who work in advertising agencies or businesses where you would like to work. In some instances, your work—at least, the creative concepts—may be better.

SEARCHING FOR YOUR FIRST JOB

Searching for your first job in advertising may take more time than you think, especially if you are not sure which job you are interested in.

Which Position Do You Want?

In advertising, medium- to large-size advertising agencies typically hire individuals for the following positions:

- Account Supervisors
- Account Executives
- Assistant Account Executives
- Traffic Managers
- Account Planners
- Creative Supervisors or Directors
- Art Directors
- Associate Art Directors
- Senior Producers
- Producers
- Copywriters
- Media Supervisors
- Media Buyers

There may be other positions, depending on the advertising agency. Let us examine the typical departments in which these positions exist as well as the roles of these positions.

Account supervisors, account executives, and assistant account executives work in the Account Services Department and are in contact with clients. In fact, they act as liaison between clients and the Creative Department and Production Department, making sure that the clients are kept abreast as to what is being done regarding their campaigns. Traffic managers are also in the Account Services Department and coordinate and monitor all jobs. They work with all departments to make sure that a campaign's production remains on schedule.

Account planners are in the Research Department and are responsible for gathering the necessary research concerning target markets and for providing the data to the Creative Department, so that the research is the basis for the clients' campaigns. Creative supervisors or directors, art directors, associate art directors, senior producers, producers, and copywriters are found in the Creative Department and are responsible for producing creative content for the print and broadcast media. Finally, media supervisors and media buyers work in the Media Services Department and apply mathematics and statistics to measure target markets, media circulations, and media costs to minimize media expenses and maximize media effectiveness.

As the above illustrates, there are numerous positions found in medium- to large-size advertising agencies. Of course, full-service advertising agencies may have other positions in addition to the above, such as assistant or junior copywriters and layout or graphic artists, to mention a few. Once you have decided on a particular position, you can concentrate on the following to make your search easier.

Where Do You Want to Live and Work?

You may desire to live near your relatives, but if they do not live in a city that has advertising agencies or other businesses that have advertising departments, you may have to move. The larger advertising agencies, companies, businesses, and media firms are located in larger cities, such as New York, Chicago, Detroit, Los Angeles, San Francisco, Boston, Minneapolis, Dallas–Ft. Worth, and so on. Generally, cities that have populations of 100,000 or more will have several advertising agencies as well as companies and businesses that have advertising departments. Of course, these cities will have one or more media firms.

Once you have decided on a place to live, start searching for advertising agencies, companies, businesses, or media firms that are nearby. Some students forget to answer this question. Instead, they search for a position and hope that the advertising agency, company, business, or media firm that has an opening is located in a city they will enjoy. This may not be wise; people may not like the city or may grow to feel isolated because they are not close to relatives or friends.

Making Contacts

One way of searching for a position in the city you have selected is by making personal contacts. For instance, you may have a professor who has helped place one or more former students at one or more advertising agencies, companies, businesses, and media firms in the city you have selected. You may know someone—a friend or a relative—who has lived or knows someone in the city you have selected. You may have made an acquaintance with someone from the city you have selected. These individuals may possibly know someone who works in advertising in an advertising agency, company, business, or media firm in the city. If this is the case, try to obtain the name of the person; the person's title or position; the advertising agency, company, business, or media firm's address; and the telephone number. Ask the person providing this information if it is all right for you to use his or her name in the letter you write. It is not unethical or unprofessional to identify the person who provided the person's name to whom you are writing a letter of introduction or cover letter. In fact, if the person knows the person well, it may help you to gain an advantage over other letters that the person may receive.

Other personal contacts may be obtained by contacting the advertising federation in the city you have selected. Generally, cities that have advertising agencies and specialty firms will have advertising federations that usually are associated with the American Advertising Federation. These federations have members who work in the advertising profession. Sometimes the directors of these advertising federations are informed about position openings and consequently can provide information about the positions that are available and whom to contact.

APPLYING FOR YOUR FIRST JOB IN ADVERTISING

Before you apply for your first job in advertising after graduating from college, you need to research the advertising agencies for which you desire to work. In short, you need to learn the executives' names, know what clients the agencies service, and have a firm grasp of the agencies' philosophies. If you desire to work for a company or business other than an advertising agency, you need similar information. Research will help you understand what the agencies are doing and how well they are doing it. It will also help you determine which agencies you would like to work for as well as provide information you may need for an interview. After all, an interview allows you to express why you are interested in the firm and how you meet the firm's needs.

Researching the Advertising Agency, Company, Business, or Specialty Firm

In order to learn about advertising agencies, companies, businesses, and specialty firms, you need to do some research. A good place to begin is at a college or university library. If a college or university library is not nearby, you may use a large public library. However, many public libraries do not subscribe to all of the publications listed below.

For information about advertising agencies, you should examine the following sources, which usually are shelved in the "Reference" section of a library:

- *Standard Directory of Advertising Agencies (also referred to as The "Red Book")*
- *The Adweek Directory: The Directory of U.S. Advertising Agencies, Public Relations Firms, Media Buyers Services and Specialized Marketing Companies*
- *Standard Directory of International Advertisers and Advertising Agencies: The International Red Book*

These sources are published annually and provide key executives' names, the agencies' addresses, and the agencies' clients, among other useful information.

For information about advertisers (companies and businesses), you should examine the third source listed above as well as the following, which usually are placed in the "Reference" section of a library:

- *Standard Directory of Advertisers*
- *Standard & Poor's Corporate Records*
- *Standard & Poor's Register of Corporations, Directors and Executives*
- *Thomas Register of American Manufacturers*

These sources are published annually and include information about a company's history, products or brands produced, address, departments, and key executives' names.

Of course, additional information about advertisers may be found in the following magazines and newspapers:

- *Advertising Age*
- *Adweek*
- *Barron's*
- *Brandweek*
- *Business Week*
- *Forbes*
- *Fortune*
- *Harvard Business Review*
- *Mediaweek*
- *New York Times*
- *Wall Street Journal*

The information found in the magazines and newspapers listed above will be more current than the information found in the annual publications. For instance, you may learn about personnel changes at advertising agencies in *Advertising Age* and *Adweek*. You may learn about new accounts for advertising agencies in both periodicals as well. Of course, other information that may be of use may be found in these publications. For instance, many of these publications list job openings.

For information about specialty firms, you should examine the following annual publications, which usually are shelved in the "Reference" section of a library:

- *Broadcasting and Cable Yearbook*
- *D & B Directory of Service Companies*
- *Editor and Publisher International Yearbook*
- *Gale Directory of Publications and Broadcast Media*
- *O'Dwyer's Directory of Public Relations Firms*

The first publication provides information about radio and television stations as well as cable companies. The second provides information about service companies throughout the United States. The third publication provides information about newspapers and firms that service newspapers, and the fourth publication provides information about various periodicals and broadcast media. The fifth provides information about public relations firms. Most, if not all, of these companies need people who know about advertising. Most, if not all, of these publications provide information about the respective businesses, including the names of key executives and the companies' addresses.

You may obtain valuable information from the World Wide Web. For instance, if you desire information about advertising agencies, you may visit the following websites:

- www.aaaa.org (this is the website for the American Association of Advertising Agencies)
- www.adforum.com
- www.ad-freaks.com
- http://advertising.utexas.edu
- www.agencycompile.com
- http://agencyfinder.com
- http://agencypreview.com
- http://Americanadagencies.com
- http://4Advertising.com

If you wish to learn about advertising agencies in specific cities, such as Minneapolis, Phoenix, San Diego, Seattle, Miami, or Los Angeles, you may visit the following websites:

- http://Minneapolisadagencies.com
- http://Phoenixadagencies.com
- http://Sandiegoadagencies.com
- http://Seattleadagencies.com
- http://SouthFloridaadagencies.com
- http://LosAngelesadagencies.com

And for information about companies and businesses, you may visit the following:

- http://annualreportservice.com (this website provides annual reports of various companies)
- http://CompaniesOnline.com (this website has a directory of over 100,000 companies with websites)

- http://businesswire.com (this website provides information about different businesses)
- http://hoovers.com (this website provides information about 9,500 public and private businesses)
- http://metamoney.com/w100 (this website provides information about the top U.S. and international companies that are on the Web)
- http://prars.com (Public Register's Annual Report Service provides annual reports for various companies)
- http://reportgallery.com (this website provides annual reports for various companies)
- http://Researchmag.com (this website provides articles and basic factual information about numerous businesses)
- http://sec.gov/info/edgar.shtml (information about businesses that have less than $10 million in assets and 500 shareholders)
- www.stockinfo.standardpoor.com (this website provides information from Standard & Poor's about various companies)
- http://wsj.ar.wilink.com (this is the annual reports service from the Wall Street Journal)

For other information about businesses and companies, you should visit "Business Connections," which is offered online by the *New York Times*: http://nytimes.com/library/cyber/reference/busconn.html.

If you desire to search for jobs in advertising online, you may visit the following websites:

- www.monster.com
- http://adagencyjobs.net
- http://tigerjobs.com

These websites are basically job banks. However, the listings are not exhaustive. Many advertising agencies do not list openings on these websites; therefore, if you are interested in a particular advertising agency, do not assume that the agency is not interested in hiring someone just because it has not listed an opening on one of the above.

The Cover Letter

Once you have found a position that you are interested in, you need to write a cover letter and résumé. Remember, both are advertisements about you.

The cover letter should be tailored to the position you are seeking; it should not be written so that it is generic—that is, written in such a way that it may be sent to any prospective employer without any changes. The cover letter provides an opportunity for you to illustrate your communication skills. It allows you to express how well you know the company to which you are applying as well as the reasons you should be considered for the position.

Let us examine the cover letter in depth. A cover letter should be typed on $8\frac{1}{2} \times 11$-inch quality bond paper. It should contain ample margins. It should be typed on one side of one page. The copy should be typed in paragraph form, and the paragraphs should be balanced on the page. The paragraphs should be brief so that they are easy to read. The writing should have a conversational but formal tone. Because a cover letter provides the first impression that prospective employers have of you, you do not want to sound informal.

Personal information—name, address, telephone number(s), fax number(s), and e-mail address—should be typed at the top of the cover letter, followed by the date. Then the name, title, name of the company, and its address should be typed, followed by the salutation.

The first paragraph should present the reason for the letter. Identify the position or particular job for which you are applying and provide the source from which you learned about the position. The source may be an advertisement in a trade magazine or daily newspaper, a friend or acquaintance, an employment service, or some other medium or person.

The second paragraph should explain why you are interested in the position and the company. Express in a positive fashion why you should be considered for the position. If you have just graduated from college, you may explain how your formal education and skills qualify you for the position. Be specific about your accomplishments. If you have relevant professional experience, you should mention this as well. In short, describe how you meet the position's qualifications. In order to write this paragraph, refer to the advertisement for the position. Use the language of the industry in which the position exists. Illustrate to the reader that you understand the industry's culture. However, do not use jargon. Use words that the reader will understand.

The third paragraph should refer the reader to your résumé, which you should enclose with the letter. Do not repeat verbatim from your résumé, however. Some prospective employees, especially those who have been working for several years, will enclose a portfolio. If this applies to you, then you should refer the reader to your portfolio as well.

The fourth paragraph should express your desire for an interview at the reader's discretion and convenience. In other words, you need to be flexible as to the time, day, and place. Include when and where you can be reached and your telephone number(s). If you intend to follow up the cover letter and résumé with a telephone call, provide the date and time. Include a sentence that encourages the reader to respond as well as a sentence that informs the reader about your eagerness to provide additional information. Close with a sentence that thanks the reader for his or her time and consideration.

When you are finished, read the letter for content and mistakes. Are the addresses and telephone numbers correct? Is the name of the person to whom it is addressed spelled correctly? Is the person's title spelled correctly? Is the punctuation correct? Is the grammar correct? Did you remember to sign your name as well as type it? Read the letter out loud. Does it sound natural? Is it easy to understand? Let others read it too. Accept their criticism and suggestions.

GUIDELINES FOR WRITING A COVER LETTER The following guidelines may help you write a better cover letter. Refer to these whenever you need to write a new one:

1. Research the position and company before you write the cover letter.
2. Address the letter to a specific person within the company. Use the person's name and title.
3. Be enthusiastic and positive in your cover letter.
4. Begin by identifying the position for which you are applying.
5. Mention where you learned about the position.
6. Identify what you can do for the company.
7. Relate your education and two or three skills and experiences to the position's qualifications.
8. Explain how your education, skills, and experiences match the requirements of the job.

BOX 15.1 ***Example of a Cover Letter***

2550 Hartville Road
Hartville, Ohio 44555

January 2, 2004

Ms. Kelli Williams
Human Services Coordinator
The Thompson Agency
5050 Thomas Avenue
Cincinnati, Ohio 42500

Dear Ms. Williams:

I understand from a classified display advertisement posted in the *Cincinnati Enquirer* that you are in need of an experienced copywriter to work on several accounts. My work experience makes me an ideal candidate, and I am very interested in learning more about the position.

In my current job at the *Hartville Courier* I sell advertising space and write advertising copy. I have helped increase the newspaper's revenue from advertising by 20 percent and have helped create hundreds of advertisements for numerous advertisers. Although I have not worked as a copywriter at an advertising agency, I believe that my education, experience, and skills have prepared me for such a position.

I would like to meet with you at your convenience to discuss the position. If you wish to arrange an interview, please contact me at the above address or by telephone at (606) 555-2455.

Thank you for your time and consideration.

Respectfully,

Mary James

Mary James

9. Mention that you have enclosed a copy of your résumé.
10. Mention that you are available for an interview. Provide the telephone number(s) and the time when the reader may contact you to schedule an interview.
11. Offer to provide additional information.
12. Thank the reader for his or her time and consideration.
13. Use active verbs.
14. Do not use the word I too often.
15. Check your letter for mistakes.
16. Make sure that the cover letter is typed on one side of one sheet.
17. Keep a copy of the letter.

AN EXAMPLE OF A COVER LETTER Box 15.1 (previous page) contains an example of a cover letter.

The Résumé

The résumé should present your credentials and qualifications in a succinct manner. It should provide information about your educational background, professional or work experience, skills, and activities or interests in one or two pages. Some résumés include additional information, such as job objective, military service, licenses, and publications, among others.

When you write a résumé, make sure that it is no more than two pages in length, especially if you have just graduated from college. On the other hand, if you have been working for several years, your résumé may be longer. In addition, make sure that it appears uncluttered. Information that is the same or similar should be grouped under boldface or capitalized headings. Have ample margins and use no more than two typefaces throughout. In fact, one typeface should be considered for the entire document.

A good résumé should be tailored to the position for which you are applying, much like the cover letter. Of course, if there is a deadline for the position for which you are applying, you may not have enough time to tailor your résumé. In this instance, you may have to send a copy of an "older" résumé.

Let us examine what a good résumé should have. First, it should contain your name, address, telephone number(s), fax number, and e-mail address at the top of the first page. Second, it may contain the following heading, JOB OBJECTIVE, followed by a brief sentence that describes what you desire to do professionally. (Some people include a summary statement at the top of the résumé instead of a job objective, and some include the job objective in the cover letter.) Third, it should contain the following headings: EDUCATION, EXPERIENCE, HONORS, SKILLS, and ACTIVITIES. Of course, some people will use different headings for the information that should be listed under these headings. Let us examine each of these headings.

Under EDUCATION, you should list colleges, universities, and other institutions. Identify by name and location (city/state), months/years attended, degrees or diplomas received, months/years the degrees or diplomas were received, majors and minors, and grade point average (if B average or above). You may list important courses completed. Some people may include subheads to separate information in this section. For instance, they may include "Other Schools," "Independent Study," or "Other." If you need to use subheads, make sure that they reflect the information they represent.

For EXPERIENCE, you should include full-time and part-time salaried jobs, internships, co-op positions, volunteer work, and freelance work. Include the month/year for each, the position by title you held, the name and location of employer, and your duties. Under HONORS, list any academic honors, such as scholarships, honors' lists, fellowships, professional awards, and community recognitions. Include titles, places, and dates received.

For SKILLS, list your various skills, such as computer languages and software applications, teaching or tutoring, leadership, and athletics, among others. Under ACTIVITIES, identify the academic, professional, and community organizations, such as clubs, committees, and special interest groups, in which you are an officer or member. You may include professional and community activities for which you have worked. Hobbies or other interests, such as travel, are optional. Usually, you should not include these unless they relate to the position for which you are applying.

Some people list references' names, addresses, and telephone numbers on their résumés, but you do not have to. You may type these on a separate sheet and give the sheet to the prospective employer after the interview.

Résumés may be chronological or skills based (functional). The former presents information in reverse chronological order—that is, the most recent is presented first. The latter presents information, such as experiences, under headings that identify the skills or qualities that are required for a particular position or profession.

Many résumés contain brief descriptions about work experiences and other activities. These descriptions should begin with verbs, and pronouns and articles should be deleted. Use nouns. In short, these descriptions should be concise and precise. If you are writing about past experiences, use the past tense; if you are writing about present experiences, use the present tense. Do not include information such as age, gender, health, marital status, religious affiliation, and political affiliation. These are not necessary.

GUIDELINES FOR WRITING A RÉSUMÉ The following guidelines should help you whenever you have to write a résumé:

1. Use quality bond paper and a computer and laser printer.
2. Maintain consistency in headings, spacing, and layout.
3. Make ample use of white space between major sections.
4. Emphasize headings and important information by using capital letters, boldface, underlines, or italics. Do not overuse these, however.
5. Use active verbs.
6. Use adjectives and nouns that describe you in a positive manner.
7. Be consistent in punctuation.
8. Put periods and commas within quotation marks. Put periods at the ends of sentences.
9. Do not use exclamation marks.
10. Capitalize proper nouns.
11. Do not switch tenses within your résumé.
12. Write out numbers between one and nine, and use numerals for number 10 and above.
13. Do not begin sentences with numerals. Spell these out or rephrase.
14. Check dates for consistency in style and accuracy.
15. Check the abbreviations of state names.

BOX 15.2 ***Example of a Résumé***

MARY JAMES
2550 Hartville Road
Hartville, Ohio 44555
(606) 555-2455

OBJECTIVE:
To obtain a full-time position as a copywriter.

EDUCATION:
Kent State University, Kent, Ohio
Bachelor of Science, Mass Communications, May 2000
Major Emphasis: Advertising Minors: Marketing; English
Overall GPA: 3.75/4.0
Honors: Dean's List

COMPUTER SKILLS:
- MS Word
- MS Excel
- MS PowerPoint
- QuarkXPress
- Adobe Illustrator

EXPERIENCE:
Hartville Courier, Advertising Sales Representative and Writer, 2000–Present

- Sell advertising space to various advertisers
- Write advertising copy for advertisements
- Assist Advertising Manager with solving clients' advertising problems
- Have helped increase newspaper's advertising revenue by 20 percent

ACTIVITIES:
Newspaper Advertising Association, Member, 2000–Present
Ohio Newspaper Advertising Association, Member, 2000–Present

REFERENCES:
Available on request.

16. Do not use more than one or two typefaces, and use a typeface that is easy to read, such as Times New Roman.
17. Check the spelling, especially of names and titles, by reading every word.
18. Allow others to read your résumé. Be open to their comments or suggestions.
19. Check the spelling of your name and address. Check your telephone number. Is it correct? Are these pieces of information at the top of the page? Are they slightly larger than other copy? Are they bolder?
20. Try to keep your résumé to one page, if possible, and print on one side.
21. The organization of information should be clear and easy to understand.
22. Make sure that the information, such as education and employment, contains dates, the names of institutions or employers, and descriptions of degrees or duties.

AN EXAMPLE OF A RÉSUMÉ Box 15.2 contains an example of a résumé. If you need additional help in writing a cover letter and résumé, you may contact your college placement office. The personnel in this office can help you prepare both, and they may know about positions that need to be filled. They can also provide helpful tips for your interview.

The Portfolio

If you want to work in advertising, even if you want to be an account executive, you should have a portfolio. A portfolio or "book" displays your creative ability. Portfolios come in all sizes. I suggest that you purchase one that is 11 × 14" or 18 × 24" and that it contain pages that allow for the inclusion of loose samples of your work. Today, professionals are using CDs, Zip disks, and even websites to display their work.

No matter which of the above forms you decide on, make sure that you create at least 10 to 20 advertisements for inclusion. Several of these advertisements should be part of an advertising campaign. In fact, you may have advertisements for more than one campaign. However, I suggest that you do not include more than two or three, especially if the advertisements for each campaign total three. Concentrate on print advertisements, such as those for magazines, not on storyboards for television commercials or scripts for radio commercials, unless you intend to interview at an advertising agency that does mostly broadcast commercials. Make sure that your advertisements are for current advertisers or advertisers that do not exist. More important, make sure that your advertisements display your creative ability and skills.

When you have done your advertisements, organize them so that the advertisements for a campaign are together, in a logical order, not spread throughout the portfolio. In addition, make sure that you have strong advertisements at the beginning, in the middle, and at the end of your book.

If you go to an interview at an advertising agency that creates advertisements for advertisers you have selected for your book, remove the advertisements for these advertisers before you go. Otherwise, your advertisements may be compared subjectively with the work the agency has created; if your advertisements do not measure up, you may not be offered the position.

GUIDELINES FOR CREATING A PORTFOLIO The following guidelines should help you create a portfolio:

1. Make sure that your portfolio is neat in appearance and carefully organized.
2. Make sure that you have your name, address, and telephone number on or in your portfolio.
3. Include an introduction and a table of contents before the advertisements begin.
4. Make sure that you have one or more copies of your portfolio, in case a prospective employer wants to keep a copy for several days.
5. The advertisements in your portfolio should be your best work.
6. The advertisements should be consistent in creative style and skill.
7. Make sure that the advertisements are relevant to the prospective employer. For instance, if the prospective employer is an advertising agency that creates advertisements for financial institutions, include advertisements that are similar in your portfolio.
8. Make sure that your portfolio begins and ends with your best work.
9. Make sure that the advertisements do not face in different directions. In short, you want to make it easy for the reader to examine each advertisement.
10. Remove any empty pages or sleeves.
11. Invite others, including various professionals, to examine your portfolio before you go to an interview. Be open to comments and suggestions.

A FINAL NOTE

Advertising is an exciting profession. It allows you the opportunity to help others by solving their marketing and advertising problems. Good luck!

APPENDIX

Graduate Programs

At the time of writing, the following universities offered a master's degree with an emphasis or major in advertising or integrated marketing communications:

- Academy of Art College (MFA)
- Arizona State University (MMC)
- Boston University (MS)
- California State University, Fullerton (MA)
- California State University, Northridge (MA)
- Emerson College (MA)
- Florida International University (MS)
- Florida State University (MS)
- Golden Gate University (MS)
- Governors State University (MA)
- Kansas State University (MS)
- Louisiana State University (MMC)
- Loyola University, Chicago (MS)
- Marquette University (MA)
- Marshall University (MAJ)
- Michigan State University (MA)
- Morehead State University (MA)
- Murray State University (MA, MS)
- Northwestern University (MS)
- Ohio University (MSJ)
- Pennsylvania State University (MA)
- Point Park College (MA)
- Roosevelt University (MS)
- San Diego State University (MA)
- San Jose State University (MS)

- St. Cloud State University (MS)
- Suffolk University (MA)
- Syracuse University (MA, MS)
- Temple University (MJ)
- Texas Christian University (MS)
- Texas Tech University (MA)
- Towson University (MS)
- University of Alabama (MA)
- University of Arkansas (MA)
- University of Colorado (MA)
- University of Denver (MS)
- University of Florida (MA)
- University of Georgia (MA, MMC)
- University of Illinois (MS)
- University of Kansas (MS)
- University of Louisiana at Lafayette (MC)
- University of Memphis (MA)
- University of Missouri (MA)
- University of Nebraska (MA)
- University of North Carolina at Chapel Hill (MA)
- University of North Texas (MJ, MA)
- University of Oklahoma (MA)
- University of Oregon (MA, MS)
- University of South Carolina (MMC)
- University of Tennessee (MS)
- University of Texas at Austin (MA)
- University of Utah (MA, MS)
- Virginia Commonwealth University (MS)
- Webster University (MA)
- West Virginia University (MSJ)
- Wichita State University (MA)

I suggest that you check other sources, such as http://GradSchools.com, http://Petersons.com, and annual publications that can be found at any major bookstore.

Selected Bibliography

Aitchison, Jim. *Cutting Edge Advertising: How to Create the World's Best Print for Brands in the 21st Century*. Singapore: Prentice-Hall, 1999.

Allerton, Haidee E. "Generation Why: They Promise to Be the Biggest Influence Since the Baby Boomers." *Training and Development*, Vol. 55, No. 11 (November 2001): 56–60.

Anderson, Axel, and Denison Hatch. "How to Create Headlines That Get Results." *Target Marketing*, Vol. 17, No. 3 (March 1994): 28–35.

Applegate, Edd, ed. *The Ad Men and Women: A Biographical Dictionary of Advertising*. Westport, CT: Greenwood Press, 1994.

Arens, William F. *Contemporary Advertising*, 8th ed. New York: McGraw-Hill/Irwin, 2002.

Asher, Donald. *From College to Career: Entry-Level Resumes for Any Major*. Berkeley, CA: Ten Speed Press, 1992.

Axelrod, Joel N. *Choosing the Best Advertising Alternative: A Management Guide to Identifying the Most Effective Copy Testing Technique*. New York: Association of National Advertisers, Inc., 1971.

Baker, Stephen. *Systematic Approach to Advertising Creativity*. New York: McGraw-Hill Book Co., Inc., 1979.

Baldwin, Huntley. *How to Create Effective TV Commercials*. Lincolnwood, IL: NTC Business Books, 1989.

Barry, Ann Marie. *The Advertising Portfolio*. Lincolnwood, IL: NTC Business Books, 1990.

Beatty, Richard H. *The Perfect Cover Letter*. New York: John Wiley and Sons, 1989.

Bendinger, Bruce. *The Copy Workshop Workbook*. Chicago: The Copy Workshop, 1993.

Benezra, Karen. "Don't Mislabel Gen X." *Brandweek*, Vol. 36, No. 20 (May 15, 1995): 32–34.

Bernbach, Evelyn, and Bob Levenson. *Bill Bernbach's Book*. New York: Villard Books, 1987.

Bernstein, David. *Creative Advertising: For This You Went to Oxford? A Personal Textbook of Advertising*. London: Longman, 1974.

Blake, Gary, and Robert W. Bly. *The Elements of Copywriting: The Essential Guide to Creating Copy That Gets the Results You Want*. New York: MacMillan, 1998.

Blatt, Dick. "In-Store Ads Compel Attention: Study Shows That In-Store Ads Disseminate Key Message in Convenience Stores." *Snack Food and Wholesale Bakery*, Vol. 91, No. 8 (August 2002): 40.

Bly, Robert W. *Ads That Sell: How to Create Advertising That Gets Results*. Brentwood, NY: Asher Gallant Press, 1988.

———. *Advertising Manager's Handbook*. Englewood Cliffs, NJ: Prentice-Hall, 1993.

———. *The Copywriter's Handbook: A Step-by-Step Guide to Writing Copy That Sells*. New York: Dodd, Mead and Co., Inc., 1985.

———. *The Online Copywriter's Handbook: Everything You Need to Know to Write Electronic Copy That Sells*. New York: McGraw-Hill, 2002.

Bogart, Leo. *Strategy in Advertising*. Lincolnwood, IL: NTC Business Books, 1996.

Bond, Jonathan, and Richard Kirshenbaum. *Under the Radar: Talking to Today's Cynical Consumer*. New

York: John Wiley and Sons, Inc., 1998.

Book, Albert C., Norman D. Cary, and Stanley I. Tannenbaum. *The Radio and Television Commercial*, 3d ed. Chicago: NTC Business Books, 1996.

Book, Albert C., and C. Dennis Schick. *Fundamentals of Copy and Layout: Everything You Need to Know to Prepare Better Ads*, 3d ed. Lincolnwood, IL: NTC Business Books, 1997.

Broadbent, Simon, ed. *The Leo Burnett Book of Advertising*. London: Business Books, 1984.

Buchholz, Andreas, and Wolfram Wordemann. *What Makes Winning Brands Different? The Hidden Method behind the World's Most Successful Brands*. West Sussex, England: John Wiley and Sons Ltd., 2000.

Burnett, Leo N. *Leo: A Tribute to Leo Burnett through a Selection of the Inspiring Words He Spoke*. Chicago: Leo Burnett Co., 1971.

Burton, Phillip Ward. *Advertising Copywriting*, 7th ed. Lincolnwood, IL: NTC/Contemporary Publishing Group, 1999.

Bushko, David, and Richard H. Stansfield. *Dartnell's Advertising Manager's Handbook*, 4th ed. Chicago: Dartnell, 1997.

Buxton, Edward. *Creative People at Work*. New York: Executive Communications, Inc., 1975.

———. *Promise Them Anything: The Inside Story of the Madison Avenue Power Struggle*. New York: Stein and Day, 1972.

Calkins, Earnest Elmo. *Advertising*. Chicago: American Library Association, 1929.

Caples, John. *How to Make Your Advertising Make Money*. Englewood Cliffs, NJ: Prentice-Hall, Inc., 1983.

———. *Tested Advertising Methods*. Englewood Cliffs, NJ: Prentice-Hall, Inc., 1984.

Cohen, William A. *The Marketing Plan*, 3d ed. New York: John Wiley and Sons, Inc., 2001.

Colley, Russell H. *Defining Advertising Goals for Measured Advertising Results*. New York: Association of National Advertisers, 1961.

Criscito, Pat. *Designing the Perfect Resume*, 2d ed. Hauppauge, NY: Barron's, 2000.

Cross, Mary. *A Century of American Icons: 100 Products and Slogans from the 20th Century Consumer Culture*. Westport, CT: Greenwood Press, 2002.

Davis, Joel. *Advertising Research: Theory and Practice*. Upper Saddle River, NJ: Prentice-Hall, 1997.

Davis, Joel J. *Understanding Yellow Pages*. Troy, MI: Yellow Pages Publishers Association, 1998.

Davis, Sally Prince. *Creative Self-promotion on a Limited Budget*. Cincinnati, OH: North Light Books, 1992.

de Bono, Edward. *Lateral Thinking for Management*. New York: American Management Association, 1971.

———. *Serious Creativity*. New York: HarperCollins, 1992.

Della Femina, Jerry, and Charles Sopkin. *From Those Wonderful Folks Who Gave You Pearl Harbor: Front-Line Dispatches from the Advertising War*. New York: Simon and Schuster, 1970.

Dobrow, Larry. *When Advertising Tried Harder: The Sixties*. New York: Friendly Press, 1984.

Dru, Jean-Marie. *Beyond Disruption: Changing the Rules in the Marketplace*. New York: John Wiley and Sons, Inc., 2002.

———. *Disruption: Overturning Conventions and Shaking Up the Marketplace*. New York: John Wiley and Sons, Inc., 1996.

Ebenkamp, Becky. "Whipple: Squeeze This!" *Brandweek*, Vol. 41, No. 36 (September 18, 2000): 28.

Farbey, David. *How to Produce Successful Advertising: A Guide to Strategy, Planning and Targeting*, 3d ed. London: Kogan Page, 2002.

Fearon, Robert. *Advertising That Works: How to Create a Winning Advertising Program for Your Company*. Chicago: Probus Publishing Co., 1991.

Felton, George. *Advertising: Concept and Copy*. Englewood Cliffs, NJ: Prentice-Hall, 1994.

———. "Pro Bono Collegio?" *Brandweek*, Vol. 42, No. 22 (May 28, 2001): 28.

Ferrell, O. C., Michael Hartline, and George Lucas. *Marketing Strategy*, 2d ed. Cincinnati, OH: South-Western Publishing, 2002.

Foote, Camerson S. *The Fourth Medium: How to Use Promotional Literature to Increase Sales and Profits*. New York: Dow Jones-Irwin, 1988.

Fraser-Robinson, John. *The Secrets of Effective Direct Mail*. London: McGraw-Hill Book Co., 1989.

Friesen, Pat. "Direct Response Creative: What to Test First." *Target Marketing*, Vol. 22, No. 5 (May 1999): 50.

Gabay, J. Jonathan. *Teach Yourself Copywriting*. Lincolnwood, IL: Contemporary Books, 2000.

Gardyn, Rebecca. "Retirement Redefined." *American Demographics*, Vol. 22, No. 11 (November 2000): 52, 54–57.

"Generation Y Challenges Retailers." *USA Today*, December 1, 2000: 9.

Gifford, Wendy. "Creating Advertising Miracles." *Writer's Digest*, Vol. 79, No. 10 (October 1999): 40–42.

Glatzer, Robert. *The New Advertising: Twenty-one Successful Campaigns from Avis to Volkswagen*. New York: Citadel Press, 1970.

Gobe, Mark. *Emotional Branding: The New Paradigm for Connecting Brands to People*. New York: Allworth Press, 2001.

Goodrum, Charles, and Helen Dalrymple. *Advertising in America: The First 200 Years*. New York: Harry N. Abrams, Inc., 1990.

Gordon, Kim T. "Slogan's Heroes." *Entrepreneur*, Vol. 29, No. 7 (July 2001): 89.

Gossage, Howard Luck. *Is There Any Hope for Advertising?* Edited by Kim Rotzoll, Jarlath Graham, and Barrow Mussey. Urbana: University of Illinois Press, 1986.

Graber, Steven. *The Everything Cover Letter Book*. Holbrook, MA: Adams Media, 2000.

Gronback, Ken. "Marketing to Generation Y." *DSN Retailing Today*, July 24, 2000: 14.

Haskins, Jack B., and Alice Kendrick. *Successful Advertising Research Methods*. Lincolnwood, IL: NTC Business Books, 1992.

Henricks, Mark. "Words to Live By: A Catch Phrase Conveys the Vision of Your Business—to Employees and to Customers." *Entrepreneur*, Vol. 26, No. 9 (September 1998): 78–80.

Herzbrun, David. *Copywriting by Design: Bringing Ideas to Life with Words and Images*. Lincolnwood, IL: NTC Business Books, 1997.

Higgins, Denis. *The Art of Writing Advertising: Conversations with Masters of the Craft*. Lincolnwood, IL: National Textbook Co., 1965.

Hilliard, Robert L. *Writing for Television, Radio, and New Media*, 7th ed. Belmont, CA: Wadsworth, 2000.

Hopkins, Claude. *Scientific Advertising*. Chicago: Advertising Publications, Inc., 1966.

Hornblower, Margot. "Great Xpectations: Slackers? Hardly. The So-called Generation X Turns Out to Be Full of Go-getters Who Are Just Doing It—But Their Way." *Time*, Vol. 149, No. 23 (June 9, 1997): 58–63, 66–68.

Humphreys, Jeffrey M. "African-American Buying Power by Place of Residence: 1990–1999." Available at www.selig.uga.edu/forecast/totalbuy/afr-amerBlack%20Buying%201999%20text.html: 1–7.

———. "Asian-American Buying Power by Place of Residence: 1990–1999." *Georgia Business and Economic Conditions*, Vol. 59, No. 1 (January–February 1999): 1–7.

———. "Hispanic Buying Power by Place of Residence: 1990–1999." *Georgia Business and Economic Conditions*, Vol. 58, No. 6 (November–December 1998): 1–8.

Ind, Nicholas. *Great Advertising Campaigns: Goals and Accomplishments*. Lincolnwood, IL: NTC Business Books, 1993.

Jackson, Tom. *The Perfect Resume*. New York: Doubleday, 1990.

Jeweler, A. Jerome, and Bonnie L. Drewniany. *Creative Strategy in Advertising*, 7th ed. Belmont, CA: Wadsworth, 2001.

Jones, John Philip. *The Advertising Business: Operations, Creativity, Media Planning, Integrated Communications*. Thousand Oaks, CA: Sage Publications, 1999.

———. *How to Use Advertising to Build Strong Brands*. Thousand Oaks, CA: Sage Publications, 1999.

Jones, Susan K. *Creative Strategy in Direct Marketing*. Lincolnwood, IL: NTC Business Books, 1991.

Kanner, Bernice. *The 100 Best TV Commercials . . . and Why They Worked*. New York: Random House, 1999.

Kaye, Barbara K., and Norman J. Medoff. *Just a Click Away: Advertising on the Internet*. Needham Heights, MA: Allyn and Bacon, 2001.

Keding, Ann, and Thomas Bivins. *How to Produce Creative Advertising: Proven Techniques and Computer Applications*. Lincolnwood, IL: NTC Business Books, 1991.

Kennedy, Joyce Lain. *Cover Letters for Dummies*. New York: Hungry Minds, 2000.

Kimeldorf, Martin. *Portfolio Power: The New Way to Showcase All Your Job Skills and Experiences*. Princeton, NJ: Peterson's, 1997.

Klein, Erica Levy. *Write Great Ads: A Step-by-Step Approach*. New York: John C. Wiley and Sons, Inc., 1990.

Koestler, Arthur. *The Act of Creation*. New York: Macmillan Co., 1964.

Kover, Arthur J., and William L. James. "When Do Advertising 'Power Words' Work? An Examination of Congruence and Satiation." *Journal of Advertising Research*, Vol. 33, No. 4 (July–August 1993): 32–38.

Krannich, Ronald L., and William J. Banis. *High Impact Resumes and Letters: How to Communicate Your Qualifications to Employers*. Manassas Park, VA: Impact Publications, 2002.

Krannich, Ronald L., and Caryl Rae Krannich. *Dynamite Cover Letters and Other Great Job Search Letters*. Manassas Park, VA: Impact Publications, 1997.

———. *Dynamite Resumes: 101 Great Examples and Tips for Success*, 3d ed. Manassas Park, VA: Impact Publications, 1997.

Laskey, Henry A., Ellen Day, and Melvin R. Crask. "Typology of Main Message Strategies for Television Commercials." *Journal of Advertising*, Vol. 18, No. 1 (Winter 1989): 36–41.

Lavidge, Robert J., and Gary A. Steiner. "A Model for Predictive Measurements of Advertising Effectiveness." *Journal of Marketing*, Vol. 25, No. 6 (October 1961): 59–63.

Lederman, Eva. *Careers in Advertising*. New York: Princeton Review, 1998.

Leigh, James H. "The Use of Figures of Speech in Print Ad Headline." *Journal of Advertising*, Vol. 23, No. 2 (June 1994): 17–33.

Leo, John. "One Tin Slogan." *U.S. News and World Report*, Vol. 130, No. 3 (January 22, 2001): 13.

Lewis, Herschell Gordon. "Automatic Self-starters." *Direct Marketing*, Vol. 57, No. 7 (November 1994): 38–40.

———. *On the Art of Writing Copy*. Englewood Cliffs, NJ: Prentice-Hall, Inc., 1988.

Lewis, Herschell Gordon, and Carol Nelson. *Advertising Age Handbook of Advertising*. Lincolnwood, IL: NTC Business Books, 1999.

———. *World's Greatest Direct Mail Sales Letters*. Lincolnwood, IL: NTC Business Books, 1996.

Lisanti, Tony. "Mean What You Say, and Say What You Mean." *Discount Store News*, Vol. 38, No. 17 (September 6, 1999): 11.

Lois, George, with Bill Pitts. *What's the Big Idea? How to Win with Outrageous Ideas (That Sell!)*. New York: Plume, 1993.

Lois, George, and William Pitts. *The Art of Advertising: George Lois on Mass Communication*. New York: Harry N. Abrams, 1977.

Lyons, John. *Guts: Advertising from the Inside Out*. New York: Amacom, 1987.

Maddock, Richard C., and Richard L. Fulton. *Marketing to the Mind: Right Brain Strategies for Advertising and Marketing*. Westport, CT: Quorum Books, 1996.

Marler, Patty. *Cover Letters Made Easy*. Lincolnwood, IL: VGM Career Horizons, 1996.

Maslow, Abraham H. "'Higher' and 'Lower' Needs." *Journal of Psychology*, Vol. 25 (1948): 433–436.

———. *Motivation and Personality*. New York: Harper and Row, 1954.

———. "A Theory of Human Motivation." *Psychological Review*, Vol. 50 (1943): 370–396.

Mayer, Martin. *Whatever Happened to Madison Avenue? Advertising in the '90s*. Boston: Little, Brown, 1991.

McKibbin, Stuart. *The Business of Persuasion: Copywriting Skills and Techniques That Get Results*. Dublin: Oak Tree Press, 2001.

McNeill, William. *First Time Resumes*. Holbrook, MA: Adams Media Corp., 2000.

Meeske, Milan D. *Copywriting for the Electronic Media: A Practical Guide*, 4th ed. Belmont, CA: Wadsworth, 2003.

Metzdorf, Martha. *The Ultimate Portfolio*. Cincinnati, OH: North Light Books, 1991.

Miller, William C. *Flash of Brilliance: Inspiring Creativity Where You Work*. Reading, MA: Perseus Books, 1999.

Minski, Laurence, and Emily Thorton Calvo. *How to Succeed in Advertising When All You Have Is Talent*. Lincolnwood, IL: NTC Business Books, 1994.

Morgan, Dana. *7 Minute Cover Letters*. Foster City, CA: IDG Books Worldwide, 2000.

———. *7 Minute Resumes: Build the Perfect Resume One 7-Minute Letter at a Time*. Foster City, CA: IDG Books Worldwide, 2000.

Morrison, Margaret A. *Using Qualitative Research in Advertising Strategies, Techniques, and Applications*. Thousand Oaks, CA: Sage Publications, 2002.

Najjar, Laurie, and Lyndsey Erwin. "The Fourth Annual Top POP Buyers Report." *Point of Purchase*, August 2002: 16–20.

Nelson, Roy Paul. *The Design of Advertising*. Dubuque, IA: William C. Brown, 1981.

Norins, Hanley. *The Complete Copywriter: A Comprehensive Guide to All Phases of Advertising Communication*. Malabar, FL: Robert E. Krieger

Publishing Co., Inc., 1980 (originally published in 1966 by McGraw-Hill Book Co).

———. *The Young & Rubicam Traveling Creative Workshop*. Englewood Cliffs, NJ: Prentice-Hall, Inc., 1990.

Nucifora, Alf. "Pay Attention: Generation Y Is Looming." *Business Journal*, May 19, 2000.

Ogilvy, David. *Confessions of an Advertising Man*. New York: Atheneum, 1963.

———. *Ogilvy on Advertising*. New York: Vintage Books, 1985.

Orlik, Peter B. *Broadcast/Cable Copywriting*, 6th ed. Boston: Allyn and Bacon, Inc., 1998.

Orr, Alicia. "The Mechanics of a Direct Mail Test." *Target Marketing*, Vol. 17, No. 5 (May 1994): 10–11.

Osborn, Alex F. *Applied Imagination: The Principles and Procedures of Creative Thinking*. New York: Charles Scribner's Sons, 1953.

O'Toole, John. *The Trouble with Advertising*. New York: Chelsea House, 1981.

Paetro, Maxine. *How to Put Your Book Together and Get a Job in Advertising*, 21st Century ed. Chicago: The Copy Workshop, 2002.

Parente, Donald. *Advertising Campaign Strategy: A Guide to Marketing Communication Plans*, 2d ed. Orlando, FL: Harcourt, Inc., 2000.

Pattis, S. William. *Careers in Advertising*. Lincolnwood, IL: NTC Business Books, 1996.

Philadelphia, Desa. "And What Does It Mean in Farsi? Ad Slogans That Are Successful in English Don't Always Travel Well." *Time*, Vol. 158, No. 23 (November 26, 2001).

Provenzano, Steven. *Slam Dunk Resumes—That Score Every Time!* Lincolnwood, IL: VGM Career Horizons, 1994.

Reeves, Rosser. *Reality in Advertising*. New York: Alfred A. Knopf, 1961.

Rieck, Dean. "Headline Writing Basics: What Every Headline Should Do and Nine Proven Ways to Do It." *Direct Marketing*, Vol. 58, No. 12 (April 1996): 44–47.

Ries, Al, and Jack Trout. *Positioning: The Battle for Your Mind*. New York: McGraw-Hill, 1981.

Ritchie, Karen. "Marketing to Generation X." *American Demographics*, Vol. 17, No. 4 (April 1995): 34–39.

———. "Why Gen X Buys Brand X." *Brandweek*, Vol. 36, No. 20 (May 15, 1995): 22–23, 26–27, 29, 31.

Roman, Kenneth, and Jane Maas. *The New How to Advertise*. New York: St. Martin's Press, 1992.

Rosen, Emanuel. *The Anatomy of Buzz: How to Create Word-of-Mouth Marketing*. New York: Doubleday/Currency, 2000.

Rothenberg, Randall. *Where the Suckers Moon: The Life and Death of an Advertising Campaign*. New York: Vintage Books, 1995.

Ryan, Robin. *Winning Cover Letters*. New York: John Wiley and Sons, 1997.

———. *Winning Resume*. New York: John Wiley and Sons, 1997.

Schmitt, Bernd H. *Experiential Marketing: How to Get Customers to SENSE, FEEL, THINK, ACT, and RELATE to Your Company and Brands*. New York: Free Press, 1999.

Schofield, Perry. *100 Top Copy Writers and Their Favorite Ads*. New York: Printer's Ink, 1954.

Schulberg, Pete, and Bob Schulberg. *Radio Advertising: The Authoritative Handbook*, 2d ed. Lincolnwood, IL: NTC Business Books, 1996.

Schultz, Don E. *Essentials of Advertising Strategy*. Chicago: Crain Books, 1981.

Schultz, Don E., Stanley Tannenbaum, and Anne Allison. *Essentials of Advertising Strategy*. Lincolnwood, IL: NTC Business Books, 1992.

Schwab, Victor O. *How to Write a Good Advertisement: A Short Course in Copywriting*. Rev. and enl. ed. New York: Harper and Row, 1962.

Seiden, Hank. *Advertising Pure and Simple: The New Edition*. New York: Amacom, 1990.

Shimp, Terence A. *Advertising and Promotion: Supplemental Aspects of Integrated Marketing Communications*. Orlando, FL: Harcourt, Inc., 2000.

Smith, Rod. "Pork's 'Startling' Tagline Ranks Fifth-Most Memorable." *Feedstuffs*, Vol. 72, No. 26 (June 26, 2000): 15.

Sroge, Maxwell. *How to Create Successful Catalogs*. Lincolnwood, IL: NTC Business Books, 1995.

Steel, Jon. *Truth, Lies and Advertising*. New York: John Wiley and Sons, Inc., 1998.

Stein, Donna Baier, and Floyd Kemske. *Write on Target: The Direct Marketer's Copywriting Handbook*. Lincolnwood, IL: NTC Business Books, 1997.

Stone, Bob. *Successful Direct Marketing Methods*, 4th ed. Lincolnwood, IL: NTC Business Books, 1988.

Stone, Bob, and Ron Jacobs. *Successful Direct Marketing Methods*, 7th ed. New York: McGraw-Hill, 2001.

Sullivan, Luke. *"Hey, Whipple, Squeeze This": A Guide to Creating Great Ads*. New York: John Wiley and Sons, Inc., 1998.

Tieszen, Lori. "The X Market." *Beverage World*, Vol. 115, No. 1630 (December 15, 1996): 98–100.

"To Arms, to Arms, Generation Y Is Advancing on the Aftermarket." *Aftermarket Business*, July 1999: 4.

Trachtenberg, Jeffrey A. "Words Still Matter." *Forbes*, Vol. 139 (May 4, 1987): 142.

Trout, Jack, with Steve Rivkin. *Differentiate or Die: Survival in Our Era of Killer Competition*. New York: John Wiley and Sons, Inc., 2000.

Twitchell, James B. *20 Ads That Shook the World: The Century's Most Groundbreaking Advertising and How It Changed Us All*. New York: Crown Publishers, 2000.

———. *Adcult USA: The Triumph of Advertising in American Culture*. New York: Columbia University Press, 1996.

Usborne, Nick. *Net Words: Creating High-Impact Online Copy*. New York: McGraw-Hill, 2002.

Valladares, June A. *The Craft of Copywriting*. New Delhi: Sage Publications Inc., 2000.

Vitale, Joseph G. *AMA Complete Guide to Small Business Advertising*. Lincolnwood, IL: NTC Business Books, 1995.

von Oech, Roger. *A Kick in the Seat of the Pants*. New York: Harper Perennial, 1986.

———. *A Whack on the Side of the Head*. New York: Warner Books, 1990.

Wallas, Graham. *The Art of Thought*. New York: Harcourt, Brace and Co., 1926.

Weinberger, Marc G., Leland Campbell, and Beth Brody. *Effective Radio Advertising*. New York: Lexington Books, 1994.

Wellner, Alison Stein. "The Census Report." *American Demographics*, Vol. 24, No. 1 (January 2002): S3–S6.

Westphal, Linda. "Before and After: Ads Made Better." *Direct Marketing*, Vol. 61, No. 5 (September 1998): 63.

Wilkinson, David. "The Brochure." *Direct Marketing*, Vol. 50, No. 1 (May 1987): 62–63, 123.

Yate, Martin John. *Cover Letters That Knock 'Em Dead*. Holbrook, MA: Adams Media, 2002.

Young, James Webb. *A Technique for Producing Ideas*. Chicago: Crain Books, [1940] 1975.

Zeff, Robbin Lee, and Brad Aronson. *Advertising on the Internet*, 2d ed. New York: John Wiley and Sons, Inc., 1999.

Zyman, Sergio (with Armin Brott). *The End of Advertising As We Know It*. Hoboken, NJ: John Wiley and Sons, Inc., 2002.

Index

Note: Page references with a *b*, *f*, or *t* indicate a box, figure or table on the designated page.

About the Author

Edd Applegate is professor of advertising at Middle Tennessee State University.